Contemporary British and Irish Poetry

An Introduction

Sarah Broom

palgrave
macmillan

First published in 2006 by
PALGRAVE MACMILLAN
Houndmills, Basingstoke, Hampshire RG21 6XS and
175 Fifth Avenue, New York, N.Y. 10010
Companies and representatives throughout the world.

PALGRAVE MACMILLAN is the global academic imprint of the Palgrave Macmillan division of St. Martin's Press, LLC and of Palgrave Macmillan Ltd. Macmillan® is a registered trademark in the United States, United Kingdom and other countries. Palgrave is a registered trademark in the European Union and other countries.

ISBN-13: 978–1–4039–0674–8 hardback
ISBN-10: 1–4039–0674–2   hardback
ISBN-13: 978–1–4039–0675–5 paperback
ISBN-10: 1–4039–0675–0   paperback

This book is printed on paper suitable for recycling and made from fully managed and sustained forest sources.

A catalogue record for this book is available from the British Library.

Library of Congress Cataloging-in-Publication Data

Broom, Sarah, 1972–
    Contemporary British and Irish poetry : an introduction / Sarah Broom.
        p. cm.
    Includes bibliographical references and index.
    ISBN 1–4039–0674–2 (cloth)—ISBN 1–4039–0675–0 (pbk.)
    1. English poetry – 21st century – History and criticism. 2. English poetry – 20th century – History and criticism. 3. English poetry – Irish authors – History and criticism. 4. Northern Ireland – In literature.
    5. Ireland – In literature. I. Title.

PR612.B76 2005
821'.9209—dc22   2005049316

10 9 8 7 6 5 4 3 2 1
15 14 13 12 11 10 09 08 07 06

Printed and bound in China

To my parents, Alison and Brian

Contents

Acknowledgements

I would like to thank my former colleagues at the University of Otago for their support during the first year of writing. I am grateful to Jim Acheson for encouraging me to begin this book, and to Dick Corballis for his assistance and advice during my time at Massey University. I would like to thank Bernard O'Donoghue and Steven Matthews for their generous support over the years, and for many stimulating and formative discussions about poetry. Thanks to Helen Farish and Subarno Chatterji for comments on sections of the book, and to Deana Rankin and Pat Palmer for discussions of Irish poetry back in Oxford days whose contours can still be traced in some of these pages. Thanks also to Selina Guinness for sharing her thoughts on the contemporary poetry scene. I am grateful to Ann Hassan for her careful and thoughtful scrutiny of the draft version, and to Kate Wallis and Sonya Barker at Palgrave Macmillan for all their help. Thanks also to the University of Auckland Library for providing library access during the final stages of this project.

I would like to thank my parents for their understanding and steadfast support over so many years, and Jen and Alex for their support. I am deeply grateful to Michael for his belief in me, his continual encouragement, and his help in every possible way. And finally, thank you to our son Daniel for reminding me what's important and *always* cheering me up.

The section on Michael Longley in Chapter 5 is adapted from an article published in *New Hibernia Review* in 2003.

The author and publishers are grateful to the following for permission to reproduce copyright material:

Bloodaxe for extracts from *Zoom* by Simon Armitage, extracts from *Propa Propaganda* by Benjamin Zephaniah, extracts from *Off Colour* by Jackie Kay, extracts from *Other Lovers* by Jackie Kay, extracts from *Carrying My Wife* by Moniza Alvi, and extracts from *A Bowl of Warm Air* by Moniza Alvi.

Faber & Faber for extracts from *Book of Matches* and *The Universal Home Doctor* by Simon Armitage, extracts from *Door into the Dark, Wintering Out, North, Field Work, Station Island, The Spirit Level* and *Electric Light* by Seamus Heaney, extracts from *Quoof, The Annals of Chile* and *Moy Sand and Gravel* by Paul Muldoon, and extracts from *Nil Nil* and *God's Gift to Women* by Don Paterson.

Farrar, Straus and Giroux for extracts from *Wintering Out, North, The Spirit Level* and *Electric Light* by Seamus Heaney.

Harcourt Brace for extracts from *The Shout* by Simon Armitage.

Gallery Press for extracts from *The Irish for No, Belfast Confetti, The Twelfth of Never* and *Breaking News* by Ciaran Carson.

Gallery Press for 'Hag' by Nuala Ní Dhomhnaill, translated by John Montague, from *Pharoah's Daughter*.

Wake Forest University Press for extracts from *The Irish for No, Belfast Confetti, The Twelfth of Never* and *Breaking News* by Ciaran Carson.

Grace Nichols and Curtis Brown Ltd for extracts from *i is a long memoried woman*, and extracts from *Lazy Thoughts of a Lazy Woman*. Reproduced with permission of Curtis Brown Ltd, London, on behalf of Grace Nichols. Copyright © Grace Nichols 1983, 1989.

Time Warner Book Group for extracts from *The Fat Black Woman's Poems* by Grace Nichols, published by Virago.

Anvil Press for extracts from 'Homesick'. 'Homesick' is taken from *Selling Manhattan* by Carol Ann Duffy, published by Anvil Press in 1997.

Carcanet for extracts from *Outside History* by Eavan Boland (1990).

W.W. Norton & Company, Inc. for extracts from 'Outside History', from *Outside History: Selected Poems 1980–1990* by Eavan Boland. Copyright © 1990 by Eavan Boland. Used by permission of W.W. Norton & Company, Inc.

The Random House Group Limited for extracts from *The Weather in Japan* by Michael Longley published by Jonathan Cape. Used by permission of The Random House Group Limited.

The Random House Group Limited for 'Leaves' from *Snow Water* by Michael Longley published by Jonathan Cape. Used by permission of The Random House Group Limited.

Michael Longley for extracts from *Gorse Fires*, published by Secker & Warburg.

Pan Macmillan for extracts from *The World's Wife* by Carol Ann Duffy, and extracts from *Jizzen* by Kathleen Jamie.

Reality Street for extracts from *Mop Mop Georgette: Selected Poems* by Denise Riley.

Tom Leonard for extracts from *Intimate Voices: Selected Work 1965–1983*, published by Etruscan Books in 2004. Copyright © Tom Leonard.

Tom Leonard for extracts from *access to the silence*, published by Etruscan Books in 2004. Copyright © Tom Leonard.

Geraldine Monk for extracts from *Selected Poems*, published by Salt.

Every effort has been made to trace the copyright holders but if any have been inadvertently overlooked the publishers will be pleased to make the necessary arrangement at the first opportunity.

Introduction

Nearly every overview or anthology of contemporary poetry in Britain and Ireland published in the last two decades has asserted the radical democratisation and pluralisation in poetry publishing and reviewing that has occurred since the 1960s. As a general trend this is undeniable. The poetry scene in the 1950s in Britain was overwhelmingly white, male, middle-class and centred around Oxbridge and London, and in Ireland (where class and regional relationships are differently inflected) it was overwhelmingly white and male. Since the 1960s and 70s there has been a gradual but radical diversification of the poetry being published and reviewed, so that women poets, poets from working-class, rural and non-metropolitan backgrounds, and poets from ethnic minorities have become prominent and recognised figures within the poetry world.[1]

Of course, this process has been tortuously slow, and often more loudly proclaimed than actualised; a glance at the critical overviews published in the 1990s, even, will show a marked under-representation of women poets and poets from ethnic minorities.[2] But it has been steady, propelled firstly by changes in the education system in Britain and Northern Ireland which extended free secondary school education to all children, allowing working-class young people access to university; secondly by feminism and movements for racial equality; thirdly by the dynamic towards devolution within the United Kingdom; and fourthly by the impact of postmodernism's valuing of diversity, hostility to hierarchies of value, and alertness to the voices of the marginalised. However, not everyone joins in with this fanfare to pluralism; poets from the avant-garde community are justified in noting that the impression of 'diversity' in poetry is too often produced by simply bringing together poets of diverse backgrounds, rather than by being truly open to diversity in poetic form. As Chapter 7 suggests, a sense of discontent over the formal conservatism of the Irish and British poetic and critical establishments seems to be growing, and this hurdle may be the next to be overcome.

This book seeks to give a sense of the state of poetry in Ireland and Britain today. It cannot hope to be all-encompassing (the number of excellent poets who had to be excluded is rather horrifying) or representative (there are styles and kinds of poetry being written which are not even covered in this book, themes which are untouched, and regions which are unrepresented), but it seeks to provide for the reader a number of different and fascinating pathways into a remarkable poetic territory. This territory is geographically delineated by the deceptively simple phrase 'Britain and Ireland'. Problematic at first glance in its bestowal of priority on Britain, this phrase is requisitioned to act as shorthand for a multiplicity of regions and nations with histories which have varied and diverged enormously over the last four or five decades. In the last decade or so, Ireland has perhaps seen even greater societal changes than Britain. Startling economic growth in the Republic has effected a complete reversal of the longstanding emigration problem, with large-scale economic immigration forcing a difficult adjustment to multiculturalism. The Republic's integration in Europe has also led to major changes in terms of social norms, with the legalisation of homosexuality (1993) and divorce (1995). The last decade in Northern Ireland, marked momentously by the Good Friday Agreement of 1998, has witnessed gradual and significant political progress, despite recurrent setbacks and stand-offs. Scotland and Wales have also experienced dramatic political change, in the establishment of the Scottish Parliament and the Welsh Assembly, and, in Scotland at least, in an increasing desire for independence. These changes in the constitutional structure of the United Kingdom, together with a growing uncertainty about the significance of 'Britishness' (despite New Labour's earnest efforts in the late 1990s to cultivate 'Cool Britannia') have also led to some growth in – and anxiety about – a new English nationalism, even as the British government starts to assess the level of interest within England for regional assemblies.

Although this book pays close attention to these devolutionary dynamics, and to regional and national difference, I have chosen for the most part not to *structure* it around national and regional divisions, because of the sense that if this train of inquiry were followed, it would inevitably dominate the book and exclude all other areas of interest. The only exception to this is the chapter on poetry that has emerged out of the conflict in Northern Ireland.

I have made this exception because the Troubles have produced a cultural context that has no equivalent or comparison elsewhere. No doubt the same could be argued for particular dimensions of other regions, but the extremity of the Northern Irish political situation over the last few decades makes it a particularly unique and compelling focus for discussion. Otherwise, I have chosen to pursue themes that draw out similarities and differences between poets from the different regions and nations of Britain and Ireland. One of these themes is in fact the idea of nation itself, in its intersection with gender and sexuality.

Some of these themes – gender and sexuality, class, race and ethnicity – are familiar, and their recurrence might be criticised by those who argue that we should move beyond 'identity politics', or by those who claim that poetry criticism should be 'saved' from cultural studies.[3] It is true that 'identity politics' can be restrictive and reductive, if one understands by this term the kind of discourses that claim absolute solidarity and uniformity around any given term of identification, whether it be 'black', 'woman', 'gay', or whatever. But this kind of identity politics has very much had its day, and political and activist discourses as well as academic discourses are these days much more likely to emphasise the multiplicity of subject positions which an individual simultaneously inhabits; the contradictory and plural identities which individuals acknowledge as their own. Meanwhile the identity labels themselves are undergoing constant revision and evolution, and those pertaining to race, ethnicity, gender and sexuality are still contentious, explosive, unpredictably fluid, and utterly central to the cultural debates of our times. The term 'class' is rather different; although it is often cited in discussions of identity politics, its history is actually quite separate, and many Marxist theorists see identity politics as undermining materialist analysis. But Marxism was the first of a series of group-based paradigms to undergo attack for reductiveness (as 'identity politics' generally would later), and now the term 'class' itself seems to be losing its cultural currency, even if the inequalies to which it refers remain. This is in itself an interesting issue, which will be discussed in Chapter 1. Terms relating to gender, sexuality and race/ethnicity, though, show no such sign of fading from public discourse, and indeed the chapters on these issues will demonstrate that for poets writing in Ireland and Britain today these issues are urgent, stimulating and profoundly important.

There is absolutely no contradiction between paying attention to such issues and paying attention to poetry as an art form. This book shows that formal diversity is thriving in Irish and British poetry; if we reach for examples we might first light upon the rap rhythms of Patience Agbabi, the classical metres of Peter Reading, the minimalist poems in Ciaran Carson's latest work, the column poems of Tom Raworth, the 'eye dialect' and poster poems of Tom Leonard, the prose poems of David Kinloch, and the rhyme pyrotechnics of Paul Muldoon's poetry. Although formal issues feature in every discussion, the final chapter gives particular attention to the question of formal difference, in its investigation of the simmering animosities between 'mainstream' and 'experimental' poetry. It also investigates the other major, but less hostile, divide in contemporary poetry: performance versus the page. Another chapter explores the nature of self, subjectivity and agency, a conceptual nexus which brings together some of the most difficult and provocative questions which face us today. While theorists and philosophers struggle to develop new concepts of self which engage with but move beyond poststructuralism's radical questioning of human agency, and when a sense of individual disempowerment is one of the dominant notes in popular culture, poets are being driven to explore the nature of the self and the scope and limits of human agency, particularly in terms of the relationship between the individual and language. This is an issue that will emerge in various different contexts in this book, but is given particular attention in Chapter 6.

Postmodernism has been one of the key terms in most introductions to critical surveys and anthologies of British and Irish poetry since Morrison and Motion's 1982 *Penguin Book of Contemporary Poetry*, which even then looked decidedly odd in its choice of poets to represent 'the spirit of postmodernism'.[4] The term itself is now starting to sound strangely dated; as Marjorie Perloff notes, ' "postmodernism" seems to have largely lost its momentum: How long, after all, can a discourse – in this case, poetry – continue to be considered *post-*, with its implications of belatedness, diminution and entropy?'[5] Perloff, a prominent American advocate of avant-garde poetry, puts her energy into tracing the continuities of contemporary avant-garde poetry with early modernism, and a sense of the continuity between modernism and postmodernism is becoming ever more prevalent, with the former term regaining currency in relation to formal experimentation. But now more than ever, it feels inadequate to attempt to herd poets together under either term. Poetry written today in Britain and Ireland often does have characteristics associated with postmodernism (for instance self-consciousness, irony, fragmentation, allusiveness, an attention to the materiality of language, a collapsing of the divisions between 'high' and 'low' culture) but it has many other characteristics too. Some of the 'I' voices we hear in contemporary British and Irish poetry *are* preoccupied with the ontological status of that 'I' – but not all. Not all eschew the lyrical in favour of irony; the best are able to combine the two in a way that confounds the categories.

The last decade has seen the usual mixture of optimism and pessimism about poetry's future. In Britain, the New Generation promotion of 1994, with its slightly foolish claim that poetry was 'the new rock'n'roll', generated a brief flurry of attention for poetry in the media and a sense of buoyancy among at least some sections of the poetry community. If poetry's profile was edged a little higher by this promotion and other innovations in the early 1990s, the publicity did not pay off in any increase in sales figures for poetry collections in general, and a panel discussion at the University of Warwick in 2002 on 'The Crisis in Poetry Publishing' emphasised the enormous difficulties facing poetry presses, given the radically decreasing space assigned to poetry by large bookstores and their tendency to fill these shelves with anthologies and a few big names.[6] Oxford University Press's decision to close its poetry list in 1998 was a symptom of the times and sent shock waves through the poetry world.

But the permanently echoing complaints about poor sales, struggling publishers, and the difficulty of reaching 'general readers' (complaints which are less prominent in Ireland, where poetry's role in cultural life still seems more secure) are balanced out by more positive signs of the state of poetry. More and more poetry is being published, even if the publishers have difficulty selling individual 'slim volumes'. Sales of anthologies are strong, especially of the more populist variety; Neil Astley's 2002 Bloodaxe anthology *Staying Alive* sold 35,000 copies in its first six months. While the financial difficulties of small presses, and presses which focus exclusively on poetry, *are* a real cause for concern, the fact is that innovative presses are still entering the field (the tang which Salt Publishing has recently added to the poetry world being a case in point). Meanwhile, strategies that bring poetry directly to potential readers and listeners, such as the internet, television and live performance, have a growing and encouraging role. The internet in particular, which has since its beginnings been crucial to the experimental poetry scene, offers the possibility of truly international exchange and awareness, something which is currently being actualised by online magazines like *Jacket* and *Contemporary Poetry Review*, as well as many online discussion lists. The readership for online publications, whether they focus on criticism or poetry, is vast compared to that for traditional little magazines, and is rapidly growing; as *CPR*'s 2004 mission statement notes, '*The Criterion*, at the height of T.S. Eliot's fame, had 700 subscribers. For the *Contemporary Poetry Review*, that is a day's audience—and it doubles each year.'[7]

Andrew Michael Roberts notes that editors of anthologies are frequently caught in 'the double bind of typicality and novelty', wanting to provide a selection of poetry which is typical of prevailing writing, but at the same time wanting to assert a new version of literary history or draw the public's attention to a new kind of writing, two desires which do not necessarily sit easily together. The other double bind he notes is that of absolute versus relative value; anthologists tend to want to represent the range and diversity of poetry, to be open to a variety of forms, yet at the same time 'few anthologists can resist the implication that, whatever other criteria of selection they have applied, some notion of pure "quality" is in operation.'[8] The author of a critical introduction such as this must face these issues and more; the choice of poets emerges in a two-way process alongside the choice of chapter themes, so that it is possible that some very good poets may be excluded simply because they are difficult to discuss in conjunction with other poets writing today. Like most anthologies and overviews, this book picks a precarious and pragmatic pathway between the different imperatives, seeking to represent a range of the kinds of poetry that have been written over the past few decades, but, within these various categories, exercising an inevitably subjective critical judgment as to which poetry is the most rewarding of close attention.

Critical texts such as this one are less able to represent novelty than are anthologies, as in seeking to provide critical writing which will be useful in teaching contexts (among others) there is a need to focus, for the most part, on poets who have published several collections and are relatively established. For this reason there is less coverage than I would have liked of the youngest and/or newest generation; future books of this kind will no doubt include the likes of Colette Bryce, Paul Farley, Leontia Flynn, Caitríona O'Reilly, Pascale Petit, Jacob Polley, Justin Quinn, Jean Sprackland and David Wheatley, to name just a few. Some of these names (but not those from the Republic of Ireland) were included (along with Patience Agbabi, whose poetry is covered in this book) in the Poetry Society's rather unconvincing effort to recreate the New Generation buzz by anointing a 'Next Generation' in 2004. Alice Oswald, while having only emerged relatively recently, has made a strong impression on the poetry world, and I regret that I have not been able to cover her work. Among more established poets, there are also many whom I would have loved to discuss, but for various reasons could not; they include Caroline Bergvall, John Burnside, Fred D'Aguiar, Paul Durcan, Lavinia Greenlaw, Vona Groarke, W.N. Herbert, Selima Hill, Medbh McGuckian, Derek Mahon, Bernard O'Donoghue, Tom Paulin, J.H. Prynne and Peter Riley. Of course there was also a need to decide how far back the book would reach. I decided to make the generation of Heaney, Harrison, Clarke, Raworth and Longley (all born 1937–39 and beginning to write during that decade of change, the 1960s) the elders of the book, which means that there are several older figures like Geoffrey Hill, Fleur Adcock, U.A. Fanthorpe, Roy Fisher and Edwin Morgan who stand behind these poets.

Because of the decision not to orient the book around national divisions, the inevitable national headcounts will reveal some imbalances. I regret the under-representation of Wales generally, and of the younger generation from Ireland, but I hope that this is compensated for by the book's thematic momentum and integrity. I have not included poetry in languages other than English, apart from poetry in Scots dialects that are accessible for English-speakers. Obviously there is a wealth of poetry in Irish, Scots Gaelic and Welsh, and in other languages, which is excluded because of this, but although wonderful translations of this poetry are often available, critical discussion which is based purely on a translated text can often feel inadequate.

This book has been written, for the most part, in New Zealand, to which I returned recently after many years in Britain. My years spent in Britain revolved around researching and teaching contemporary Irish – to begin with – and British poetry. They took me through Leeds, Oxford and London, with considerable time spent in Ireland along the way, and then back to New Zealand where I have been teaching contemporary British and Irish poetry to New Zealand students. My particular position as insider/ outsider has, I hope, given me a unique perspective on contemporary British and Irish poetry; a perspective which values difference and diversity and is sensitive to the ways in which links and connections may be formed between different contexts. I have now spent twelve years thinking and writing about British and Irish poetry, and I would suggest that the poetry's capacity to hold and reward my interest and commitment, as it compels the interest of many other readers who do not come from either Ireland or Britain, is a testament to the strength, richness and depth of what is being written in Britain and Ireland today.

Notes

1 The poetry world in Ireland is still overwhelmingly white, something which will no doubt change as immigration alters the ethnic mix of Irish society.

2 David Kennedy, for instance, states 'I have chosen not to write about Black British or Afro-Caribbean poetry not only because it seems inappropriate for a white critic to do so but because these poetries are still being theorised through perspectives of language and difference.' This is perplexing; the logic of the first part of this statement would surely exclude him from writing about women's poetry as well, while waiting for some moment of completion in 'theorising' seems like a hopeless and self-defeating strategy (*New Relations: The Refashioning of British Poetry 1980–1994* (Bridgend: Seren, 1996), p. 8). Likewise, Neil Corcoran devotes only two pages to the history of 'Westindian-British poetry', noting that it would be 'presumptuous' for him to tell this story, which is 'as yet better told elsewhere' (*English Poetry Since 1940* (Harlow: Longman, 1993), p. xvi). Such anxieties, while understandable, have too often been used as an excuse for perpetuating the marginalisation of this poetry.

3 See, for example, Edna Longley's comment that 'the language of poetry criticism must stop making concessions both to "identity-discourse" … and to cultural studies.' 'Not Blinkbonny Enough', *Thumbscrew*, no. 13 (Spring/ Summer 1999), pp. 4–9 (p. 9).

4 Blake Morrison and Andrew Motion (eds), *The Penguin Book of Contemporary British Poetry* (London: Penguin, 1982), p. 20.

5 Marjorie Perloff, *21ˢᵗ-Century Modernism: The 'New' Poetics* (Malden, MA: Blackwell, 2002), p. 2.

6 'The crisis in poetry publishing: The Warwick debate', www2.warwick.ac.uk/ fac/arts/english/undergrad/modules/second/en238/small_presses/poetry_ in_crisis/, accessed 11 October 2004. In the discussion Esther Morgan

expresses perplexity at 'why ... this raised profile, all this activity at literature festivals, the rise of performance poetry etc, *hasn't resulted in greater sales'*.

7 www.cprw.com/missionstatement.htm, accessed 13 October 2004.

8 Andrew Michael Roberts, 'The rhetoric of value in recent British poetry anthologies', *Poetry and Contemporary Culture: The Question of Value*, ed. Andrew Michael Roberts and Jonathan Allison (Edinburgh: Edinburgh University Press, 2002), pp. 101–22 (pp. 102–3).

1

'Wanna yoo scruff': Class and Language

Tony Harrison, Tom Leonard, Don Paterson

The poets included in this chapter all come from working-class backgrounds in which poetry seemed a most unlikely career choice or leisure pursuit, but whereas Paterson's first memorable experiences of poetry as an adult were encounters with the poetry of Tony Harrison, and in particular his sonnets about his working-class family background, Harrison himself saw no such role models around him, and had to work out for himself that the Cockney Keats and the Northern Wordsworth could be used as models in quite different ways than had been suggested to him hitherto. For Leonard and Harrison, the sense of the necessity of battling against a class-bound literary establishment has been a dominating and driving force. Paterson's poetry, with few exceptions, takes on a much less confrontational stance, something which may be partly due to his sense of coming after poets like Harrison, Leonard and Douglas Dunn, and may also be related to the very different political climate of his formative years.

'Class' in recent years has started to sound like a rather old-fashioned term, as politicians avoid it and Marxist class-based analyses have fallen out of fashion in academia. But although the discourses are changing, economic and social stratification remains, and for this reason it is interesting to compare Paterson, a working-class poet who grew up in the Thatcher years, with Harrison and Leonard, two poets who experienced the heyday of working-class activism in the 1970s. The 1970s were also a time of innovation and excitement for theorists interested in the role of literature in society, as Marxist theory began to engage with

10

structuralism. Raymond Williams's *Marxism and Literature* (1977) and Terry Eagleton's *Criticism and Ideology* (1976) were just two of the books that reflected and inspired a new commitment to reading literature in relation to its particular historical and material conditions. Recent cultural materialist critiques of poststructuralism, heavily influenced by Williams, reflect the continued strength of this critical tradition in Britain and Ireland. 'Class' may be a more problematic concept than it once was, but the social and historical orientation associated with the Marxist critical tradition is still a vigorous force within literary and cultural studies.

Tony Harrison

Tony Harrison is a poet unlike any other on the contemporary scene, not least because of his ability to make verse work in genres and arenas in which it has recently had very little success. His contribution to the revival of verse drama has been enormous, and his success in producing 'film poems' for television is a lesson in what can be done with and for poetry with vision and determination. In recent years he has published very few collections of stand-alone poetry, but has produced verse in plenty for theatre and film works. It is necessary, then, to consider Harrison's poetry for film and theatre, but at the same time his oeuvre has become so extensive that it is only possible to do justice to a small number of his works in the space of this chapter. In order to give a sense of the range of his work, I will discuss, alongside a number of his shorter poems, the long poem *V.*, which was made into a film-poem and broadcast on television, and I will also briefly explore one of Harrison's theatre works, *The Big H*. Harrison is also unusual among contemporary poets in Britain and Ireland in his dedication to metrical, rhyming verse. Looking back to models like Donne, Marvell, Milton, Gray and Wordsworth, rather than to his immediate precursors in the twentieth century, Harrison has shown incontestably that metrical rhyming verse can be forcefully contemporary and can work strikingly in contexts such as television that might seem inherently opposed to such 'old-fashioned' forms. In a society that was perhaps in danger of forgetting the power, in performance, of poetry that exploits aural effects, Harrison has been a welcome presence.

Harrison was born in 1937, and his poetic career kicked off with *The Loiners*, published in 1970. In a later autobiographical poem Harrison's mother is remembered as weeping for weeks after she saw the collection, exclaiming '*You weren't brought up to write such mucky books!*'.[1] *The Loiners* ('Loiners' means people from Leeds) is important in that it reveals a Harrison who is more modernist, less direct and less evangelical in his approach than the later and more well-known Harrison. The collection also reveals Harrison's early preoccupation with themes he was later to develop: social inequality and marginalisation, sexuality, colonialism, imperialism – and the anger and violence that are linked to all of these. There is, however, a much greater focus on sexuality than in later collections, and as Luke Spencer argues, *The Loiners* demonstrates very clearly a problem that persists in much of Harrison's later work. Despite Harrison's attempt to consider the linkage between colonialism and sexuality in poems like 'The White Queen' and 'The Song of the PWD Man', there is still a failure to address the overlap between sexuality as a liberating mode of self-expression and self-expansion, and sexuality as a mode of domination and oppression. As Spencer comments, ' "The Nuptial Torches" is the only poem which treats a woman as a moral subject with her own voice; in many other poems, such as "Newcastle is Peru", 'the woman's body functions as an object of his gaze and as a terrain for his appropriation.'[2] Like Spencer I would argue that this issue of the treatment of women in Harrison's poetry is an interesting fault-line that emerges in much of his work, and does at times undermine the persuasiveness of his efforts to confront other issues such as that of class.

Rather than discuss *The Loiners* in any detail, however, I would like to move on to the constantly metamorphosing sequence whose core was originally published as *From The School of Eloquence and Other Poems* in 1978. In 1978 the sequence contained eighteen sonnets, and this was expanded to fifty in *Continuous* and sixty-three in the *Selected Poems* of 1984. The core of eighteen poems contains what came to be iconic lines like the scholarship boy leaning out his window to shout to his friends, '*Ah bloody can't ah've gorra Latin prose*' (*SP*, 116). This line takes us directly to what I am most interested in pursuing in relation to Harrison's poetry: his exploration of the relationship between language, literature and power. Harrison's poetry draws persistently on his own experience as a working-class boy who gained a scholarship to

Leeds Grammar School and was thus thrown into an environment dominated by upper-middle-class values in which his accent and his origins were viewed as 'vulgar' and 'low'. His ambivalence about the effect that his subsequent education had on him (he went on to study classics at Leeds University and began a PhD) provides the material for many poems and the emotional fuel for much of his writing.

One of the epigraphs which Harrison chose for *The School of Eloquence* comes from E.P. Thompson's book *The Making of the English Working Class*, and the quotation explains the origin of the phrase 'The School of Eloquence' as one of the cover names for the London Corresponding Society, an eighteenth-century radical working-class organisation which had as one of its aims the development of literacy among the working classes. In using this phrase Harrison is aligning himself with a long tradition of republican and reformist working-class movements, and drawing attention to the centrality of language in the struggle for political power. The sonnets from *The School of Eloquence* reveal Harrison's ambivalence towards the lack of eloquence and literacy in his family and community background; on the one hand it is experienced as frustrating and disempowering, while on the other hand it is celebrated as an unpretentious and energetic directness:

> What t'mob said to the cannons on the mills,
> shouted to soldier, scab and sentinel
> 's silence, parries and hush on whistling hills,
> shadows in moonlight playing knurr and spell.
>
> It wasn't poetry though. Nay, wiseowl Leeds
> *pro rege et lege* schools, nobody needs
> your drills and chanting to parrot right
> the *tusky tusky* of the pikes that night. (*SP*, 113)

Here, in 'The Rhubarbarians', a kind of alternative eloquence is proposed, linked to violent rebellion as well as to the drive for reform and social change. Against the 'tusky tusky' of the pikes are set the drills of Greek and Latin grammar which shaped Harrison's life at Leeds Grammar School. The dense, jagged, alliterative lines of the first two stanzas and the lyricism of the third ('parries and hush on whistling hills, / shadows in moonlight playing knurr and spell') evoke the complexity of the poet's emotional investment in the history of working-class collective action.

Interestingly, the attempt to convey this in a poetry which leans in the third stanza towards romanticism is itself undermined by the brusqueness of the fourth stanza which rejects this poeticisation: 'It wasn't poetry though'. The poem is complex in its ironies; while one might not need the 'drills and chanting' of a grammar school education simply to 'parrot' the 'tusky tusky' of the pikes, the poem itself, with its supple variations on the iambic and its poised sound effects, has clearly benefited from that very classical education, and its evocation of working-class resistance cannot be classed as simple 'parroting'.

Harrison's attitude towards his grammar school experience, which he explores obsessively in the *The School of Eloquence* sonnets, has been considered by Ken Worpole in the broader context of the impact of the grammar school system on working-class communities. Worpole argues that the scholarship system could be seen as 'one of the most effective pre-emptive attacks on the possibility of a popular working-class socialist politics in this century', and backs this up by quoting from various mid-century teachers who saw grammar school education as a way of 'communicating middle-class values to a "new" population' and by noting that most of the scholarship children moved away from their roots in the Labour party to become Conservative voters.[3] The overall positive or negative impact of the grammar school system on working-class communities is clearly a contentious issue, but Harrison's poetry certainly reflects his ambivalence towards the system in terms which match Worpole's description of the '11-plus' examination as something which 'swept through hundreds of thousands of homes each year like an icy wind, and which in many places destroyed the cementing ties of family and class relationships, literally dividing families and friends against each other, sometimes forever'.[4]

Harrison's poetry is deeply marked by the sense of a permanent division between himself, as only son, and his parents, which he sees as produced by the way in which his grammar school education changed him. As 'Book Ends' puts it, 'what's still between's / not the thirty or so years, but books, books, books' (*SP*, 126). His poetry also reveals a preoccupation with the way in which the grammar school teachers denigrated his own working-class roots, particularly with regard to language. Along with the television play *The Big H*, which I will be discussing later, 'Them & [uz]', from the *The School of Eloquence* sonnet sequence, is Harrison's most forthright approach to this experience. The poem recounts the refusal of a school English teacher to let the young Harrison read Keats's 'Ode to a Nightingale' because of his regional accent with its dropped 'h's, glottal stops and flat vowels. He begins '*mi 'art aches*' only to be cut off by the English teacher with 'Mine's broken, / you barbarian, T.W.!' (*SP*, 122). The teacher relegates the young T.W. Harrison to the 'low' end of literature: 'Poetry's the speech of kings. You're one of those / Shakespeare gives the comic bits to: prose'. In response, the poem's speaker declares his determination to 'occupy / your lousy, leasehold Poetry' (123). As many critics have noted, the poem's very form achieves a radical challenge to the conventions of the tradition which Harrison seeks to occupy; a line like 'RIP RP, RIP T.W.' clearly aims to startle, while the use of phonetic spelling for the word 'us' draws the reader's attention cleverly to the issue of the kind of pronunciation he or she is using in reading the *rest* of the poem either silently or aloud.

Like many of Harrison's poems, 'Them & [uz]' puts its erudition on display as a kind of taunting gesture towards the schoolteachers and other authorities who relegated him to 'the comic bits'. Harrison has said that he began to use metre as a way of occupying literature; as Douglas Dunn puts it, the ironies of Harrison's poetry derive from the application of

> pentametric metricality and full rhymes – the philistine standard of verse – to subjects that otherwise subvert or denounce the mistaken political, social and literary expectations that those who uphold that standard tend to invest in it.[5]

As its exemplar of determination overcoming disadvantage the poem presents Demosthenes, the Greek orator who overcame his childhood stutter by learning to speak distinctly with pebbles in his mouth, and strengthened his voice by speaking against the noise of the ocean. The fact that the poem begins with the Greek cry αἰαῖ (followed by the 'ayay' with which Leon Cortez and other stand-up comics greeted their audience[6]) immediately signals its status as 'high' literature and its participation in the tradition of classically educated English writers – that very tradition from which his grammar school teachers considered him naturally excluded. The poem demonstrates, however, that this tradition is far less homogeneous than the upper middle classes would perhaps like to believe; Keats was a Cockney and Wordsworth's poems are written to be spoken with a regional accent. Poetry as text too often elides geographical and class differences which oral poetry would expose; even readers who do not speak 'R.P.' tend to assume that a poem should be read in 'R.P.' (or at least they mostly did so in the seventies – one should not underestimate the impact that the poetry of Harrison and others has since had on readers' assumptions and expectations). Harrison's poetry makes sure that this assumption is challenged, particularly by using rhymes that only work if one reads the poem with a Northern accent.

However, at times Harrison's poetry seems to reveal an anxiety that is still hostage to some of the establishment values he is battling against. For example, the line '[uz] can be loving as well as funny' seems rather out of place in a poem that is supposedly proclaiming the normality and ordinariness of the use of '[uz]'. Suggesting that the pronunciation can be loving *as well as* funny seems defensive, as if he accepts as valid the perspective of the teachers or middle-class students who find his accent funny.[7] Likewise, as Luke Spencer has commented, the inclusion of the final couplet about his 'one mention in the *Times*' comes across slightly awkwardly, as if a persistent anxiety about 'making it' forces him to give this sign of acceptance too much prominence, even if ironically. As Spencer puts it, the 'one mention in the *Times*' is 'a symptom of enhanced social status which shifts the poem towards a Hoggart-like emphasis on making the grade (with or without one's original accent intact) and away from questions about the nature and value of "the grade" itself'.[8]

The couplet does, however, highlight Harrison's self-conscious anxiety about being lauded by the establishment and the difficulty of clinging to 'my own voice' in the face of praise as well as denigration. 'Turns' fears the possibility of poetry being a sycophantic betrayal of class solidarity:

> He never begged. For nowt! Death's reticence
> crowns his life's, and *me*, I'm opening my trap
> to busk the class that broke him for the pence
> that splash like brackish tears into our cap. (*SP*, 149)

Harrison's poetry shows a continual conflict between the desire to 'occupy' poetry, to break down its traditional gentilities and carefully constructed borders, and the fear that any commitment to the literary world is a betrayal of his roots. As he has gone on writing the anxiety has diminished and his exuberance – and at times ferocity – has increased; this seems to be partly due to his success with verse drama and film-poems, which has enabled him to reach much wider audiences than would have been possible with poetry in book form alone.

The most publicised of these ventures into media outside the printed word was *V.*, which Harrison published as a poem in 1985 and which was made into a television film and broadcast on Channel 4 in November 1987, after loud debate in the media over the appropriateness of its screening. The debate was overtly over the so-called 'obscenity' of the poem, but Blake Morrison argued in *The Independent* that the outraged Tory MPs were

> right to believe that the poem is shocking, but not because of its language. It shocks because it describes unflinchingly what is meant by a divided society, because it takes the abstractions we have learned to live with – unemployment, racial tension, inequality, deprivation – and gives them a kind of physical existence on the page.[9]

V. is disturbing, and it *is* partly to do with the battering which the reader receives from the violent language which punctuates the poem. However, this has less to do with the discomfort of taboo-breaking than with the misogyny in the repetition of 'cunt' as the sign for the objects of the skinhead's aggression and contempt. Commentators pointed out that the poem is sparked by the poet's anger at the words sprayed on his parents' grave: 'Harrison knows the words are offensive. They offend him and he knows that they will offend others. They do, however, exist in the reality of the graveyard in Leeds, and he has tried, as he shouts at an imaginary skinhead, "to give a higher meaning to your scrawl".'[10] Actually, it is only 'United' that is painted on his parents' grave, and Harrison's poet persona is not so offended by the words that he refrains from using them himself: 'another hand / has added, in a reddish colour, CUNTS. // Which is, I grant, the word that springs to mind, / when going to clear the weeds and rubbish thrown / on the family plot by football fans, I find / UNITED graffitied on my parents' stone' (*V.*, 11–12). Likewise, when he argues with the skinhead the poet figure is just as prolific with his terms of abuse: ' "Listen, cunt!" *I* said, "before you start your jeering / the reason why I want this in a book / 's to give ungrateful cunts like you a hearing!" ' (19). The language in fact comes across as a rather desperate attempt to connect with the skinhead, who receives the effort contemptuously. The broader point, of course, is that the skinhead is in fact the poet's alter ego, the figure representing his working-class past, the Leeds he has left behind, the person he could have become had he not gone to grammar school, the rebel who enacts his rebellion in vandalism and violence rather than directing it into poetry: 'He aerosolled his name. And it was mine' (22). But neither the educated, gentrified poet figure nor the skinhead show any awareness of the misogyny involved in the constant use of 'cunt', and nothing in the poem draws attention to this.

The ending sees the poet figure proclaiming his return 'Home, home to my woman' (26) in an attempt to envisage an alternative unity which can stand against the bitter 'United': 'Turning to love, and sleep's oblivion, I know / what the UNITED that the skin sprayed *has* to mean' (30). It means, apparently, the unity and one-ness found in sexual love and commitment: 'the bride / I feel united to, *my* bride is coming / into the bedroom, naked, to my side. // The ones we choose to love become our anchor / when the hawser of the blood tie's hacked, or frays' (31). But this rather too facile answer to the poem's sense of division is interrupted by the skinhead yelling '*Wanker!*', and the final stanzas of the poem emphasise that the poet's efforts towards imaginative and inter-personal resolution are always undermined and shadowed by the voice of the sceptical, the angry and the dispossessed, the poet's unconscious or repressed self: 'the skin's UNITED underwrites the poet, / the measures carved below the ones above' (31).

This idea is very effectively troped in the retrieved image of the empty mining pit that underlies the cemetery. *V.* was written during the miners' strike of 1984, and the epigraph at the beginning of the poem (and film) is a quotation from Arthur Scargill, president of the National Union of Miners, who led the strike: '*My father still reads the dictionary every day. He says your life depends on your power to master words.*' In the film version of *V.* (directed by Richard Eyre) footage of the miners' strike is used to accompany the stanza that asserts the poet's identification with the working class and the miners:

> class v. class as bitter as before,
> the unending violence of US and THEM,

personified in 1984
by Coal Board MacGregor and the NUM (11)

The empty mine recalls both exploitation, class conflict, and a context of working-class solidarity which is in danger of being lost after the mine closures and the failure of the miners' stand of 1984. The presence of the mine under the poet's grave symbolises the instability and the riskiness of poetry in a context of such splittings of identity and identification: *'Beneath your feet's a poet, then a pit'* (33).

V. is a direct and open effort to confront the issues of alienation, unemployment and social anger in contemporary Britain. The *'V'* of the title puns on 'versus' and 'verses' as well as recalling the victory 'V' sign which appears in several of Harrison's poems about the second world war and the victory celebrations which were darkened for him by his emerging and subsequent knowledge of the events which precipitated 'VE' day and 'VJ' day. It thus points out the degree to which antagonism and aggression – even violence – are dominant in mainstream culture, from football to world wars, rather than simply being linked with certain socio-economic groups. In the film version the initial image sequence, which comes after a specially recorded chatty introduction by Harrison and before the beginning of the poem proper, includes a brief image of Thatcher giving the V sign, accentuating the issue of the miners' strike as well as suggesting that Thatcher's government was waging war on its own people. In the poem, the speaker's efforts towards a far too easy withdrawal from the arena of conflict into a cosy and self-satisfied world of domestic harmony are quite deliberately *undermined*, and the poem certainly leaves us with no answers to the fracturing of society, apart from the doubtful hope of continuing dialogue. One aspect of the poem which remains problematic is its presentation of the female; while the desire to retreat into a domestic idyll is critiqued as escapist and impossible, the poet's possessive approach to his 'woman' and the strict association of woman with hearth and home is not critiqued or linked to the poem's use of 'cunt' as a term of abuse.

Generally, though, *V.* recognises the way in which obscene language becomes the only possible language for the linguistically impoverished and angry. It also continues to explore the poet's ambivalence about his own increased eloquence, which takes him so far away from the skinhead that he has to compensate by joining in with the obscenities. The skinhead taunts him for his (undoubtedly gratuitous) sprinkling of French phrases:

> *So what's* a cri-de-coeur, *cunt? Can't yer speak*
> *The language that yer mam spoke? Think of 'er!*
> *Can yer only get yer tongue round fucking Greek?*
> *Go fuck yourself with* cri-de-coeur! (17)[11]

Here, as elsewhere in Harrison's work, 'correctness' in speech and the ability to speak the language of the privileged is a double-edged sword. This idea is rather shockingly and brutally confronted in *The Big H*, a musical drama developed for television that was broadcast on BBC 2 in 1984.[12] *The Big H* is a nativity play in which comedy is bizarrely but successfully combined with horror. It is a virtuosic play on the missing 'h' of Leeds speech; the resistance to efforts to replace his 'h's on the part of Boy 12 comes to represent resistance to all tyranny.

The central figure for violent oppression in the play is Herod. This nativity play reminds us that the story of Jesus is in fact a very violent one, and confronts us with what it really meant for Herod to order his soldiers to kill all boys under the age of two. In *The Big H* schoolteachers succumb to their 'inner Herod' and their initially repressed aggression towards students turns surreally into a literal killing spree, as certain of the students become 'the Prel', Herod's death squad, sent out to murder toddlers in an effort to eliminate potential rebelliousness before it even emerges. 'The Prel' is derived from the Leeds motto, *Pro Rege et Lege* (for king and law), and the play blatantly identifies the cultural tyranny of the effort to repress differences in speech with acts of physical violence and war (H-bomb, Hiroshima, Hanoi, Hamburg) and extremities of state control (H-block).

The play has moments of pure comedy, such as when the recalcitrant Boy 12 is engineered into the wrong place in the line so that he will be forced to deal with the letter 'H', but for most of the play the overtly comic mode, with its puns, ubiquitous alliteration and bizarre transformations, is startlingly used to convey real horror, as we recoil from the succession of gruesome descriptions of ways in which toddlers might be hurt and killed. This section is spoken by the three Herods, each taking alternate lines:

> Teeny-weenies under two, all tots still at their mothers' tits.
> Cherished chubby little cherubs, choke and chop to little bits,

Bazooka all bambinos that are newly born in Bethlehem.
If you have to murder millions then go ahead and
      murder 'em.
Millions of bloody babes I'll butcher and I'll barbecue,
Boil the buggers down to bones and bubbly barley
      sugargoo.[13]

This is supposed to echo comic children's verse, suggesting that the culture which professes to nurture children is in fact secretly aggressive – even murderous – towards them, or at least towards their potential difference and capacity to challenge authority.

The play ends, however, on a more positive note, as Boy 12, the innocent and persecuted dropper of 'aitches', steps forward to protest: 'Sir! / It's 'orrible, sir! I'm sick of all this 'orror!' (*BH*, 357). He manages to transform the three Herods into Wise Men, the twelve Mams sing alleluia, and the play ends with a special birth at Leeds Maternity Hospital:

    the cops have problems with the traffic flow
    as loads of folk come to Leeds to see
    the North's most noted Nativity,
    and the lions lay down with the lamb,
    and the lions lay down with the lamb! (361)

The genuine hope and exuberance of this last sequence of the play is qualified by the final line, spoken by Boy 12, who is busy writing his thirty thousand lines, 'Christ is Born Today', and who has learnt to be wary: 'And he'll grow up to be a teacher!' (361). Overall, the play is certainly not optimistic, given its pointed emphasis on the repetition of violence, tyranny and authoritarianism throughout history, and this final line emphasises the way in which hope can turn to devastation. As Herod's Mam says earlier in the play, 'when I see what 'e became / I wished 'e'd died in me' (340).

The Big H was just one of the many works for television, film and the stage which Harrison produced in the eighties and nineties. Throughout that time his reputation as a public poet, willing to engage vociferously and controversially with current events, grew steadily. Other poetry besides collaborative, dramatic, or translation work was collected, for the most part, in two books: *The Gaze of the Gorgon*, in 1992 (which included the text of the title film-poem as well as other poems, all except two previously published) and *Laureate's Block and Other Poems*, published in 2000. *Under the Clock* (London: Penguin, 2005) was published just as this book was being completed. During this period Harrison has demonstrated a continued and intensifying concern about war and atrocity, as well as artistic freedom. Although much of his poetry is still overtly political, Luke Spencer's comment on the individualism of Harrison's later stance is apt:

> the most recent work, for all its political courage and continuing sense of history, is largely characterised by a stance that is markedly individualistic in its libertarianism. There is still an exemplary social significance in the predicament of Salman Rushdie, or in Harrison's encounters with redneck Americans and know-nothing Brits; but there is no longer the sort of interaction between public and private which can represent personal experience as profoundly political or collective experience as an imperative incitement to personal commitment. Retreat from the brutality of contemporary life and the threat of nuclear extinction is a typical response from *V.* onwards.[14]

Although there may be exceptions to this, it is true that, as Spencer says, a poem like 'The Act', in which the poet-speaker encounters the rough Newcastle squaddies on the plane between Newcastle and Belfast, does not probe 'what has made these men what they are' and does not question 'whether they should be patrolling the streets of Belfast at all'.[15] Nor does it venture the kind of difficult dialogue between viewpoints that *V.* attempts, but wishes, for the Ulster poets to whom it is dedicated, a kind of safe retreat into domestic pleasure. We no longer see Harrison agonising over his separation from the working-class culture he is observing; there is a degree of emotional distance from the displaced aggression the squaddies express that contrasts starkly with *V.* and earlier poems.

Laureate's Block and Other Poems combines rather privately oriented poems about family, illness, friendship and leisure with documentary poems about Bosnia and manifestos such as the title poem, 'Laureate's Block', which was published in the *Guardian* during the period preceding the announcement of the new Poet Laureate, after Ted Hughes's death. Harrison's name had been mentioned in relation to the position, and he was eager to declare his contempt for this idea. In a review for the *Guardian* of the subsequent collection, *Laureate's Block*, Robert Potts describes the title poem as 'hubristic' and goes on to criticise Harrison's technique severely:

> There is much to dislike in the volume, but the worst thing about it is that the verse is bad. Harrison has been lauded so often for his technical skill, his facility with metre as a classicist and his ability to use the demotic alongside the elevated, that fewer and fewer people notice how cloth-eared he has become.[16]

Although this is much more descriptive of 'Laureate's Block', which is clearly meant to (and does) give the impression of being dashed off on the spur of the moment, than it is of some of the other poems in this volume, there is some truth in this criticism. One feels, at times, that Harrison has trapped himself within the predominantly iambic metrics and tight rhyme schemes that he has previously used with such success. He *has* truly 'occupied' the forms that have dominated English literature for centuries, and he has transformed our thinking about their capacity and potential in a contemporary context. Nevertheless, it is fascinating to speculate on what kind of poetic – and political – project might potentially emerge if Harrison allowed himself, at this late stage in his career, to experiment more in his use of form, perhaps even in the manner of Peter Reading, whose use of multiple complex metrical forms in combination with prose and free verse gives his poetry a keenness that Harrison's has, latterly, sometimes lacked.

Tom Leonard

Tom Leonard (b. 1944) shares Harrison's commitment to challenging the authoritarianism of the cultural elite and the repression of difference by those in positions of power. Harrison and Leonard also share a focus on the school as the site of cultural domination. Recently Leonard has found himself in the ironic position of providing materials on the internet for students who are studying his poetry for GCSE, despite the fact that he has argued strongly against the way in which literature is currently taught in schools. In 'The Proof of the Mince Pie', first published in *Scottish International* in 1973, Leonard argues that the education system in Britain requires students to simulate 'middle-class modulations' and reflects in its structure 'an essentially acquisitive attitude to culture',[17] a belief that literature is something that can be acquired through school and university education, just as a middle-class accent can be 'bought' by parents paying for private school education. The role of the literary critic, says Leonard, is 'to categorise, that the bourgeoisie might safely possess'; an exam demands that a student show his or her mastery or possession of the literary text rather than allowing any meaningful and challenging engagement with it (*IV*, 66). Such views are bound to induce a perhaps salutary sense of awkwardness for literary critics attempting to write about Leonard's own work, but they also suggest ways in which the education system can change for the better. In 'Poetry, Schools, Place', for example, he argues that 'the first right that ought to be maintained in the presence of a work of art is the right to silence, though this right to silence is precisely what the present educational system attempts to reject' (*Reports from the Present*, 24). The right to non-response, or to a response which takes the form of silence, is certainly something which should be acknowledged and valued as part of teaching practice, rather than valuing students' 'ability to speak convincingly of a personal encounter that has not usually taken place' (24).

The major collections of Leonard's work (*Intimate Voices: Selected Work 1965–1983* (1984), *Reports from the Present: Selected Work 1982–1994* (1995), and *access to the silence: poems and posters 1984–2004* (2004)) make it impossible for the reader to separate his prose work from his poetry. They contain essays, poems, poster-poems, cartoons, dramatic dialogues, and pieces that defy categorisation. They deliberately present poetry not as an esoteric, isolated art form but as a kind of conversational musing, a mode of entertainment, a political gesture, an everyday event, a form that exists side by side with and interacts with other disparate modes of writing. This is all part of Leonard's effort to retrieve poetry from behind the bastions of privilege, from its reification as an aesthetic object which can be categorised, explained and thus possessed. Leonard's poetry certainly resists conventional responses.

One of Leonard's most effective poetic strategies has been his use of a phonetically transcribed urban Glaswegian dialect or sociolect. At first glance these poems can be fairly opaque to the reader, and Leonard's speakers make no concessions: 'if yi canny unnirston thim jiss clear aff then / gawn / get tay fuck ootma road' (*IV*, 14). In the 1960s when this poem was first published,

Leonard's style was something very new. It is true that MacDiarmid and other writers of the so-called Scottish Renaissance had made it perfectly acceptable to write in Scots, while Highland writers were continuing the long tradition of literature in Scottish Gaelic. Both literary Scots and Gaelic had been mobilised within the Scottish nationalist movement, and were valued as signifiers of 'authentic' Scottish culture and history. However, Leonard's Glaswegian poetry was an entirely different matter, confronting deeply held prejudices against the urban vernacular. In his introduction to *Radical Renfrew*, Leonard quotes a schoolteacher from the 1930s who laments the state of 'the Doric of the populous centres of the country': 'It is not Scots at all, but a thing debased beyond tears. It is a mongrel patois due to lower class immigration from Ireland, from Lancashire mills, and the meaner streets of Glasgow.'[18]

As this quotation shows, the purists were particularly disturbed by Glasgow, which had absorbed a variety of linguistic influences due to its huge intake of people (including many Irish) during the industrial revolution, when Glasgow was called the 'second city of empire'. In the 1960s and 1970s Leonard and other writers set out to challenge these still persistent prejudices by writing a Glaswegian literature using the language really spoken in Glasgow. Leonard's phonetic spelling, differing deliberately from the traditional Scots spelling even when the pronunciation seems identical, has been influential in the decades since. Novelists James Kelman and Alasdair Gray, who, along with Leonard, were part of the writers' group run by Philip Hobsbaum in Glasgow in the 1970s, draw on similar techniques to evoke the difference and energy of Glaswegian speech. Leonard has commented on the key difference between himself and MacDiarmid, a writer he admires:

> One way I fundamentally differ from him is in wanting to use a language descriptive of what actually is linguistically, rather than prescriptive of what ought to be, or historically was: the difference between us is a common one between writers in a post-colonial state.[19]

Leonard, then, is certainly aware of his role in the development of Scottish culture, but because of the traditional disdain for Glaswegian Scots, his use of phonetic spelling, along with

Glaswegian slang and the distinctive syntactical features of Glaswegian speech, points at least as urgently to the issue of class as to that of nationality. Implicitly it exposes the limitations and elitism of Scottish nationalism, but more broadly it challenges all versions of 'correct' language, whether English, Scottish, or anything else. Moreover, Leonard does this with a humour that is simultaneously subtle and rough-edged, and with a mixture of warmth and edgy aggression.

Whether the reader belongs to the particular class of people that has acquired the asset of British 'R.P.', speaks the Glasgow dialect represented in the poems, or speaks some entirely different form of English, he or she has probably nevertheless been conditioned to expect that when a writer uses 'eye-dialect' to represent a character's speech, the writer is marking the character's difference and usually social inferiority. Usually the reader's assumption (right or wrong) is that the author him or herself does not speak with the accent or dialect indicated. Writers from Shakespeare to D.H. Lawrence are encountered in this way. In reading Leonard's poems we may at first apply this experience and expect the poet to be treating his characters as interesting sociolinguistic phenomena. In a review of Albert Mackie's *Talking Glasgow*, Leonard demonstrated that it is this above all that he wants to avoid:

> It's another of those 'warm-hearted' linguistic racist affairs, where all of 'us' good middle-class or ex-working-class folk can sit back and have a good laugh at how 'they' working-class Glaswegians talk ... Not a 'fuck' or a 'cunt' will disturb the pleasant time to be had by the reader ... Nowhere will real linguistic aggression or anger show alongside the of-course-always-bowdlerized 'humour'; the natives here are not even allowed the luxury of getting restless.[20]

Certainly Leonard's dialect poems make it difficult for the reader to assume a comfortably patronising stance toward the speakers. They also make it difficult to assume any single stance, as the poetry ranges so extremely from aggressive inarticulacy to warm expressiveness. Readers may have to confront their own prejudices and assumptions – perhaps the assumption, for example, that someone who speaks in a working-class dialect will not have the education to refer casually to Bertrand Russell, metaphysics, or Samuel Beckett, as the speaker in *Ghostie Men* does. The reader may take these poems – or the prose piece 'Honest' – as an indication that the appropriate stance towards the speakers is one of valorisation and affirmation, since the poems emphasise that culture and literacy are not merely the domain of the rich or those with middle-class accents. But that same reader may then be startled by poems like 'The Good Thief', which displays overt sectarianism ('ma right insane yirra pape / ma right insane yirwanny us jimmy'), 'Pffff', a chilling poem whose ending reveals that the woman whom the speaker blames for turning him on in the middle of the street is just a schoolgirl ('bluddy blaizir oanur tay / stullit fuckin skool'), or 'No Light', in which a speaker blandly recounts a knife attack on someone with the wrong kind of accent (' "i've not *got* a light," / hi sayz, dead posh') (*IV* 9, 56, 59). These poems demand that the reader take the speaker as he is, with no explanation or toning-down of aggression for a middle-class readership.

Some of Leonard's poems, such as 'The Good Thief', seem to distance the speaker from the poet (in this case through the title), while in others the poet is clearly identified with the speaker, as in 'right inuff': 'ma wife tellt mi jist-tay-get-inty-this-poem tellt mi' (*IV*, 120). The identification of poet and speaker in some poems, along with the wit and cleverness of some of the speakers, prevents readers from adopting a patronising attitude, and forces them therefore to confront and take seriously the challenge of the aggression, violence and prejudice which some of the poems also contain. We are given the impression of a poet who is passionate about giving voice to a full and diverse community of people, whose anger and aggression is presented as just as valid and important an expression of their reality as their meditations on language and love – of which there are many.

The poetry also seeks to demonstrate the expressiveness of Glasgow patois, but at the same time it conveys a sense of inarticulacy, or anxiety about the process of communication:

A Summer's Day

yir eyes ur
eh
a mean yir

pirrit this wey
ah a thingk yir
byewtifl like ehm

fact
fact a thingk yir
ach a luvyi thahts

thahts
jist thi wey it iz like
thahts ehm
aw ther iz ti say (*IV*, 41)

The speakers' insecurity about their own expressive capacity
often leads to a directness which is more expressive than any
more complex formulations would have been. Leonard makes it
clear where this anxiety about expression comes from; his most
well-known poem cleverly uses reported speech to contrive to
have a BBC presenter explaining in an urban Glaswegian accent
why he is in fact reading the news in a BBC accent:

coz yi
widny wahnt
mi ti talk
aboot thi
trooth wia
voice lik
wanna yoo
scruff. (*IV*, 88)

The poem has a humorous effect but at the same time makes
provocative suggestions, such as the idea that whenever someone
with a working-class accent listens to the television news the main
'message' he or she receives is not about the news but about his or
her own inferiority, and about the intransigence of the social link
between authority and language. Leonard's speakers vary in their
response to this kind of message, but many are cheerfully brusque
in their dismissal of it: 'ach well / all livin language is sacred /
fuck thi lohta thim' (*IV*, 120).

Leonard's poetry draws attention particularly to the plight of
working-class men. Many of his speakers in the Glaswegian
dialect poems are obviously male, and draw attention to specifically masculine experience. In *Ghostie Men* they show a sophisticated understanding of feminism, linking it to colonialism ('thaht
basturd therr / niz imperialist cock' (*IV*, 106)), but they suggest at
the same time that the life of a working-class man might not be

particularly privileged or satisfying:

    aye
    moanz aw thi time noo
    stucknthi hooss
    tied tay thi wainz
    unfulfillt

    no lik me thoa
    bagza overtime
    page three tay wank owr
    weekend nthi boozirz
    smashd ootma mind

    happy iz larry
    fulfillt iz fuck
    (*IV*, 116)

The first stanza suggests an old-fashioned male grumpily resistant to his wife's new concern with personal fulfillment and wanting to maintain the status quo, but the second and third stanzas make us reconsider this view as the speaker emerges as someone who is perhaps open to his wife's sense of lack of fulfillment but wants to take the argument further to question the satisfactoriness of traditional male roles.

Like Harrison's, Leonard's speakers use language which could be considered misogynist, but interestingly they use far less. The comparison suggests perhaps Harrison's anxiety about establishing his speakers' working-class credentials, and his consequent over-reliance on swearwords to do so. Leonard shows a greater awareness than Harrison of the implications for women of men's frustration and aggression, and he does not seek to reify the female into any kind of abstraction as Harrison does at the end of *V*. The poems which deal with sexuality are immersed in the concrete and seek to reverse gender stereotypes playfully, as when the male speaker in one poem says to his lover 'treat me izza sexual objict / mawn / roll doon ma wighz / slowly' and asks her 'huvyi any wee thingz / any wee hangups / dont feel daft / ahl hing thim upfur yi' (*IV*, 121). The sequence *Nora's Place*, written somewhat later and using conventional spelling, takes the point of view of a woman who is barely coping with the everyday pressures of hungry children, no money, a relationship which is faltering, a drinking habit and a debilitating anxiety: 'who on earth / tries to control their breath / on their way to the shops' (*RP*, 132).

In *access to the silence*, his new compilation of 'poems and posters' over two decades, Leonard includes 'Hesitations', a dialect sequence which in its visual presentation differs from any of the previous dialect poems. The first four poems in the sequence might seem to be of a kind with poems from *Ghostie Men*, but the fifth and sixth depart from this model with the inclusion of lines and arrows, and the seventh and ninth poems scatter letters and phonemes around the page. The significance of the arrows and lines is difficult to determine; they seem almost arbitrary products of the frustration of the attempt at expression, with phrases such as 'nah its' and 'a mean' preceding them.[21] The dispersed text is also resistant to interpretation, with the few recognisable semantic units in the first poem also suggesting a struggle with the process of expression – 'if its', 'ach' (*as*, 24). The second dispersed poem has more recognisable units and is suggestive of argument or dialogue: 'how?', 'don't be ridiculous!', 'a tellt yi that' (26). In their use of visual and disjunctive techniques associated with experimental poetry, these poems challenge our idea of what 'a dialect poem' looks like and does.

Leonard's poetry might be considered to share some of the interests of postmodernism in that its use of phonetic spelling draws attention to the materiality of language and complicates the notion of 'voice' in poetry. In the prose piece 'Honest' a writer mulls over the issue of speaking/writing:

> But ifyi write down 'doon' wan minute, nwrite doon 'down' thi nixt, people say yir beein inconsistent. But ifyi sayti sumdy, 'Whaira yi afti?' nthey say, 'Whut?' nyou say, 'Where are you off to?' they don't say, 'That's no whutyi said thi furst time.' They'll probably say sumhm like, 'Doon thi road!' anif you say, 'What?' they usually say, 'Down the road!' the second time – though no always. Course, they never really say, 'Doon the road!' or 'Down the Road!' at all. Least, they never say it the way it's spelt. Coz it *izny* spelt, when they say it, is it? (*IV*, 73)

Leonard's work seeks, as in this passage, to make the reader conscious of the conventional nature of sign systems like spelling and pronunciation, and in this sense he approaches postmodern concepts of language. The dialect poems in 'Hesitations' powerfully make us aware of the intransigent materiality of language, as the letters and phonemes seem to acquire a perplexing life of their own, making the scriptor resort to arrows and lines in an effort to create meaning. Poems such as 'The Rainbow Of' (*IV*, 81–5) create a sense of defamiliarisation through repetition, while the poster-poems in the 'Foodies' sequence help us to dislodge common words and phrases from their numbed familiarity:

> *a gastronomic epaulette :*
>   a chip on the shoulder
> *an old man's toenail clipping :*
>   a chip off the old bloke
> *a single European currency :*
>   the Brussels Sprout
> *what Goethe cried out on his deathbed :*
> (*as*, 120)   More chips! More chips!

Leonard's sense of the importance of typeface and spacing, his use of cartoons and other visual elements, and his fragmentation – in some poems – of word, phrase and sentence, might suggest that, in common with many postmodernist poets, he seeks to destabilise the notion that 'voice' is the fundamental of poetry. But many of the dialect poems in particular *do* appear to seek to capture the spoken word – or a particular variety of it – more accurately, and more realistically, than text has so far been able to do. It would be more accurate to suggest that Leonard at once allows the voice to inhabit poetry in a new way *and* creates a reading experience that is profoundly textual in nature. This strategy leads to provocative questions concerning the conventional nature of all language and the imbrication of language with systems of power. This latter point is more urgent for Leonard than questions about the nature of the self, but his poetry is incisive in its portrayal of the way in which modes of speech and shared discourses shape, define, empower and disempower the individuals who use them. To observe glibly that Leonard's poetry shows that the self is constructed by language is not enough; Leonard's poetry shows 'speakers' who grasp – somehow – an agency and an energy within a discourse which threatens to define them as 'non-speakers', and it therefore provokes us to pursue the question of the nature and scope of human agency.

Don Paterson

Although Harrison and Leonard are both still writing, they are perhaps most strongly identified with their work of the 1970s and 1980s, the years during which they first made an impact on the poetry-reading public. The significance of 'class' has changed radically for writers coming into their own after these decades. Don Paterson, a Scottish poet from a working-class background who was born in 1963 and published his first collection in 1993, is fascinating in this respect, because his poetry shows the influence both of Harrison and of Scottish poets like Leonard who explored the potential of urban Scottish speech. Paterson has repeatedly asserted the importance of Harrison's poetry in his initial impulse to write poetry seriously: 'I came across Tony Harrison – those elegies about his mum and dad – that really blew my mind. I read for a year after that.'[22] Paterson, who left school at sixteen and never went to university, embarked on a disciplined trajectory of poetry writing (he says that he began by reading the dictionary from cover to cover and equipping himself with the kind of education in technique which he had felt he lacked as a musician[23]) that resulted in remarkably rapid recognition. He was chosen as one of the New Generation poets the year after his first collection, *Nil Nil*, was published, and he has gone on to win a number of poetry prizes, including most recently the T.S. Eliot prize and the Whitbread poetry prize for *Landing Light* (2003). His most recent publication is a book of aphorisms, *The Book of Shadows*, which has thus far had a mixed critical reception.

Class has a much more muted presence in Paterson's poetry than it does in Harrison's and Leonard's work. This is characteristic of Paterson's generation. He is nineteen years younger than Leonard, and twenty-six years younger than Harrison. Whereas they experienced, as young men, a sense of excitement, belief and momentum in left-wing circles over issues such as labour activism, welfare, and equal access to education, Paterson's generation, in their twenties in the 1980s, experienced a rapidly changing labour market in which distinctions between working-class occupations and others were less clear, and a political environment in which the traditional left seemed to have lost its way. This has been accompanied by a decline in the perceived currency of the word 'class' itself. Within sociology there is an ongoing debate on whether 'class' is now an outmoded concept. In Britain the decline in the perceived importance of class as a concept can be linked directly to Thatcher's ideological emphasis on the individual as citizen and consumer rather than on people grouped together in classes, and to her success in defeating the trade unions and thus undermining working-class solidarity. However, it is also related to the fall of communism in Eastern Europe (since a politics oriented around class is often associated with Marxism), the rise of postmodernism (which has attacked the 'grand narratives' like Marxism which depend on class, and which undermines the notion that people have a primary class-based identity), and recent shifts in labour patterns that blur the traditional boundaries of class categories.

To talk in terms of class can seem, today, divisive and regressive; this is certainly how Thatcher sought to paint it. Even the Labour party, dependent as both main parties are on 'middle Britain', is much more likely to talk of 'communities' than of classes,[24] though both Tony Blair and his Conservative predecessor John Major announced their determination to achieve a 'classless society', thereby acknowledging that this task was still ahead of them.[25] Social and economic inequalities in contemporary Britain are plain to see, and recent research shows that the amount of mobility between different economic groups is not improving:

> As far as we can tell, the rate of social fluidity, meaning the social mobility that is not structurally inevitable on account of class differentials in birth rates and changes in the proportions of positions at different levels, is roughly the same at the beginning of the twenty-first century as it was at the beginning of the twentieth.[26]

None of the traditional models or narratives of class may be adequate for our twenty-first-century reality, but economic and social stratification is unquestionably still with us.

Poets of Paterson's generation have emerged in a social context in which class is not loudly spoken of, in which its significance is uncertain and ambiguous, but in which it is still insidiously present. Some assert their radical separation from the earlier anxieties of Harrison and others. W.N. Herbert, for example, says that

> I remember once in the Poetry Workshop … there were several poets who were strongly interested in this, with Tony Harrison

for example, with the whole sort of angst of becoming middle class through education. I never felt any angst about it! I never felt there was any sundering whatsoever.[27]

This may be true for Herbert, but as we read through Don Paterson's oeuvre, noting some intriguing interview comments and prose assertions, we begin to feel that *his* relationship with the previous generation, and indeed with the whole issue of class, is much more complex.

'An Elliptical Stylus', from *Nil Nil*, comes across as a deliberate declaration of affinity with, and also difference from, poets of an earlier generation. It takes off in a direction familiar from Harrison's sonnets and Heaney's 'Digging'; the poet-son remembering the working-class father and ruminating on continuities and differences between the two generations. Paterson's narrative differs from those precursors in that the remembered experience is also an artistic one of sorts – the father hears the quality of sound produced by the elliptical stylus on the uncle's turntable, and wants to buy one 'for our ancient, beat-up Phillips turntable'. Father and son meet with smirking condescension at the shop:

> We had the guy in stitches: 'You can't ...
> er ... you'll have to *upgrade your equipment.*'[28]

Paterson's next move grafts postmodern self-reflexivity onto the kind of explicit announcement of intention characteristic of Harrison, as the speaker proposes, in parentheses, to eavesdrop on an alternative poem, 'Fidelities', which he would have written had he been the son of the shop owner or manager. The italicised poem fragment plays, of course, on the words 'elliptical stylus'; just as the father leaves the stylus *'balanced / somewhere between ellipsis and precision'*, so the son lowers the pen to the page and waits *'for it to pick up the vibration'* (*NN*, 20), crafting a poem with the values of restraint, precision, clarity, balance.

There is an interesting twisting of the parable of Heaney's 'Digging', here; firstly, it is the sardonically presented poem fragment which imitates it, rather than the 'real' poem, and, secondly, it is used to present the middle class's safe inheritance of middle-class values, rather than being used to exemplify the working-class son's simultaneous break from and imitation of his father's skills and values. The poem then returns to the primary speaker, who records his father's hurt and then declares his refusal to

> cauterize this fable
> with something axiomatic on the nature
> of articulacy and inheritance,
> since he can well afford to make his *own*
> excuses, you your own interpretation.
> But if you still insist on resonance –
> I'd swing for him, and every other cunt
> happy to let my father know his station,
> which probably includes yourself. To be blunt. (21)

The precursor poems are acknowledged here in the poem's reluctance to provide the expected closure with a comment on 'the nature / of articulacy and inheritance'.

Paterson differs from his models in his direct address to the reader; Harrison's sonnets might implicate the reader in a general address like 'So right, yer buggers, then! We'll occupy / your lousy leasehold Poetry' (*SP*, 123), but Paterson's characteristic approach is to grab the individual reader by the collar and insist upon the idea of the poem as a personal exchange between poet-speaker and actual individual reader (an idea which in other Paterson poems is simultaneously asserted and undermined). The phrase 'well afford', implying wealth, links the reader with the smug shop owner, while the ending makes this aggressively clear. The poem imitates Harrison's sonnets in its confrontational stance towards the literary establishment and its assumption that 'received' poetry is inherently linked with class, but it is even more directly aggressive towards the reader. Paterson's poem also imitates Harrison's approach in its formal ironies; the working-class poet-speaker demonstrates his capacity to appropriate, mockingly, the tone of gentle nostalgia which he associates with middle-class verse, and in its entirety the poem, with its fluid iambics and interweaving rhymes (note the '-ance' and '-tion' rhymes which link stanzas three and four), demonstrates a commitment to appropriating traditional form; not least, of course, in that final very Harrisonian rhyme 'cunt'/'blunt' (we might note in passing that the gender politics of Paterson's poetry, while more self-conscious than Harrison's, are sometimes equally disturbing).

The mockery of the italicised passage is made more cutting by the fact that we know from the rest of *Nil Nil* that Paterson himself is master of 'an elliptical style', something that the quoted passage seems to espouse but not embody. The poem in context seems to assert Paterson's capacity as poet to be both blunt and elliptical, and all in a very self-aware manner, fully cognisant of precursors in all directions. In his sonnets Harrison is self-conscious of his position as a working-class poet in relation to the literary establishment; Paterson is self-conscious of his position in relation to a whole series of poems *about* being a working-class poet in a class-bound literary culture. The choice of a shop manager (or perhaps even shop assistant) as the representative of the dominant classes serves to reinforce the poet-speaker's credentials as '*real* working-class'.

An interview comment reveals Paterson's anxiety that middle-class readers will find the poem 'palatable':

> the poem … was intended as a deliberate inversion of the current practice of inviting the audience to 'share' the experience; I'm terrified some well-heeled wee bugger will come up to me afterwards and tell me how much he enjoyed it. I think there are some grudges that have to be renewed annually: poetry is a good way of making palatable things that should remain indigestible, making certain kinds of crime easier for both the perpetrator and the victim to live with. There are a lot of sub-Harrison types who see their poetry as lending dignity to the working-class experience, as commemorating it in the proper fashion, when what they're really dealing with is their own embarrassment with their social origins, and their awkwardness in using the language of their superiors. It's depressing to see the working classes patronise *themselves* in this way. But I do worry about talking too openly about this sort of thing – even brilliant poems like Dunn's 'The Come-on' and O'Brien's 'Cousin Coat' worry me; part of me thinks, no, no, you're telling the bastards too much, this should be circulated between ourselves, as in-house memoranda or something … paranoia, like I said. I suppose the Elliptical Stylus poem is really about my own inequality to the task, masquerading as frustration with the form.[29]

Certainly this poem is unusual within Paterson's oeuvre, and clearly this anxiety about self-exposure and exploitation (like

Harrison's shame at 'opening my trap / to busk the class that broke him') contributes to the relative reticence of Paterson's poetry on the issue of class.

'Blunt' and 'elliptical' are words that describe Paterson's poetry particularly well. His poems can be enigmatic in a Muldoonian manner, but in Paterson's poetry this is at times contrasted with an expansive lyricism (most evident in *The Eyes*, Paterson's versions of Machado (1999), and in *Landing Light*, which has obviously benefited from the Machado experience) and also, at times, with a rough humour that seems to assert the poetry's difference from the 'refined' style which 'An Elliptical Stylus' associates with middle-class poetry. In the 'Prologue' to Paterson's second collection *God's Gift to Women*, for example, we have Paterson's characteristic address to the reader, this time readers as a collective in the congregation for which a poem is 'a little church'. This is an amusing comparison of poetry to a sermon read to confined and bored listeners, attempting 'spiritual transport': 'Be upstanding. Now: let us raise the fucking *tone*.'[30] This is a signal that Paterson intends to disrupt the genteel monotony which poetry so often lets itself doze into.

Stylistically, however, Paterson takes a different route in this direction from either Harrison or Leonard. His style is remarkably varied throughout the three collections of his own poems that he has published, and even more varied if one counts the 'versions' included in *The Eyes*. Whereas in Harrison's and in Leonard's poetry we get the sense that the presentation of non-standard urban speech in poetry is something new and radical, something that must be pushed through in the face of resistance, Paterson clearly enjoys a freedom generated by the work of these earlier figures. He moves between diverse idioms in both English and Scots: the Scots-inflected English of a short poem like 'Filter' ('Whatever I do with all the black / is my business alone' (*NN*, 3); the lyrical, ballad-influenced rhythms of '00:00: Law Tunnel' ('I will go to my mother / and sing of my shame / I will grow up to father / the race of the lame' (*GGW*, 7); the childish Scots-inflected English of '11:00: Baldovan' ('me and Ross Mudie are going up the Hilltown / for the first time ever on our own' (*GGW*, 12); the urban Scots of 'Homesick Paterson, Live at the Blue Bannock, Thurso' ('Sure enough, jist the wey Eh'd left her, / / nursin a half o Irn Bru and tequila, / fannin hersel doon wi the *People's Friend*' (*GGW*, 22) and of 'Postmodern' ('Onywiy, three weeks later, the boy / thinks, Ach, the wife's oot, Eh'll hae another squint / at thon video again' (*GGW*, 51); and the more traditional Scots of poems like 'Form', 'Twinflooer' and 'Zen Sang at Dayligaun' (all from *Landing Light*).

Paterson does have a kind of 'default idiom', which is a predominantly English idiom with some Scots vocabulary and phrasing, and within this context the Scots poems appear as refreshing interludes. His primary style is not oriented towards speech patterns in the way that Tom Leonard's is; he employs a linguistic register which is much more 'literary' in its range, and places emphasis on formal patterning. It is influenced most noticeably by Muldoon, Longley and Derek Mahon, with Harrison a fading presence as the poetry develops. One could wish, perhaps, for a further development of the Scots poetry, which does tend to be limited to chatty narrative on the one hand, and lyrical meditation on the other; the layered intricacy of a poem like 'The Alexandrian Library' or even 'Nil Nil' is missing from the Scots poems. Paterson has commented in interview on his sense of the lack of a 'middle way' in Scots between 'the basilect, that's to say a tongue my mother was anxious for me not to speak' and literary Scots: 'The middle way doesn't exist, the tongue in which intelligent Scots could discuss politics, or culture, or whatever; and it *can't* exist until we reappropriate a classical vocabulary, something long denied to us through our political and cultural disenfranchisement.'[31] Leonard's inclusion of 'intellectual' vocabulary in his dialect poems may be seen as one possible response to this state of affairs.

Though less obviously than for Leonard, class is still an issue for Paterson in the poems which use non-standard forms. 'Postmodern', for example, is a poem written in urban Scots about a man who accidentally records the reflection of himself masturbating as he watches and tapes a porn video. Paterson has said 'it was a squib but it was actually trying to make a semi-serious point about self-reflection.'[32] Why does Paterson choose to write this poem – narrate the story – in an urban, working-class Scots idiom? Surely because it invites the middle-class reader to apply his or her prejudices about working-class men, and then encounter those prejudices guiltily as he or she absorbs the poem's point about self-reflection. At the same time, of course, the poem mocks the grandiosity of postmodernism's ruminations by literalising the idea of self-reflection, and by mocking the academic reader: 'Dye no' get it? Will Eh hae tae *explain* it tae ye?' (*GGW*, 51).

'Homesick Paterson, Live at the Blue Bannock, Thurso', is also interesting because of the inclusion of Paterson's own name in the title. If we know that Paterson himself is a musician as well as a poet it becomes clear that Paterson is proffering an alternative version of the poet persona to the reader, and perplexing us with the question of how much the poet we know as Don Paterson, who writes lines like 'To the God of absence and of aftermath, / of the anchor in the sea, the brimming sea' (*GGW*, 56), also identifies with the 'Hameseek' Paterson who says things like 'he'd the sort o puss ye'd never tire o hittin' (*GGW*, 21). Although Paterson's poems do not foreground the link between language and class as forthrightly as Leonard's and Harrison's, such movement between idioms unsettles easy assumptions about class categories.

Paterson's poetry might also be seen to reflect Britain during and after Thatcher's period in power in its stark portrayal of a kind of impoverished urban existence in poems like the first part of 'The Alexandrian Library'. Ken Roberts describes (in 2001) the effect of post-1970s economic changes on the working class:

> It has shrunk in size and it has been disorganized by the spread of unemployment and job insecurity ... The good jobs that remain have become less secure and the workers in these jobs are now under greater pressure in the workplace. Meanwhile, sections of the working class have been impoverished. They are concentrated in the inner-cities and on 'sink' council estates which have spectacularly high levels of unemployment, single parenthood and crime rates, and low educational standards.[33]

Surely this is the kind of ravaged image of contemporary Britain – specifically, Scotland – that is reflected in the first part of 'The Alexandrian Library', in *Nil Nil*. This is not, however, documentary social realism; 'The Alexandrian Library', taking inspiration from Borges's story 'The Library of Babel', is a weird and surreal tale of the search for the 'great' book or poem. In Paterson's words, the poem is attempting 'to imagine what would be in that great book rather than actually trying to write it': 'perhaps when you do stumble across the great book it's not so great; but when you imagine the great book then it is, and to talk about that you might end up writing it by default.'[34]

The poem is written in the second person, so that the reader is drawn inexorably into the gyre of the poem's trajectory, which

proceeds as a disturbing dream through strangely blighted
worlds: a desolate train journey on a closed-down line, a tene-
ment and allotments, and the faintly comical and exhausted cultural detritus of Harry Sturgis's second-hand bookshop. Finally,
we are spun back through 'Planck-Time / Absolute Zero / Albedo
Fuck-All' to the world of 'Mare Insomniae' where the reader/poet
is awake and alone:

> And you listen:
> but it is only the milk-train
>
> or your heart,
> pounding over the points. (*NN*, 33)

This impressive poem demands in-depth analysis of the kind I
cannot provide in this chapter; I will restrict myself to commenting merely on the way in which the imagery of impoverishment
and urban decay is central to the poem.

The initial train ride, itself on a disused line, passes through a
landscape of desertion:

> You pass the closed theme-park, a blighted nine-holer,
> the stadium built for a cancelled event
> now host to less fair competition:
> a smatter of gunfire pinks at your cheek
> as it leans on the glass. Now the line curves
> over pitheads and slagheaps, long towns with one street
> where only the kirk strains much above ground-level. (26)

When the human inhabitants of this landscape are finally encountered, they are equally desolate:

> you set off on foot
> for the northernmost tip of a council estate,
> for the last Pictish enclave, where beaky degenerates
> silently moon at the back of the shops
> while girls with disastrous make-up and ringworm
> stalk past with their heads down and arms folded.
> You are drawn inside the stone mouth of a tenement
> where a young woman, soaping it out on her knees,
> watches you try the blue door by the bin-recess
> before shaking her head, then nodding you over. (26–7)

This is some form of dream, and as such it is a representation of the hinterland of the mind. Paterson's stance is not that of the liberal commentator or documentary realist who approaches urban decay and impoverishment from the outside, as something to be noted, pitied and remedied; instead, these scenes are part of an internal landscape, the territory of memory within which the 'you' of the poem struggles to make the connections, to 'recollect something important' (27). There is a kind of fear and disgust, along with an element of mockery, in his portrayal of the 'beaky degenerates' and the 'girls with disastrous make-up and ringworm'.

This scene has little in common with the working class of Harrison's sonnets or even the angry but still engaged unemployed of Harrison's *V.*; this is instead a hopeless underclass, an excluded class that inhabits a surreal underworld. This is interesting given that there was much debate during the nineties over whether Thatcher's policies had created a new 'underclass' of excluded citizens in Britain. It is also fascinating that whereas both Harrison and Leonard frame the issue of poverty and exclusion in the context of the need for change, and actually seek in their poems to effect change, Paterson's poetry mostly avoids such activist implications. There is no sense that anything will change because of the journey into 'the dream-warren'; merely that the memory will remain to haunt as 'that part of the mind that the mind cannot contemplate' (33).

Paterson's comments on the poem are interesting if slightly glib:

> The search for some kind of absolute autochthony, something I'm pretty obsessed with, becomes exactly that – a very physical, very daft journey to this Pictish enclave … then when that's failed, when it's discovered that there's only this wee black hole at the centre of things, the focus of the search becomes the lost library, for continuity.[35]

The word 'autochthony' is perhaps helpful; it emphasises the way in which the poem searches for a specifically Scottish rootedness. The poem looks for this in a working-class context – note the 'pitheads and slagheaps' (26) – but is confronted with the complete devastation of any sense of community, while the desire for an absolute nativeness is mocked in the vision of the 'last Pictish enclave' (26). There is more to the poem, though, than the simple failure to find absolute rootedness or continuity; the anxiety which is reflected in the image of the 'horror' which pursues, 'stamping and snorting behind you' (31), also suggests a fear of regression or descent, a fear of losing one's safe and carefully acquired distance from poverty and the absurd low-brow banality of Harry Sturgis's bookshop. In this sense it can be seen as a comment on the relationship between the upwardly mobile and the excluded in contemporary Britain.

When one reads Paterson's introduction to *New British Poetry* (discussed also in Chapter 7) one begins to think that some of the anxiety may belong to Paterson himself, and in a rather unexamined sense. Despite his efforts to underline his own working-class credentials in this introduction, he comes across as strenuously defending a non-threatening, populist/establishment poetics which is content to depend on a purely middle-class readership. His strangely inflated sense of persecution by the 'Postmoderns' seems to rest on their prestige within the academy (despite the fact that, as Andrea Brady points out, the majority of the poets included in his own anthology work or have worked in universities[36]), while his ideological opposition to them centres on the fact that they believe in the possibility of art being revolutionary, and in 'the false and very un-British paradigm of artistic progress'.[37] Whatever we make of that, Paterson's alternative paradigm, a British mainstream characterised by a 'happy accommodation', a tradition which displays 'a relatively seamless evolution', is surprising in the strenuousness of its effort to smooth over the differences and conflicts within the history of British poetry.[38] Rather intriguing, as well, is his remark that the eventual number of *Poets Against the War* (1500) published in the Nth Position e-book 'would seem to undermine the usefulness of the designation "poet" '.[39] Such comments contribute to an image of Paterson as strangely anxious about the possibility of any erosion of his own status as 'poet', whether by the proliferation of poetry on the internet or by any increase in the status of experimental poetry in universities. Perhaps this prose piece was written in haste – mistakes such as the failure to give the correct title for Keith Tuma's *Anthology of British and Irish Poetry* suggest that not much editing was done – but it certainly does make one wonder about the extent to which Paterson's poetry *might* perhaps be shaped by an anxiety about attaining a specifically middle-class status as 'poet'. It is notable that despite the intensity of an early poem like 'An Elliptical Stylus', explicit treatment of class has almost vanished from Paterson's later work. Sean O'Brien suggests in *The Deregulated Muse* that what Paterson 'does *not* write will also exert an effect on his poems'.[40] Perhaps, however, the built-up pressure is being deflected into his prose.

Conclusion

Class is an issue for many more poets covered in this book besides the three I have chosen to focus on here. Peter Reading is of particular significance, I think, as a critic and lamenter of the state of social and economic relationships in contemporary Britain, as my discussion of his work in Chapter 7 can only begin to show, while issues of class are also crucial for many poets within the experimental community. But Tony Harrison, in particular, will be probably remembered as the poet who, in the twentieth century, did the most to break down the elitism and class-bound nature of poetry in Britain.[41] Crucial to his achievement has been his concentration not only on the content and style of his poetry, but on the media through which it reaches the public. The success of film-poems like *V.* has led to a much greater receptiveness on the part of television production companies to the idea of using poetry on television; Simon Armitage and Jackie Kay are just two of the poets who have recently been able to make and broadcast what one might call 'documentary film-poems'.[42] But despite the impact which Harrison's forays into different media have made, it is perhaps the early sonnets from *The School of Eloquence* that other poets will look to most frequently, as both a revelation and a critique of the cultural, social and economic chasms in British society.

Notes

1 Tony Harrison, *Selected Poems*, 2nd ed. (London: Penguin, 1987), p. 166. Henceforth referred to as *SP*.

2 Luke Spencer, *The Poetry of Tony Harrison* (Hemel Hempstead: Harvester Wheatsheaf, 1994), pp. 37, 40.

3 Ken Worpole, 'Scholarship boy', *Tony Harrison*, ed. Neil Astley (Newcastle upon Tyne: Bloodaxe, 1991), pp. 61–74 (pp. 62–3).

4 Worpole, 'Scholarship boy', p. 62.

5 Douglas Dunn, 'Formal strategies in Tony Harrison's poetry', *Tony Harrison*, ed. Astley, pp. 129–32 (p. 130).

6 Spencer, *The Poetry of Tony Harrison*, p. 73.

7 Interestingly, John Haffenden, in an interview with Harrison, attempted to question him about the defensiveness in this line, but Harrison's reply doesn't address this, suggesting that he does not see this quality in it. *Tony Harrison*, ed. Astley, pp. 227–53 (p. 233). Interview originally published in *Poetry Review*, vol. 73, no. 4 (1984), pp. 17–30.

8 Spencer, *The Poetry of Tony Harrison*, p. 74.

9 Blake Morrison, *The Independent*, Sunday 24 October 1987. Quoted in the Bloodaxe edition of *V.* and relevant journalism: Tony Harrison, *V.*, 2nd ed. (Newcastle upon Tyne: Bloodaxe, 1989), p. 56. All future references to *V.* will relate to this edition.

10 Ian Hislop, *The Listener*, Thursday 29 October 1987. Quoted in *V*, p. 62.

11 I have used the spelling and punctuation of the original Bloodaxe edition of *V.* for this stanza, as the later edition seems to include errors.

12 Because the televised version of this play is so difficult to get hold of, I will be discussing the text only.

13 Tony Harrison, *The Big H*, in *Dramatic Verse 1973–1985* (Newcastle upon Tyne: Bloodaxe, 1985), pp. 321–61 (pp. 354–5). Henceforth referred to as *BH*.

14 Spencer, *The Poetry of Tony Harrison*, p. 127.

15 Ibid., pp. 120–1.

16 Robert Potts, 'Bathetic fallacies', Guardian, 26 February 2000, http://books.guardian.co.uk/reviews/poetry/0,,140635,00.html, accessed 7 October 2004.

17 Tom Leonard, *Intimate Voices: Selected Work 1965–1983* (London: Vintage, 1995, first published 1984), p. 65. Since individual volumes of Leonard's work are relatively difficult to access, references to his poetry will be to the three major collections of his work, *Intimate Voices*, *Reports from the Present*, and *access to the silence*. *Intimate Voices* will henceforth be referred to as *IV*.

18 Tom Leonard, *Reports from the Present: Selected Work 1982–1994* (London: Cape, 1995), p. 53. Henceforth referred to as *RP*.

19 Dan Stephen, 'Talking to Tom Leonard', *Variant*, vol. 2, no. 5 (Spring 1998), pp. 27–8 (p. 28).

20 Tom Leonard in *Aquarius*, no. 12 (1980), p. 124. Quoted in Edwin Morgan, *Crossing the Border: Essays on Scottish Literature* (Manchester: Carcanet, 1990), p. 326.

21 Tom Leonard, *access to the silence: poems and posters 1984–2004* (Buckfastleigh: Etruscan Books, 2004), pp. 22–3. This collection overlaps with *Reports from the Present*; both include the sequences 'Situations Theoretical and Contemporary' and 'Nora's Place'. Henceforth referred to as *as*.

22 Matt Seaton, 'It's a slow process', *Guardian*, 30 March 2004, www.guardian.co.uk/g2/story/0,,1127411,00.html, accessed 7 October 2004.

23 Christina Patterson, 'Don Paterson: Playing the beautiful game', *Independent*, 9 January 2004, http://enjoyment.independent.co.uk/books/interviews/story.jsp?story=479285, accessed 7 October 2004.

24 As David Cannadine puts it, Tony Blair 'has expressed no ambition to promote class consciousness or incite class conflict. On the contrary, these venerable part nostrums are the "great absence" from his political vision and his political vocabulary. Like John Major, only more so, he is primarily interested in talking about community, consensus and conciliation, and

class gets in the way of such talk.' *The Rise and Fall of Class in Britain* (New York: Columbia University Press, 1999), p. 13.

25 Quoted in ibid., pp. 185, 187.

26 Ken Roberts, *Class in Modern Britain* (Basingstoke: Palgrave (now Palgrave Macmillan), 2001), p. 15.

27 W. N. Herbert, interview in Verse, vol. 7, no. 3 (1990), pp. 89–96 (p. 90). Quoted by David Kennedy in *New Relations: The Refashioning of British Poetry 1980–1994* (Bridgend: Seren, 1996), p. 19.

28 Don Paterson, *Nil Nil* (London: Faber, 1993), p. 20. Henceforth referred to as *NN*.

29 Don Paterson, interview with Raymond Friel in *Talking Verse*, eds Robert Crawford, Henry Hart, David Kinloch and Richard Price (St Andrews and Williamsburg, VA: Verse, 1995), p. 193.

30 Don Paterson, *God's Gift to Women* (London: Faber, 1997), p. 1. Henceforth referred to as *GGW*.

31 Don Paterson, interview with Raymond Friel, p. 192.

32 John Stammers, 'Private enterprise for the public good', interview with Don Paterson, *Magma*, vol. 12 (1998), http://magmapoetry.com/poem.php?article_id=42, accessed 7 October 2004.

33 Roberts, *Class in Modern Britain*, p. 118.

34 Stammers, interview with Don Paterson.

35 Don Paterson, interview with Raymond Friel, p. 197.

36 Andrea Brady, ' "Meagrely provided": A response to Don Paterson', *Chicago Review*, vol. 49, nos 3&4, and vol. 50, no. 1 (Summer 2004), pp. 396–403 (pp. 397–8).

37 Don Paterson and Charles Simic (eds), *New British Poetry* (Saint Paul, MN: Graywolf, 2004), p. xxiv.

38 Paterson and Simic, *New British Poetry*, p. xxiv.

39 Ibid., p. xxviii.

40 Sean O'Brien, *The Deregulated Muse: Essays on Contemporary British and Irish Poetry* (Newcastle upon Tyne: Bloodaxe, 1998), p. 266.

41 Class clearly operates differently in Ireland, Scotland and Wales than it does in England, and this chapter has sought to bring this out to some extent through the discussion of Scottish writers. However, the intersections of class with issues of nationalism, religion, language and the relationship to England are perhaps even more complex in Ireland, because of the greater intensity of the colonial/postcolonial relationship between Ireland and Britain in the twentieth century. The Irish context would require a separate discussion.

42 Armitage has written (and in some cases presented) a number of verse pieces for television, including the documentaries *Drinking for England* (1998) and *Saturday Night* (1996) and the film-poem *Xanadu* (1992). Jackie Kay's documentary *Twice Through the Heart* was broadcast on BBC television in 1992.

2

'My tongue is full of old ideas': Race and Ethnicity

Benjamin Zephaniah, Jackie Kay, Moniza Alvi

Patience Agbabi's poem 'The Black The White and The Blue' gives a snapshot of prejudice in London life. PC Edward White, 'East End born East End bred', is both racist and guiltily gay; as one of the 'boys in blue' he beats up black and Asian men, but after his night-time transformation into a 'West End fag' he is himself the target of violence:

> West End fag West End fag
> stabbed in the back by an East End lad
> son of a racist left him for dead
> boy in blue is covered in red
> Black man Asian man
> kisses his lips and holds his hand
> *Nigger Paki Queer*
> when will we walk the streets without fear?[1]

The poem is compelling in performance, delivered by Agbabi in a rhythmic staccato style with powerful use of pauses. The repetition and parallelism are crucial in the poem's communication of the incessant return and repetition of violence and prejudice as well as the damage inflicted by repetitive derogatory labelling. Agbabi is one of Britain's most exciting performance poets,[2] and, in common with many other performance poets in Britain, she takes advantage of the direct and personal connection between poet and audience in the performance context to make forceful comments on political issues. One of the issues that is central to her work, and to the writing of the three poets discussed in detail in this chapter, is race.

'Race' is currently one of the most problematic terms around. For several decades there has been widespread agreement among scholars that racial categories have no basis in genetic difference.[3] Given this recognition, and given that racial discourses have historically been overwhelmingly destructive, should we not seek to move away altogether from thinking in terms of 'race'; should we avoid couching our arguments in terms of racial categories, despite the fact that they are still pervasive in popular and political discourse? This is the argument put forward by Paul Gilroy in *Against Race*, as he argues for a new humanism that rejects racial categorisations entirely. But Gilroy also admits that this may be difficult even – perhaps especially – for those groups who have previously been oppressed by racialised discourse:

> When ideas of racial particularity are inverted in [a] defensive manner so that they provide sources of pride rather than shame and humiliation, they become difficult to relinquish. For many racialized populations, 'race' and the hard-won, oppositional identities it supports are not to be lightly or prematurely given up.[4]

There are various responses to this situation on the part of academics, most of them involving the careful enclosing of 'race' within quotation marks to signal its contentious nature. One response has been the gradual shift in both popular and academic discourse towards a preference for the term 'ethnicity' over 'race'. 'Ethnicity' implies cultural rather than biological commonality; it is also much more fluid than 'race', as one's ethnic identification might change according to context. Ethnicity clearly sits better with postmodern concepts of identity formation than race does, as it involves some element of self-definition and its categories are not absolute but created and shaped as part of a process of social interaction. Interestingly, however, the term 'race' often seems exactly the right one to use in the context of poetry in Britain today; this is because many poets are concerned to reveal the pervasiveness and persistence of racism which is based overtly on physical characteristics.

This chapter does not cover any poets who would identify as 'white' and have no familial links with cultures outside the British Isles. This I regret, as it is important not to convey the message (all too often encountered) that race is something that is of sole concern to non-white communities and individuals. 'White' people all too often see others as racially marked, and themselves as not 'raced'. Recent theoretical work is doing much to examine the concept of whiteness and its operations in society. However, in making decisions about coverage for this book, I was confronted with a very large group of 'non-white' poets (or poets who have a familial connection with a non-Western culture) writing compellingly and passionately about race and ethnicity, and a paucity of 'white' poets making it a central theme in their writing. Given the limitations on space within this book and this chapter, the inclusion of a 'white' poet whose work is not centred on the issues at hand, at the cost of excluding another for whom the issues of race and ethnicity are crucial, seemed wrong. Nevertheless, I acknowledge that this decision leaves a gap in my discussion.[5]

Thirty years ago it would have been obvious that the main problem facing black and Asian poets in Britain was one of marginalisation and invisibility. Today there is another and quite different danger: that of appropriation and commodification by the academic and literary establishment. Marginality was perhaps never trendier than it has been over the last decade, and it is hard work finding a poet who does not present him or herself as 'in-between', hybrid, marginal or 'other' in some aspect of his or her life. Such a climate poses risks. As bell hooks says, 'Often this speech about the other annihilates, erases. No need to hear your voice when I can talk about you better than you can speak yourself.'[6] This comment points to the danger that poets and their poetry might be snapped up by literary and cultural critics as mere tools or materials in an authoritative discourse in which the dominant voice is in fact the critic's. Self-exposure might be exploited. As Heidi Safia Mirza argues, 'We undertake journeys of self-discovery, which are then appropriated and recorded as objective knowledge, "original context", and "specificities". The dominant culture achieves hegemony precisely by its capacity to convert and recode for the authoritative other.'[7] These comments must make us as critics self-conscious of our own role in the dominant culture; clearly such texts as my own must seek not to 'recode' in such a way that the real disruptiveness of the original voices is downplayed or repressed.

There is certainly a danger of co-opting and commodification – as Patience Agbabi puts it in 'The Rap-Trap', 'Slack went / the rhymes / when you signed on the dotted line'.[8] But Lola Young argues that in Britain, at least for black women artists and intellectuals, the problem is still one of underexposure rather than commodification.[9] It may be that some few figures have received accolades and attention but the large majority of black and Asian poets still struggle to be published and reviewed. One poet who *has* achieved success on many mainstream platforms is Benjamin Zephaniah, and he has been the focus of arguments suggesting that the literary establishment only rewards those black poets who are perceived as harmless and non-threatening. Kwame Dawes quotes Zephaniah's appreciation of the British Council's liberalism in paying him to 'travel the world, … speaking my mind as I go, ranting, praising, and criticizing everything that makes me who I am', and responds that,

> As a British representative he is a curiosity, a figure whose ranting against Britain allows Britain to declare its wonderful liberal sensibility. Where Linton Kwesi Johnson is sometimes vilified and feared for his hard-hitting reggae verse, Zephaniah is loved. Perhaps this may merely be a product of personality, but I suspect there is a great deal more going on there. One sometimes has the impression that Zephaniah is seen as harmless. Who knows if this is true? But what I miss in him is the irony to recognize that he may actually have been co-opted by the very system he denounces.[10]

This is the kind of criticism that may be directed rather too easily at individuals who have managed to achieve unprecedented mainstream acceptance, but it is nevertheless a serious charge, and I will seek to test its validity in the coming pages. The fact that we are having this debate at all, however, shows that black British poetry is no longer indubitably 'marginal'. In fact, R. Victoria Arana argues that avant-garde black British poets 'do not see themselves as "speaking back" to a hegemonic center; they consider themselves the new leaders, the ones who are doing the speaking out, issuing the orders, steering the nation into the new millenium.'[11] Arana's argument is a little strained at times, but clearly the coming of age of a new generation of black and Asian Britons who do not see themselves as immigrants and have their own 'centres' of cultural life has generated a confident and thriving arts and music scene which is recognised almost universally as being at the forefront of British cultural life.

So far I have been using the term 'black' as if it is unproblematic, but it is of course supremely contentious. In 1989 Stuart Hall, a leading cultural studies theorist, proclaimed 'the end of the innocent notion of the essential black subject'.[12] Although the term 'black' has never been uncontentious, since the 1980s there has been a new recognition of

> the extraordinary diversity of subjective positions, social experiences and cultural identities which compose the category 'black'; that is, the recognition that 'black' is essentially a politically and culturally *constructed* category, which cannot be grounded in a set of fixed trans-cultural or transcendental racial categories.[13]

The struggle to formulate a non-essentialist concept of blackness that can still operate as a vehicle for political activism is ongoing.

In this chapter I have been using the phrase 'black and Asian' as shorthand for the majority of poets in Britain who have a familial connection to a non-Western culture. Obviously this is deeply problematic. 'Asian' is as difficult a term as 'black', being used to refer to people from vastly diverse cultures, and referring to entirely different groups in different parts of the world. Some Asians have taken on aspects of 'black' culture, and have embraced the term 'black' as something with which they identify, while many Caribbean poets of Indian origin are immersed in both 'black' and 'Asian' culture. Clearly the phrase 'black and Asian' leaves many cultural groups out entirely, and ridiculously obliterates differences even between those people who would identify as one, the other, or both. Other poets who are labelled 'British Asian' or 'black British' would prefer simply to be called 'British', disliking the constant referencing of race/ethnicity and feeling far more British than anything else. At the same time these terms are positive signifiers of identity for many people. Clearly they need to be used with the greatest caution and an awareness of their potential clumsiness – and with a sensitivity to the historical shifts in the usage of the terms.

Of all the immigrant communities in Britain, the Caribbean community has been the most prominent in the poetry scene, and British poets of Caribbean origin have consistently made issues of race, ethnicity and culture central to their writing. Edward Kamau Brathwaite in the sixties and Linton Kwesi Johnson in the seventies and eighties were the first poets of Caribbean origin to make a major impact on British poetry publishing, and Johnson in particular remains a vital role model for young black poets today. Both Brathwaite and Johnson were influenced by black music genres; Brathwaite by jazz and blues, and Johnson by reggae. It was Brathwaite who coined the term 'nation language' as a positive, politically assertive replacement for 'creole', 'patois' or 'dialect', all of which had negative connotations. Brathwaite's arguments for the use of 'nation language' (including the memorable phrase 'The hurricane does not roar in pentameters'[14]) have influenced writers from other postcolonial contexts to write in non-standard English. Linton Kwesi Johnson's innovation was primarily in his adoption and transformation of the Jamaican DJ's habit of 'chatting' or 'toasting' to the instrumental versions of reggae singles. Johnson coined the term 'dub poetry' himself in an effort to draw attention to the poetic nature of much of this improvisation by DJs, but it caught on as a label for his own poetry.[15]

Linton Kwesi Johnson's first books and albums were produced in a climate of growing social and political tension around the issue of race. Johnson, who was a member of the Black Panthers and the Brixton-based Race Today collective, saw – and still sees – his art as a poetry of protest, which derives its power and passion from a heritage of creative expression under conditions of oppression. He sees the reggae rhythm as inherently revolutionary, emerging out of a history of black suffering:

> muzik of blood
> black reared
> pain rooted
> heart geared[16]

Johnson's success in combining politics, poetry and music made him an important role model for many younger artists, including Benjamin Zephaniah.

Benjamin Zephaniah

Benjamin Zephaniah was born in 1958 in Handsworth, Birmingham, to Jamaican parents. Apart from some childhood years spent in Jamaica, he lived in Birmingham until he moved to London in 1980. After a rough adolescence and two years in jail he emerged into the performance poetry and reggae scene, emulating LKJ in his determination to speak and sing about everyday life in Britain. As well as poetry and novels for children and teenagers, he has published six collections of poetry for adults: *Pen Rhythm* (1980), *The Dread Affair: Collected Poems* (1985), *Inna Liverpool* (1988), *City Psalms* (1992), *Propa Propaganda* (1996), and *Too Black, Too Strong* (2001). Here I will be concentrating on the three most recent collections, which contain Zephaniah's strongest poetry. Zephaniah has also released several reggae albums, and he performs his poetry widely.

Zephaniah's poetry and prose conception of 'blackness' is interesting in relation to the theoretical debate around that term. In the poem 'As a African' he uses the term 'African' rather than 'black', but his perspective answers calls for an inclusive definition of blackness: 'As a African', 'I was a Arawak, / A unwanted baby, / A circumcised lady, / I was all a dis / An still a African'.[17] In the preface to *Too Black, Too Strong*, he says that

> When I say 'Black' it means more than skin colour, I include Romany, Iraqi, Indians, Kurds, Palestinians, all those that are treated black by the united white states. I can hear cries of 'What?' already, but I have to say the suffering I have witnessed means that my conscience allows me to include the battered White woman, the tree dwellers and the Irish; the Irish after all are the largest immigrant group in Britain, and I still remember the notices that said 'No Blacks, No Irish, No Dogs'. My Black is profound.[18]

Zephaniah's stance approaches theoretical perspectives like that of Lola Young, who argues for a political notion of blackness which is 'fundamentally about recognizing oppression and struggle' and should be 'read *against* an essential notion of blackness related to the gradation of skin colour or "racial" origins: "black" used in its inclusive term could refer to a range of ethnic and national groups.'[19] Zephaniah's articulation of this kind of idea does risk eliding the differences between the kinds of oppression and persecution suffered by various groups, but it also offers a powerful platform of solidarity.

Given the fact that black male activism (and art) has often been slow to address the sexism within its own culture, it is important to note Zephaniah's frequent focus on sexism within all cultures. 'As a African' draws attention to the practices of female genital mutilation in African and other cultures, while 'The Woman Has to Die', also in *Too Black, Too Strong*, attacks the practice of punishment by death for a woman who chose her own lover in a Muslim culture. 'She's crying for many', in *City Psalms*, is a heartfelt plea for a woman being beaten by her male partner. Most readers would probably assume that the woman is black, since the speaker calls her his 'sista' and says that 'She is flesh of me flesh / I am bone of her bone' (55), but if we take seriously Zephaniah's claim to identify with all battered women equally as 'black' in the political sense, perhaps we cannot assume anything about her race. Here, as in many other poems ('Man to Man', for instance), the culture of macho aggression which encourages male violence is criticised: 'So yu are "De Man", / Easy man, if yu can, / Dat's me sista yu beating upstairs' (*CP*, 55). Sometimes there is a tendency to essentialise femininity into a kind of universal, idealised womanhood; this is particularly noticeable in relation to motherhood, as in 'To Ricky Reel', a poem about the Asian victim of a 1997 racial attack in Kingston, London: 'every time I see your mother / I think of womanhood' (*TBTS*, 22). But this kind of univeralisation is perhaps a feature of Zephaniah's poetry generally, rather than something specific to his treatment of women. Zephaniah constantly moves from the individual to the general, from personal detail to political principle, from the specific case to the general pattern. This is what makes his poetry so relentlessly activist; he foregrounds both individual experience and the broader political and cultural structures in which these experiences are embedded and by which they are produced.

It is interesting that Kwame Dawes's concern over the possibility that Zephaniah is being 'used' by the British establishment was expressed in a review of *Too Black, Too Strong*, Zephaniah's 2001 collection, as this is perhaps the collection in which Zephaniah is *most* critical of British policy both abroad and at home. Dawes's argument reflects the postmodern anxiety that, in Foucauldian terms, apparent acts of subversion are appropriated by or even produced by the powerful in order to create the appearance of freedom, agency, and the power to rebel. These acts of apparent subversion are controlled and limited, and actually work to reinforce the dominant ideology and existing power structures. Whether or not any 'real' agency or subversion can actually be achieved is of course hotly debated among cultural theorists and philosophers, but what Dawes misses in Zephaniah, as we saw, is 'the irony to recognize that he may actually have been co-opted by the very system he denounces'.[20]

I would suggest, however, that while irony might be the fashionable response to such a recognition, Zephaniah is not a postmodern poet in this sense. He *is* clearly aware of the danger of co-opting and appropriation, but his response is not ironic because he does not contemplate the possibility that this is inevitable; instead he asserts the poet's responsibility and capacity to remain independent:

> Smart big awards and prize money
> Is killing off black poetry
> It's not censors or dictators that are cutting up our art.
> The lure of meeting royalty
> And touching high society
> Is damping creativity and eating at our heart. (*TBTS*, 15)

In the preface to *Too Black, Too Strong* he argues that there are some things which really do disturb the establishment, and it is the poet's duty to address these issues:

> I am told that things could be easier for me if I 'played the game' but I could never stand on a platform and honestly say that the height of my career was receiving a OBE, and in an environment where the artist is scorned for being political, I have to confess that I still believe that there are things that are more important than me or my poetry. We are allowed to shock, we can be outrageous, or if we want to act like we care we can do Band Aid, Live Aid and Comic Relief, but when we want to confront the dictators, the arms traders and deal with the 'cause', we are confronted with a cut in our grants or a tearing-up of our contracts. (*TBTS*, 12)

It would be fascinating to know whether Zephaniah (who did refuse an OBE when one was offered to him in 2003) has *really* had any contracts torn up; certainly he notes in the headnote to 'The Men from Jamaica are Settling Down' that the poem began as a commissioned piece for the BBC but was rejected because it was 'too "political" and too "confrontational" ' (*TBTS*, 36).

There *is* a real danger that public praise and acceptance will effect a kind of containment of a poet like Zephaniah, but the poetry itself does bear witness to his continuing determination to confront and expose issues which really do have the capacity to discomfort those in power. He is relatively unusual among well-known British poets in his focus on British policy abroad; only Tony Harrison, among mainstream poets, shows such a level of engagement, though more concern is present in the experimental scene. Zephaniah's isolation in this respect may be behind his comment that 'the artist is scorned for being political'. Among other things, he has attacked British involvement in the arms trade, the bombing of Iraq, and the ruling of Hong Kong without any kind of democratic representation ('Great Baton you great hypocrite, talk of democracy? / Chinese people hav nu vote in yu Chinese colony' (*CP*, 33)). One of his most effective satirical political poems is 'Kill them before Ramadan', in which Britain comes under specific attack:

> Great hypocrites shed your plutonium tears,
> Make yourself believe that you regret your actions.
> Why should you not believe that
> Your great Britain is mighty independent
> And that every missile is on target,
> And every target is military,
> And all those innocent victims
> Are not really innocent victims?

The poem's title phrase reappears as a chilling refrain:

> We must be merciless.
> Before their Korans open their hearts
> Before their hearts are filled with their beliefs
> We should do the right thing,
> We must
> Kill them before Ramadan. (*TBTS*, 33–4)

Back home he is persistent in his sharp attacks on institution-alised racism in the police force, injustice in the legal system, British policy in Northern Ireland, and the effects of capitalism and consumerism. Comments on specific incidents such as the Stephen Lawrence case, and mention of particular politicians like Thatcher, Major and Blair, ensure that his protests are focused and hard-hitting – readers or hearers cannot take them as a vague taste of 'rebellion' without being forced to think about the details of the case. In 'What Stephen Lawrence Has Taught Us', for instance, we are confronted with Zephaniah's contemptuous description of the murder suspects – 'We know who the killers are, / We have watched them strut before us / As proud as sick Mussolinis' – and then with direct questions challenging the system: 'What are the trading standards here? / Why are we paying for a police force / That will not work for us?' (*TBTS*, 20). Other poems, like 'Self-Defence' (alluding to LKJ's 'All Wi Doin is Defendin'), demand or announce direct action:

> Ain't no Black in de Union Jack,
> We stand an defend any attack,
> Too many parents are crying,
> Because their children are dying,
> And we can't get any protection
> From a force wid racist connections,
> As LKJ did say
> We must stand and drive dem away,
> Self defence is no offence
> We will do what must be done.[21]

In this sense, then, Zephaniah cannot easily be seen as 'harmless' – he tackles more difficult political issues than any other poet currently writing in Britain, and he tackles them with extreme directness. Moreover, he advocates action. Of course, some poems are weaker than others; some of the poems that attempt satire, such as 'The SUN', do struggle. Occasionally, as Dawes remarks, we might feel Zephaniah 'seeking for posturing rather than for deeply-worked observation'.[22] But when they do work, the poems are compelling, and particularly so in performance.

This leads us on to the issue of the style and form of Zephaniah's poetry. 'Dis Poetry', in *City Psalms*, announces that

> Dis poetry is not afraid of going ina book
> Still dis poetry need ears fe hear an eyes fe hav a look

Dis poetry is Verbal Riddim, no big words involved
An if I hav a problem de riddim gets it solved.

Earlier in the poem we are told that 'Dis poetry is not Party
Political / Not designed fe dose who are critical', and later,

Dis poetry is quick an childish
Dis poetry is fe de wise an foolish,
Anybody can do it fe free,
Dis poetry is fe yu an me,
Don't stretch yu imagination
Dis poetry is fe de good of de Nation (*CP*, 12)

Clearly the phrase 'Not designed fe dose who are critical' is
a swipe at literary critics, while Zephaniah's proud assertion that
his poetry *doesn't* stretch the imagination is bound to rub those
same critics up the wrong way. Poetry these days is *supposed* to be
challenging – even if many critics wouldn't say that they want
poetry to be 'difficult', most believe that it should challenge the
reader's preconceptions, that it should surprise and stretch the
reader or audience.

In the specific context of West Indian writing, there is a history
of argument over whether poetry which is primarily oriented
towards entertainment and performance, and which draws on the
oral tradition, should be given attention as 'serious' poetry.
Mervyn Morris, in 1965, was the first to champion Louise Bennett,
or 'Miss Lou', a dialect poet whose often humorous performance
poetry had previously been disregarded by critics and excluded
from anthologies. In 'On reading Louise Bennett, seriously',
Morris argued that this state of affairs was due to a middle-class
bias against performance poetry, humorous poetry, and poetry
using creole.[23] Zephaniah is clearly making the same kind of argument when he pre-empts or addresses criticism by arguing
(in 'Dis Poetry' and other poems) that his poetry derives from an
alternative tradition – a tradition which values and requires the
body and rhythm, which is not primarily oriented towards the
intellectual but towards humour, emotional uplift, and energising
people for action. Obviously the use of creole or nation language
is not always combined with an orientation towards performance,
and vice versa; Dabydeen's creole poems are very much oriented
towards the reader, and Zephaniah's collections show a gradual

reduction in the number of poems which use some form of dialect, coupled with a continually strong orientation towards performance. But the oral creole tradition in its many forms, including the language traditions within reggae, has clearly energised and underpinned Zephaniah's performance-oriented aesthetic.

Other influences can be seen, however, in 'Naked', a poem which relies upon visual layout on the page as well as aural impact, and which makes a strong statement about race. This is one of several poems (another is the clever rewrite of Larkin's 'This be the verse') based on allusion or parody; in this case the relationship to Ginsberg's 'Howl' is immediately signalled through the lay-out, as Zephaniah adopts Ginsberg's long indented 'paragraph' lines (although Zephaniah's are broken up by more punctuation). Ginsberg saw 'the best minds of my generation destroyed by madness, starving hysterical naked, / dragging themselves through the negro streets at dawn looking for an angry fix'.[24] Zephaniah draws our attention to the similarities between himself and Ginsberg as figures of libertarianism and countercultural rebellion, between Rastafarian spirituality and Ginsberg's Hebrew/Buddhist mysticism, and he takes from Ginsberg (who likewise took from Whitman) the expansive, prophetic, all-encompassing 'I' voice. The speaker of 'Naked' moves from the specifically personal ('Dis is my mother. She read a poster on a / hot tin street in Jamaica that told her / that Britain loves her' (*TBTS*, 48)) to the expansive and mystical:

> Dis is me. Dreadlocks I. Rastafari. Rastafari.
>   Behold, how good and how pleasant
>   it is for revolutionaries to dwell together
>   in the house of the lord. (49)

Although Zephaniah doesn't include Ginsberg's phrase 'negro streets', it is in the back of our minds as we read 'Naked I am, fixed / in reality, not looking for a fix, / not pickpocketing in Piccadilly. // I pay tax, they force me to pay for my oppression' (48). There is a rejection here of the escapism, perhaps even the childishness, of some aspects of Beat culture – an avowal, instead, of the need to encounter squarely the realities of society rather than seek modes of escape, and an effort to direct attention towards the specificity of racial oppression by the state which the

Beats, in the USA, viewed as generally, universally oppressive. A line like 'I pay tax, they force me to pay for my oppression', gains a bitter, dark quality by being set out in isolation on the page in a poem full of long paragraph-like stanzas.

'Naked' is also interesting in its exploration of the dangers of self-revelation:

> Dis is me naked, revolting in front of you, I'm
>   not much but I give a damn. Lovers look
>   at me, haters look at me as I exhibit
>   my love and my fury on dis desperate
>   stage. (47)

This seems to chime with Audre Lorde's comment that 'the transformation of silence into language and action is an act of self-revelation, and that always seems fraught with danger.'[25] Zephaniah responds to this sense of danger, this exposure to hostile as well as friendly eyes and ears, with a self-assertion that takes risks in its swift movement between vulnerability, militancy and prophecy. His poetry ranges widely in its tone, with laughter and anger being the dominant notes, and he has been successful in renewing the highly politicised dub poetry aesthetic to speak for, to, and about a generation of black and Asian Britons who reject nostalgia and marginality and assert their centrality to contemporary British culture, or even reject the notions of the centre and the margin altogether:

> I am not half a poet shivering in the cold
> Waiting for a culture shock to warm my long lost drum
>   rhythm,
> I am here and now, I am all that Britain is about
> I'm happening as we speak. (*TBTS*, 64)

Jackie Kay

Jackie Kay's poetry reflects a similar frustration with the perception that those who are not white must in some sense be outsiders in British – and in her case, particularly Scottish – life. 'In my country' is written from the perspective of a presumably black narrator who is watched by an unknown woman 'as if I were a superstition;//or the worst dregs of her imagination'. The predictable question, *'Where do you come from?'* is answered by the narrator's weary but emphatic, ' "Here," I said, "Here. These parts." '[26] In the face of such persistent marginalisation by the dominant culture, one response is the longing for an alternative culture to identify with – for example, Zephaniah's 'long lost drum rhythm'. Zephaniah affirms the effort to create a new black British culture through incorporation of aspects of the culture of the black diaspora (e.g. Rastafarianism, reggae) but he rejects nostalgia for a lost identity. Jackie Kay explores similar ideas in her poem 'Pride', in *Off Colour*, in which a speaker who shares basic biographical details with Kay (brought up in Scotland, Nigerian biological father) meets a black man on the train – a man who transfixes her with a powerful evocation of her African roots:

> 'That nose is an Ibo nose.
> Those teeth are Ibo teeth,' the stranger said,
> his voice getting louder and louder.
> I had no doubt, from the way he said it,
> that Ibo noses are the best noses in the world,
> that Ibo teeth are perfect pearls.[27]

The poem ironically investigates the feeling named in the title, 'pride', which the speaker has seen on the faces of 'a MacLachlan, a MacDonnell, a MacLeod'. This comparison, especially in the context of Kay's other poetry, reminds us of the exclusive aspect of family, tribal or national pride, while the man's refusal to consider that the Ibos might have characteristic faults as well as virtues points towards ethnic and cultural supremacism. At the same time, a more positive and empowering 'pride' might emerge out of the sense of validation which comes from belonging, knowing and being known: 'I found my feet. / I started to dance. / I danced a dance I never knew I knew. / Words and sounds fell out of my mouth like seeds' (*OC*, 64). The final two lines, with their suggestion that the whole episode might have been imagined, leave us aware primarily of the powerful desire for a sense of cultural belonging and the validation of community, while also suggesting that such dreams of the absolute homecoming might have their dangers in escapism and exclusivity.

Jackie Kay, who was born in 1961, emerged strongly into the field of British poetry with the publication of *The Adoption Papers* in 1991, and has since published *Other Lovers* (1993) and *Off Colour* (1998), as well as various fiction. *Life Mask* (Tarset: Bloodaxe, 2005) was published just as this book was being completed. She cites the importance of Scottish poets like Liz Lochhead and Tom Leonard in giving her the confidence to write in a distinctively Scottish voice, and the parallel influence of black American women poets like Audre Lorde, Nikki Giovanni and Ntozake Shange in helping her to explore her experience of blackness (and in Lorde's case, the experience of being black and lesbian).[28] The title sequence of *The Adoption Papers*, which is strongly autobiographical, charts the life of a child with a black Nigerian father and a white Scottish mother, who is adopted by a white Scottish couple. It is just as interesting for its investigation of issues like motherhood, childbirth and the development of the mother–daughter relationship as it is for its exploration of the dynamics of a mixed-race family and the experiences of a black child in a very white Scottish society, but the latter issues are those I will explore here.

This free-verse sequence very effectively juxtaposes the voices of the biological mother, the adoptive mother, and the adopted child, strikingly drawing our attention to issues of identity and the way in which the narratives which make up our lives can be shared, combined, and transformed in the subjectivity of others. 'The Adoption Papers' powerfully evokes the experience of being perceived as essentially different simply because of skin colour – different from one's parents, and different from one's schoolmates. The degree of racial prejudice in Scottish society is exemplified most strikingly in the adoptive mother's account of the way in which the adoption authorities did not even contemplate the possibility that the couple might be happy to adopt a non-white baby:

> They told us they had no babies at first
> and I chanced it didn't matter what colour it was
> and they said *oh well are you sure*
> *in that case we have a baby for you* –
> to think she wasn't even thought of as a baby,
> my baby, my baby[29]

The dehumanisation involved in racism is evident here. In the same 'chapter' of the sequence we see a teacher demonstrate strongly essentialist and reductive notions of race and apply them cruelly in front of the class:

> We're practising for the school show
> I'm trying to do the Cha Cha and the Black Bottom
> but I can't get the steps right
> my right foot's left and my left foot's right
> my teacher shouts from the bottom
> of the class Come on, show
>
> us what you can do I thought
> you people had it in your blood.
> My skin is hot as burning coal
> like that time she said Darkies are like coal
> in front of the whole class – my blood
> what does she mean? (*AP*, 25)

If 'Pride' had left us with any uncertainty about how ironically Kay views the speaker's dream of dancing 'a dance I never knew' with her lost Ibo family, this poem's portrayal of the oppressiveness and stupidity of the notion that 'it's in your blood' makes it clear that such ideas are deeply problematic.

In 'The Adoption Papers' the girl is dismissive of 'the old blood questions' asked by dentists and doctors and those who 'keep trying to make it matter, / the blood, the tie, the passing down / generations' (29). But she admits her 'contradiction': 'I want to know my blood' (29). The next stanza, however, takes us away from the abstract problem of family lineage and reminds us of the actual, literal blood element of 'descent' – 'it is the well, the womb, the fucking seed'. For the speaker, the problem of 'blood' becomes literalised so that it means the stories of the women who gave birth in order for her to exist:

> Here, I am far enough away to wonder –
> what were their faces like
> who were my grandmothers
> what were the days like
> passed in Scotland
> the land I come from
> the soil in my blood. (29)

Blood, then, becomes associated with a narrative of birth and growth and the places in which that happened, rather than an abstract lineage or scientific classification. It is interesting that the claim that Scotland is 'the land I come from / the soil in my blood' still seems dependent upon, or at least associated with, her heritage of actual biological ancestors who lived in this place – the 'grand-mothers'. Thus, although Kay presents an alternative social con-structionist view of belonging by emphasising the degree to which the child's identity is created and shaped by nurture and her social context, she also shows the child reverting back to a longing for a biologically based sense of belonging, even if this is framed in terms of the continuity of women's experience rather than in terms of abstract genealogical categories.

The emphasis on nurture and cultural context in the develop-ment of ethnic identity is seen in the way in which the girl experi-ences her colour as something strange and defamiliarising:

> I can see my skin is that colour
> but most of the time I forget,
> so sometimes when I look in the mirror
> I give myself a bit of a shock
> and say to myself *Do you really look like this?* (27)

At the same time, however, there is a somewhat uncertain effort to cultivate a kind of alternative 'black' identity by listening to Pearl Bailey and Bessie Smith and supporting Angela Davis, a commu-nist activist imprisoned in the USA in the 1970s. It is the girl's father who brings home the badge saying 'Free Angela Davis', and this underlines the links between racism and the persecution of communists; the Angela Davis badge signals that the girl and her family are determined to fight for freedom and against prejudice.

The interest in the social construction of ethnicity is paralleled in Kay's work by an interest in the way in which racism emerges. In 'Race, Racist, Racism', a poem that is unusually abstract and experimental in comparison to Kay's other work, she explores the idea that racism is essentially a discourse: 'Say the words came first' (*OC*, 21). Different sections within the poem explore differ-ent aspects of this idea. Section 2 evokes the voice of a victim of racism who seeks to control her or his experience of racism by believing that, because language is always context-dependent and subject to interpretation, 'When it happens it is down to me'; 'It is all my fault for reading / something into nothing'. There is a strange masochism operating here, and the imagery (as in other sections of the poem) is disturbing: 'I can say the names as well as you. / Lick the whip around my thick lips.' On the other hand, section 3 probes the way in which the idea that racism is a discourse may be used to evade responsibility for racist behaviours. In a striking metaphor, racism arrives as a 'gift' on a boat (just as the West Indies workers arrived in the fifties) and infects the tongues of the people:

> out of their mouths came the gift's curse,
> the slow slurred abuse, eyes staring,
> till not a tongue in the country was clean,
> till every mind was stained with its stain.
>
> Who could help then?
> What doctors could come to scrub a tongue
> to disinfect a mind, to stop a plague.
> Nobody knew how to cure it.
>
> And it is true: many people died. (22)

It is an apt metaphor because it reverses the imagery of infection, impurity, contamination and so on which conservative Britons used (and still use today) to describe the absorption of non-white immigrants into the country, by applying this imagery to racism itself. It is also effective because it captures the potency of prejudice, which cannot be simply 'scrubbed away' because it becomes a part of the structure of subjectivity itself.

The fourth section records the way in which the language of race is contested; the male character asserts his refusal to identify with the word 'black', preferring any other colour word: 'I will be grey or brown or red. / I will be yellow or tan or beige. // I will be oak or hazelnut or coffee. / I will be toffee. I will be donkey. / But I will not be black, said he. / So you will be donkey, said I' (23). This plays out the familiar argument as to whether by rejecting the term 'black' one is in a sense affirming the racist culture's identification of black as inferior, and whether the reappropriation and thus transformation of the term is instead the best way forward. The speaker's suggestion that 'you will be donkey' implies that he will not emerge from his subordination through his strategy of rejection. The last two sections of the poem are very interesting, the fifth section glancingly and tellingly alluding to mass murder, and the sixth asserting the speaker's right and power to take an active role within language and the construction of ideas:

When the day breaks I will be there to break it.
When the new moon rises, I'll rise with it.
When the west wind blows, I'll puff and huff.
When the time comes, I'll say 'enough'.

I'll write 'The End' when it's the end of the story.

Say the words came first. (23)

The attention to the detail of idiom and metaphor implies that language needs to be carefully analysed for its assumptions and hidden meanings; at the same time, the examples chosen suggest the claiming of power and agency.

Jackie Kay's poetry is determined to chart the experience of living in a racially divided society, and, more than Benjamin Zephaniah, she probes the ways in which this affects and shapes the most intimate relationships. In 'Photo in the Locket' from *The Adoption Papers* she explores a lesbian relationship between a black woman brought up in Scotland and a white woman brought up (it seems) as part of the colonial class in Africa. The relationship is at first dogged by the legacy of anger and guilt that derives from historical relations between black and white in Africa and in Britain and is played out in their relationship. The two women are haunted by ways of thinking which they want to reject: 'Yesterday I said a terrible thing. / My tongue is full of old ideas. / Sometimes they slip like falling rocks' (47). As it progresses, however, the relationship becomes a nurturing context in which to explore, share and transform their complex inheritance:

Now, some of your memories are mine.
We move on. We don't forget.
We change not like amoebas
more like plants keeping the same stem. (49)

Kay's poetry is valuable in its ability to investigate the way in which race, colour, ethnicity and cultural history are experienced as powerful dynamics within sexual and familial relationships. While her style, which frequently echoes speech, might on occasion seem a little too plain, often Kay achieves complex effects through techniques such as the splitting and juxtaposition of voices in 'The Adoption Papers'. Her later work in particular shows her developing her talent for a conversational style by choosing to write more dramatic monologues, sometimes using Scots. She has noted her feeling of affinity with the Scottish love of performing poetry and her desire to be part of that Scottish 'tradition that wants to see the drama that is in poetry',[30] and her successful foray into television (*Twice Through the Heart*, 1992) clearly reflects this dedication to exploring poetry's dramatic potential.

Moniza Alvi

Like Jackie Kay, Moniza Alvi probes the experience of identifying with two different ethnic communities. Alvi's father was Indian and Muslim, and he and his family fled to Pakistan at the time of Partition, when he was a young man. Her mother was English, and the family moved from Lahore to England soon after Moniza's birth in 1954. Although Alvi did not return to Pakistan until after the publication of her first book, *The Country at My Shoulder*, there was considerable family contact, meaning that as Alvi grew up in Hatfield she spent a lot of time imagining Pakistan and India. Pakistan and India have a much stronger, more palpable presence in Alvi's poetry than Nigeria does in Kay's poetry, so that the sense of a double or divided existence is intensified. This sense of division is most prominent in her first two collections, *The Country at My Shoulder* (1993) and *A Bowl of Warm Air* (1996), although it is also apparent in *Carrying My Wife* (2000) and *Souls* (2002). *How the Stone Found Its Voice* (Tarset: Bloodaxe, 2005) was published just as this book was being completed. Her poetry has always been open to the surreal and allows itself to be led by metaphor, and in her later work this has developed into an ability to take hold of strange, defamiliarising perspectives on reality, as in the whimsically metaphysical *Souls*.

One of the most interesting features of Alvi's poetry is her original use of the body in her exploration of ethnicity, race and identity. While one poem, 'Blood', engages with the traditional ways of representing the 'raced' body, most of her poems take us far away from these kinds of discourses and seek to open up another way of conceiving ethnicity through the body. The focus is turned away from the body as object for the observer's gaze, or as the carrier or product of certain genes and 'blood'. Instead, space and size become crucial, and the body shrinks and expands in its different relations to country, geography and place. For example, in 'The Sari' the body is small, the body of a baby who is at first inside her mother looking out 'through a glass porthole' at a world that is hot and brown. The people she sees outside unravel a huge sari, a sari which 'stretched from Lahore to Hyderabad', takes in the Arabian sea, and is 'threaded … with roads, / undulations of land'. When she is born the people 'wrapped and wrapped me in it / whispering *Your body is your country*'.[31]

The italicised phrase introduces a motif that is explored in many different poems. It is an idea that is produced, perhaps, by the experience of dislocation and multiple allegiances; if one is separated from a meaningful place, a home, how can one concretise it in one's mind? The only concrete link with that place is the body, which after all was physically there. The enfolding of the body in the sari enables it to bear symbolically the imaginary imprints of the rivers, the stars, the roads, the undulation of the land, so that the body is at once self and 'country'. 'Country' denotes culture, people, belonging and identity, as well as place. The very next poem, 'Map of India', maps 'country' onto the body again, but this time the relative sizing is reversed – the body is huge and the country is small; the map of India is like a flap of skin, it is 'manageable – smaller than / my hand, the Mahanadi River / thinner than my lifeline' (*CMS*, 37). Here India is at once a separate body and part of the speaker's body – the hand *becomes* India and the lifeline the river. But the description of India as 'manageable' in this mapped form concedes the difference between the internalised view from a distance and the real thing.

The desire to imprint upon the body the fullness, multifariousness and complexity of the 'real thing' is expressed in 'Rolling', in Alvi's second collection *A Bowl of Warm Air* (1996), in which the sizing is reversed again as the speaker's body rolls 'like a map / like a bale of cloth' though 'India's / hundred millions', just like 'the holy man … / who rolls for eight months / to a Himalayan Shrine'.[32] As she rolls she gathers 'all the smells and sounds / like a shawl around me' (*BWA*, 23). The poem reveals a feeling of dissatisfaction with the extent of the body's closeness to the country; there is a need for greater immersion, for an engagement so full that it leads to bruising and exhaustion, but which leaves the speaker satisfied that she is really a part of the country – its contours are imprinted on the body.

A similar need is found in 'The Wedding', also in *A Bowl of Warm Air*. The speaker describes a wedding that seems to have been the result of a traditional arranged match; a marriage that was desired by the speaker as a way of becoming one with the country. The ceremony is unsatisfactory – it 'tasted of nothing / had little colour' – and towards the end of the poem we see why:

> I wanted to marry a country
> take up a river for a veil
> sing in the Jinnah Gardens
>
> hold up my dream, tricky
> as a snake-charmer's snake.
> Our thoughts half-submerged
>
> like buffaloes under dark water
> we turned and faced each other
> with turbulence
>
> and imprints like maps on our hands. (9–10)

The imprints are the henna markings of the traditional art of hand-painting, done before a wedding, and more abstractly they are the imprints of background, the markings of personal and cultural history, which Alvi often imagines as mapped onto the body. The actual marriage feels unsatisfactory because the desire for a traditional marriage has really emerged out of a sense of longing for a literal union with a 'country' in which the body would become one with land and culture. While the bridegroom fails to provide this, the poem's ending still has a positive note to it; there is no simple union, but there is immersion – immersion in the turbulence of difference, as the bride and groom confront each other and each other's pasts in the confused intensity of their initial strangeness. The implication is that although the body cannot find complete oneness with country, culture and land, it *can* tell the story of its history; it *does* bear the marks of its past.

Alvi's perspective is interesting from the point of view of the discussions over race and ethnicity. In a sense she retrieves the body from its banishment along with essentialist and biologically based conceptions of race. She brings it back not as the bearer of particular racial traits which underlie cultural conditioning, but as a vehicle for engagement, memory and change. The body tells the story of its history; a history that can be developed, added to, through an engagement with other cultures. A tension marks the poetry over the issue of how far transformation is possible, whether of the body or the self more generally. Thus in 'An Unknown Girl' the speaker's hands are hennaed by a girl in the evening bazaar, which produces 'new brown veins' and then, when the dry brown lines are scraped off, an 'amber bird' on the palm (the poem's layout in the centre of the page seems to imitate the wandering lines of the henna). But the henna 'will fade in a week', and the poem ends with a sense of loss and longing for permanence:

> When India appears and reappears
> I'll lean across a country
> with my hands outstretched
> longing for the unknown girl
> in the neon bazaar.
> (*BWA*, 15)

Here bodily transformation is used as an image for transformation of the self more generally, and the fading of the henna markings symbolises the limitations of her capacity to engage, on both an emotional and a physical level, with India. Even during the hennaing there is an awareness of the coming loss: 'I am clinging / to these firm peacock lines / like people who cling / to the sides of a train' (14). Any engagement with place and people for Alvi has to be physical as well as intellectual and emotional; thus the wonderful image of rolling all over India in order to literally batter herself with its reality. The body is not figured as any more intransigent or immutable than the mind: both carry their history, their story; both are eager to engage with and be immersed in otherness; both are figured as encountering limitations on their ability to do so.

Thus for Alvi identity is more about ethnicity than race – biological commonality gives no guarantee of connection with a culture – but her view of ethnicity includes the body as an integral part of the person, and a bearer of personal history. 'The Boy from Bombay', from Alvi's most recent collection *Souls*, tells the story of an Indian child adopted by a Swiss family who, years after his adoption, looks in the mirror and imagines himself back in India; he imagines a parallel world, an alternative self. The body has the capacity to be different things and live different stories, but it is not just a vessel that can be filled with any chosen ethnicity.

All our experience is lived through and in the body and the body remembers its past: 'He sleeps – one fist clenched / on a fragment of India'.[33]

In 'Blood', from *Carrying my Wife* (2000), Alvi confronts the alternative view of the body and race, that which describes a person's racial identity in terms of fractions relating to 'blood': 'half-English', 'one-sixteenth Indian', and so on. Like Jackie Kay, who responds to this by calling blood 'the well, the womb, the fucking seed', Alvi also personalises and sexualises the concept:

> Was I more Indian or more English?
> I blurred, as I would forever
> when my blood seeped regularly
> into the outer world.[34]

Menstruation is here presented as a process that acts as a continual reminder that the body is not separate, autonomous, closed off from the external world. The reminder is at times awkward and difficult to take ('I'd even run with that strangeness, / awkward in the egg-and-spoon race'), but it serves to undermine the idea that 'race' is contained in the body, that the body is a sealed carrier of genetic material and that its racial or ethnic identity is fixed. Instead it suggests that the blurring, the sense of instability, which is experienced during menstruation, might provide an image for the potential for (possibly disturbing) transformation and change in the ethnic identity of the embodied self. In this sense Alvi's poetry provides an interesting intervention into the debate on the role of the body in ethnicity. She does not emphasise ancestors or genetic inheritance, instead emphasising potential lives, multiple narratives of identity. But whereas a take on ethnicity that emphasises social construction might typically ignore the body, for Alvi the body is central; through the body we experience both the limitations which personal history places on transformation, and the possibilities of engagement.

Conclusion

In a sense all three of these poets are involved in creating hybrid identities which bridge and cross borders – borders of 'race', culture, place and time. Homi Bhabha argues that the kind of literature that explores such 'interstitial' states is representative of our global condition:

> where, once, the transmission of national traditions was the major theme of a world literature, perhaps we can now suggest that transnational histories of migrants, the colonized, or refugees – these border and frontier conditions – may be the terrains of world literature.[35]

The celebratory tendency of such postcolonial paradigms (and in particular, the emphasis on the possibilities for agency which are inherent in the 'in-between' condition of migrants and diaspora peoples) has been criticised by theorists like Radhakrishnan, who notes that the poststructuralist 'celebration of "difference" is completely at odds with the actual experience of difference as undergone by diasporic peoples in their countries of residence'.[36] Bhabha has also been criticised for a tendency to make the post-colonial subject into a kind of 'Everyman', blurring differences, for example, between those who migrate and those who do not. Certainly when we consider the three poets in this chapter, differences between them seem much more prominent than similarities – only Zephaniah has a strong sense of belonging to a diasporic community, for instance, while Alvi's relationship to Pakistan and India is mediated through family and friends there rather than a migrant network, and Kay presents herself as almost entirely cut off from her African heritage. While all three poets do certainly convey a sense that their complex ethnic inheritance gives them an oblique relationship to the norms and structures of British culture which is positive and freeing, this is counterbalanced in Zephaniah and Kay's poetry in particular by the hurt and trauma which racism inflicts, and the loneliness of a marginalisation which is forced rather than chosen (this last aspect being seen most clearly in Kay's poetry). But while all three poets do at times dwell on this experience of marginalisation, it would seem wrong to make this term too central in our description of their work. All three poets express a strong and – one might venture – *comfortable* sense of British identity and belonging which paradoxically exists alongside the other more discomforting experiences of racism and exclusion, and alongside the sense of belonging elsewhere as well.

'Postcolonial' writing is frequently associated with postmodernist concerns and techniques. But in this sense the poets discussed in this chapter perhaps conform less to the 'postcolonial' paradigm than David Dabydeen, whose poetry I discuss in Chapter 6. Zephaniah, Kay and Alvi explore the experience of hybridity, but not to the point at which the speaking subject is at risk of dissolution, as he is in Dabydeen's *Turner*, with its fear of the failure of representation. Dabydeen does not use the radically disjunctive poetic forms associated with Language poetry, but he does incorporate many features characteristic of postmodernism, with his use of the destabilising 'authorial' voice in the introduction to *Slave Song*, and the multiple levels of reference and allusion in *Turner*. For Kay, Zephaniah and Alvi, the speaking subject is at times conflicted, uncertain and divided, but the reader's conventional trust in the authenticity of the personal voice (even if it is the voice of a clearly dramatised 'character') is not usually undermined. Zephaniah, in particular, cultivates the sense of a direct and authentic 'truth-speaking' voice in order to both seduce and confront the audience of a poem in performance.

All three poets draw powerfully on their personal experiences to explore the resonances and complexities of being British, English, Scottish. A discussion of their poetry in the context of issues such as 'race' and 'ethnicity' serves to remind us of the inadequacy and clumsiness of our attempts to reach towards descriptions for our feelings of belonging and difference, and the difficulty of operating within a critical and publishing system whose first instinct is towards labelling and categorisation ('Black', 'Asian' etc). Poets are constantly working within and against these systems of representation, some of which may be helpful, some unhelpful. Denise Riley, in an excellent book on precisely this issue of self-description, puts it this way:

> It's rare for the self, in an untrammelled agony of exquisite choice, to invent its own names. The daily fact of societal description 'from the outside' – how I'm reported by others, what's expectantly in place, already chatting about me before I appear on stage – is integral to the dialectic of self-description.[37]

Categorisation, whether by self or other, may create solidarity, but it may also blur difference. In Riley's words, 'If intricate and fine-grained accounts are thickened into a single sanitised

identification, then histories, under the kindly guise of being facil-
itated, are obliterated.'[38]

Notes

1 Patience Agbabi, *R.A.W.* (London: Izon Amazon, 1995), pp. 26–7. In the
  original text the line *'Nigger Paki Queer'* is handwritten in rough capitals.
2 See Chapter 7 for a longer discussion of Agbabi's work in the context of
  performance poetry.
3 Current thought on the issue is reflected, for example, in the fact that an
  undergraduate sociology textbook entitled *Race and Ethnicity in Modern
  Britain* published in 1995 devotes almost no space to a discussion of the
  issue of the biological validity of 'race', stating in its first paragraph that a
  founding assumption of its argument is 'that there are no races, in the biological sense of distinct divisions of the human species'. David Mason, *Race
  and Ethnicity in Modern Britain* (Oxford: Oxford University Press, 1995), p. 1.
4 Paul Gilroy, *Against Race: Imagining Political Culture beyond the Color Line*
  (Cambridge, MA: Harvard University Press, 2000), p. 12.
5 This chapter will also consistently refer to 'Britain' as the relevant context, as
  I do not discuss any Irish poets. Ethnicity/race has, of course, always been
  an issue in the relationship between England and Ireland, as witnessed by
  writings like Matthew Arnold's on the inherent differences between the
  Celts and the Anglo-Saxons. English imperialism in Ireland was often
  framed by racial discourses. This dimension of the race/ethnicity issue is
  one that I do not have space to pursue in this chapter. Apart from the regular
  exchange of people between Britain and Ireland, the Republic of Ireland has
  until recently been rather homogeneous. It is only in the last decade that
  large numbers of immigrants from all over the world have forced the Irish of
  the Republic to confront the idea of an ethnically mixed and not exclusively
  white Irish nation. Immigration to Northern Ireland (particularly from
  China and South Asia) has a longer history, but in both North and South
  these changes are only just starting to filter through into poetry.
6 Susheila Nasta, 'Beyond the Millennium: Black women's writing', *Women:
  A Cultural Review*, vol. 11, no. 1/2 (April 2000), pp. 71–6 (p. 76).
7 Heidi Safia Mirza, 'Introduction: Mapping a genealogy of Black British
  feminism', in *Black British Feminism: A Reader* (London: Routledge, 1997),
  pp. 1–28 (pp. 19–20).
8 Agbabi, *R.A.W.*, p. 51.
9 Lola Young, 'What is Black British feminism?', *Women: A Cultural Review*,
  vol. 11, no. 1/2 (April 2000), pp. 45–60 (p. 57).
10 Kwame Dawes, 'Review of *Too Black, Too Strong*', *World Literature Today*,
  vol. 76, no. 2 (2002), pp. 159–60 (p. 160).
11 Victoria Arana, 'Black American bodies in the neo-millenial avant-garde
  black British poetry', *Literature and Psychology*, 48.4 (2002), pp. 47–81 (p. 48).
12 Stuart Hall, 'New ethnicities', in *Stuart Hall: Critical Dialogues in Cultural
  Studies*, ed. David Morley and Kuan-Hsing Chen (London: Routledge,
  1996), pp. 441–50 (p. 443) (first published 1989).

13 Hall, 'New ethnicities', p. 443.

14 Edward Kamau Brathwaite, *History of the Voice: The Development of Nation Language in Anglophone Caribbean Poetry* (London: New Beacon Books, 1984), p. 10.

15 Johnson, however, emphasises the difference between his own poetry and DJ 'chatting', saying that DJs improvise words to existing music whereas he writes the words first, in a less improvisational way, and the music 'emerges' from the poem, so the words remain the primary focus.

16 Linton Kwesi Johnson, *Dread Beat and Blood* (London: Bogle-L'Ouverture, 1975), p. 57.

17 Benjamin Zephaniah, *City Psalms* (Tarset: Bloodaxe, 1992), p. 28. Henceforth referred to as *CP*.

18 Benjamin Zephaniah, *Too Black, Too Strong* (Tarset: Bloodaxe, 2001), p. 13. Henceforth referred to as *TBTS*.

19 Young, 'What is Black British feminism?', p. 55.

20 Dawes, 'Review of *Too Black, Too* Strong', p. 160.

21 Benjamin Zephaniah, *Propa Propaganda* (Newcastle u. Tyne: Bloodaxe, 1996), p. 76.

22 Dawes, 'Review of *Too Black, Too* Strong', p. 160.

23 Mervyn Morris, 'On reading Louise Bennett, seriously', *Jamaica Journal*, vol. 1, no. 1 (1967), pp. 69–74. Quoted in *The Routledge Reader in Caribbean Literature*, ed. Alison Donnell and Sarah Lawson Welsh (London: Routledge, 1996), pp. 194–7.

24 Allen Ginsberg, *Selected Poems 1947–1995* (London: Penguin, 1996), p. 49.

25 Audre Lorde, quoted in Young, 'What is Black British feminism?', p. 57.

26 Jackie Kay, *Other Lovers* (Newcastle upon Tyne: Bloodaxe, 1993), p. 24.

27 Jackie Kay, 'Pride', in *Off Colour* (Newcastle upon Tyne: Bloodaxe, 1998), p. 62. Henceforth referred to as *OC*.

28 Laura Severin, 'Interview with Jackie Kay', *Free Verse* 2 (2002), http://english. chass.ncsu.edu/freeverse/Archives/Spring_2002/Interviews/interviews. htm, accessed 17 February 2005.

29 Jackie Kay, *The Adoption Papers* (Newcastle upon Tyne: Bloodaxe, 1991), p. 24. Henceforth referred to as *AP*.

30 Severin, 'Interview with Jackie Kay'.

31 Moniza Alvi, *The Country at My Shoulder* (Oxford: Oxford University Press, 1993), p. 36. Henceforth referred to as *CMS*.

32 Moniza Alvi, *A Bowl of Warm Air* (Oxford: Oxford University Press, 1996), p. 22. Henceforth referred to as *BWA*.

33 Moniza Alvi, *Souls* (Tarset: Bloodaxe, 2002), p. 68.

34 Moniza Alvi, *Carrying my Wife* (Newcastle upon Tyne: Bloodaxe, 2000), p. 47.

35 Homi K. Bhabha, *The Location of Culture* (London: Routledge, 1994), p. 12.

36 R. Radhakrishnan, *Diasporic Mediations: Between Home and Location* (Minneapolis, MN: University of Minnesota Press, 1996), p. 174.

37 Denise Riley, *The Words of Selves: Identification, Solidarity, Irony* (Stanford, CA: Stanford University Press, 2000), p. 7.

38 Ibid., p. 11.

3

Gender, Sex and Embodiment

Simon Armitage, Carol Ann Duffy,
Grace Nichols

Carol Ann Duffy's poem 'Pope Joan' takes the voice of the woman who, in popular history, is said to have occupied the papal chair at some point during medieval times. She was only revealed as a woman when she gave birth in public during a procession, after which she was reputedly stoned to death. Duffy's Pope Joan learns the hermetic secrets of the papacy, for centuries a male-only preserve, and becomes accustomed to a position of spiritual authority. But her experience at the pinnacle of spiritual power serves only to lead her to 'believe / that I did not believe a word',[1] and she confides to her audience, 'daughters or brides of the Lord',

> that the closest I felt
>
> to the power of God
> was the sense of a hand
> lifting me, flinging me down,
>
> lifting me, flinging me down,
> as my baby pushed out
> from between my legs
> where I lay in the road
> in my miracle,
> not man or a pope at all. (*WW*, 68–9)

This poem, which I will discuss later in the chapter, highlights the relationship between 'performed' gender and 'material' sex and

75

in so doing draws our attention to a nexus of fascinating and troublesome arguments in contemporary theory. Postmodern popular culture, as well as postmodern academic discourse, has tended to undermine the binary oppositions associated with gender: male/female; masculine/feminine. While this tendency has in part been driven by feminist theory, it has also produced difficulties for feminism, since the very category upon which feminism was founded – 'woman' – can no longer be relied upon to remain stable.

The earlier feminism of Simone de Beauvoir and others accentuated the difference between sex and gender, arguing that sex was biological and given, and gender was cultural and societally produced. Gender was the problem, and it could be solved; restrictive, marginalising and disparaging ways of conceiving of femininity could be challenged and changed, because they were culturally produced. In current theory, however, the female as well as the feminine is at issue. Theorists like Judith Butler have argued that we cannot imagine 'sex' as a passive surface (nature) onto which 'gender' (culture) is imposed; since one's sex is always experienced in and through culture, 'it appears not only that sex is absorbed by gender, but that "sex" becomes something like a fiction, perhaps a fantasy.'[2] But is there any sense in which the body has a sexed material existence prior to or outside discourse? What role does our embodiment play in our experience of sex and gender? These questions are of intense interest to many today, as theorists search for a model of the self and of sexuality that acknowledges the role of social construction and discourse in shaping our sexual identity, but at the same time recognises the profundity of the human experience of embodiment.

Another recent trend has been a growing interest in masculinity, including in literary criticism. From a situation in which most critical studies that focused on gender were written by women and either focused on women writers or the portrayal of women in texts by male writers, we have moved to a point where masculinity is a much more fashionable topic than femininity. Clearly it is a positive thing that masculinity should be displaced from its position as the unproblematic norm and should be as much open to question as femininity. Recent contemporary British and Irish poetry by men has shown a marked interest in the experience of masculinity, and in this chapter I will focus on Simon Armitage's poetry as exemplary of this. The other two poets included in this chapter, Carol Ann Duffy and Grace Nichols, have a greater focus than Armitage on the body, and discussion of their poetry will allow us to explore the notion of embodiment in greater depth.

Simon Armitage

Simon Armitage, one of the most prominent poets in the Poetry Society's New Generation Poets promotion of 1994, has had enormous popular success. The Huddersfield poet, who cites fellow Yorkshiremen Ted Hughes and Tony Harrison as influences, is doing much to fortify the Northern poetry scene. His appeal derives partly from the distinctive persona many of his poems present. The trademark Armitage 'voice', bearing the influence of Auden, Larkin and Muldoon, is cool and clever yet also humble and capable of vulnerability – and it is a voice that is for the most part decisively masculine. In fact, in *Zoom!*, his first collection of poems, published in 1989, many of the poems explicitly present themselves as from a masculine viewpoint, and the rest give no indication that they are *not* positioned within a male subjectivity. In later collections there are a few poems that clearly have female speakers, but these are rare. Despite the consistently masculine viewpoint in Armitage's poems, we are prevented from lapsing into a state of inattentiveness regarding gender by Armitage's fascination with the contours and contradictions of masculinity. In fact, much of Armitage's poetry seems to reflect a way of thinking about gender that has become prominent in recent years: the idea of gender as *performance*.

Judith Butler, in *Gender Trouble*, is the most influential exponent of this concept. For Butler, the conceptualisation of gender as performative, as a '*stylized repetition of acts*', works to undermine the idea that masculinity and femininity relate to or reveal any kind of essential sexual identity.[3] She argues that all we are doing when we act, think and speak in 'gendered' ways is repeating available cultural fictions or scripts which provide us with ways to 'do' or 'perform' masculinity and femininity, or maleness and femaleness. These performances actually 'produce' gender and indeed sex. The question then arises: can we act to change the culturally available scripts, or are we doomed to eternal repetition without agency or choice? This question of agency is a very complex one for contemporary theory, as we will see in Chapter 6.

For Butler, limited scope for agency is produced by the conflicts between different gender injunctions. For example, society might expect a woman 'to be a good mother, to be a heterosexually desirable object, to be a fit worker, in sum, to signify a multiplicity of guarantees in response to a variety of different demands all at once. The coexistence or convergence of such discursive injunctions produces the possibility of a complex reconfiguration and redeployment ...'.[4] Furthermore, performing gender in a parodic way can draw attention to the constructed nature of gender roles, and this in itself is a way of exercising agency.[5] The notion of performative gender has proved a useful tool in theory, even for those who are less severely constructionist than Butler, as most of us are. This theoretical discussion about gender as performance corresponds to (and perhaps emerges out of or contributes to) a popular interest in the notion of performing gender (note the proliferation of self-conscious and parodic 'performances' of gender and sexuality in music videos, films and TV shows).

If we read Armitage's poetry with the concept of performative gender in mind, I think we notice an interest in the performance of masculinity that is refreshingly different – different in the sense that it challenges prevalent versions of masculinity without relying on well-worn strategies like campness. *Zoom!*, Armitage's first collection, published in 1989 when Armitage was twenty-six, is the most striking in this respect. *Zoom!* contains a babble of different versions of masculinity. Sometimes the speaker is the person successfully performing a given cultural script, other times he is failing to perform it, or subverting the available roles and discourses through, in Butler's terms, a kind of 'reconfiguration and redeployment'. In 'All We Can Do' the mechanic with the 'bush-baby eyes' who comes to pick up the speaker and his female partner when their car breaks down is comfortable and competent in his version of masculinity, as he 'cleans the dip-stick / under his armpit' and 'couples' the vehicles together for the trip home, during which the woman sits 'with him / in the glass-backed cab, captive / to his fabulous tales / of strippers / at the Top Cat Club / and bearings that sheared / to the width of a tissue'. Meanwhile, the speaker steers and brakes 'in the car behind, / misreading the tangents / of the pavements and corners / as the gold / of each streetlight / burns / through your hairstyle'.[6] Assuming the maleness of the speaker, the poem acquires its tension from the sense of exclusion the speaker feels as the other two play along with conventional gender roles – the active, talkative, competent male rescuer, and the passive and admiring 'princess' (note the glass-backed cab, the gold light on the hair). But note that he is actually only imagining their conversation, fantasising that his partner (who was in fact driving their car when they broke down, negotiating a merger of 'masculine' and 'feminine' as she 'nurses' the car into the forecourt like a baby) collapses into a traditionally feminine role when she encounters the mechanic's competence in performing a dominant (in both senses) version of masculinity. The speaker approaches self-satire in his vision of the mechanic bragging about strippers and bearings, and the dominant tone is an amused fascination with gender games.

In *Zoom!* one of the key markers of competent 'performance' of cultural scripts is the confident use of idiom. Armitage's male speakers sprinkle their speech with metaphors and exclamations, many of which make specific reference to 'masculine' activities and sexuality. In 'All Beer and Skittles', a poem about growing up into a rather bullying masculine world, the title sets the tone for a poem packed with idiom and cliché. The speech world of the poem, both in the context of the narrator's own thoughts and in reported speech, is both rough and colourful: 'the details have clouded / like a plasterer's bucket', 'He had a hair up his arse / at the best of times', ' a warning against making / a poor fist of it', 'This job, he assured me, / was a piece of piss', 'he found the over-flow dripping / like a barmaid's apron / and the putty as dry as a Wesleyan wedding', 'He knew his son was all mouth and trousers' (Z, 16–18). All of these expressions evoke a world that is traditionally masculine in its outlook, the world that the boy is negotiating his place in. The most colourful – and ludicrous – of the expressions, however, is the one that is used to classify the boy as insufficiently heterosexual/masculine:

In any case, I fitted the bill,
me being the type who'd still suck his thumb
if dropped head first
in a barrel of bosoms. (Z, 18)

Despite this dismissal, the following stanza gives us proof (on those macho terms) of the boy's 'masculinity', as he talks of leaving and going to the army because of 'a girl in the village getting herself pregnant'. His conclusion to the narrative talks of having learned his lessons: 'about eating shit / and the pecking order, / and the thickness of blood / and the thickness of water' (18). What strikes us about these 'lessons', as full of clichés as they could be, is their inadequacy as either explanation or conclusion. The poem as a whole appears strangely vacant, made up of quotations and repetitions, full of cliché and echoed idiom; it gives us the feeling that the boy, despite his sense of superiority towards Gideon and his father, has been entirely trapped within their language and conventions. In Butler's terms, the boy is learning to 'do' masculinity through his retelling of the 'script' represented and spoken by Gideon and his father, and his life with 'the boys in the barracks' equates to a simple continuation of this. There is no sense that, in Butler's terms, the boy is achieving a kind of agency through a redeployment of existing discourses; the emotional blankness of the narration, and the simple repetition – rather than reconfiguration – of clichés, suggests otherwise.

Another way of being masculine is amusingly spotlighted in 'Very Simply Topping Up the Brake Fluid', also in *Zoom!*. As in 'All We Can Do', the poem portrays a mechanic. In this case, the entire poem is spoken by the mechanic as he talks a female customer through topping up the brake fluid in her car. His talk is superbly patronising and benevolent, and part of the humour lies in imagining the possible range of unspoken responses from the woman, from fury and resentment to gratitude and amused tolerance. The presence of a woman seems to give the mechanic sudden license to express himself differently, so that even the most mundane of actions gains a kind of elegance:

> Now you're all right
> to unscrew, no, clockwise, you see it's Russian
> love, back to front, that's it. You see, it's empty.
> Now, gently with your hand and I mean gently,
> try and create a bit of space by pushing
>
> the float-chamber sideways so there's room to pour,
> gently does it, that's it. (Z, 30)

The mechanic's fascination with the woman's difference and his sense of her 'softness' is revealed in his amusingly solicitous advice on ablutions:

> Lovely. There's some Swarfega in the office
> if you want a wash and some soft roll above
> the cistern for, you know.

His talk while she is presumably away washing her hands provides a marked contrast to the rest – 'Now, where's that bloody alternator?' – while the final lines underscore the deeply condescending nature of the whole: 'If you want / us again we're in the book. Tell your husband' (30).

Ultimately, the poem's focus is the way in which women might experience male language. We can imagine the disruption in this scenario if the tutee refused to 'do' femininity in the expected manner; the mechanic's gentle courtesy is founded entirely on the assumption that the woman will be passive and grateful, to which expectation she at least appears to conform. It is a poem, then, about the pressure to meet a given performance of masculinity with an appropriate performance of femininity. The poem's implied ironic stance is signaled partly (as is often the case in Armitage's poetry) by the humorous effect of the contrast between content and idiom, on the one hand, and poetic form (in this case neat quatrains) on the other.[7]

In other poems in *Zoom!* Armitage seems to work towards possible reconfigurations of masculinity. For example, in poems about encounters with men who are marginalised in society, he writes about a kind of male intimacy that often goes unrepresented; an intimacy which is not sexual or 'matey' but has the quality of the familial. In 'Simon Says' the narrator is pulled into an encounter with a deaf and dumb man on the tube:

> His eyes roll. He touches his pale milky fingers
> to my lips and tests the weight of each word, he
> catches every word. We are sat on the floor
>
> to play this game: he puts his hand against
> his drawing pad and makes me trace again and again
> with a crayon the outline of its simple shape. (*Z*, 40)

In this poem there is no specific reference to masculinity, but in 'A Painted Bird for Thomas Szasz', a complex poem about marginalisation and scapegoating in society, Armitage presents a scene which takes its shape from the familiar depiction of encounters between gay men, but in this case is doing something rather different. The language of attraction, fascination, compulsion and desire is there, but in rather surprising contexts. The first line might seem amusing – 'It was his anorak that first attracted me' (*Z*, 44) – but as the poem goes on it reveals its seriousness, as the isolation of the watched man (a 'bus-spotter' obsessed with transport) becomes clear. The speaker is cautiously willing to enter into some kind of communication or relationship with the man:

> He caught me watching the reflection of his face
> so he exhaled onto the surface of the glass
> and wrote his name on it. Billy. I passed by him,
> breathing in, and he smelt like a wet dog, drying.

The corporeality of this encounter – the speaker *chooses* to breathe in as he walks past – signals the way in which the imagery of sexual attraction has been appropriated and transformed in order to evoke a kind of attraction which centres around care and empathy. The vulnerability of the man is signaled further by the imagery of the final stanza:

> I also saw him, once, in the covered precinct
> pissing himself through his pants onto the concrete
> and fumbling with the zip on his anorak.
> He bothered me, and later I had to walk back
> across where the dark circle of his stain had grown
> and was still growing, slowly, outward, like a town.

The title of the poem elucidates for us the nature of Armitage's focus; Thomas Szasz is a psychiatrist famous for his rejection of the medicalisation of mental illness and his advocacy of rights and responsibilities for those whom the system marks as 'insane'. 'The Painted Bird' is the title of the epilogue to Szasz's book *The Manufacture of Madness*, and it in turn refers to a book called *The Painted Bird* by Jerzy Kosinski. The story which Kosinski tells and Szasz retells concerns a disturbed and angry man who paints birds in order to mark them out as different from their fellows, thus causing them to be scapegoated and killed. Szasz relates this to labeling and diagnosis within the mental health system:

> As Lekh paints his raven, so psychiatrists discolor their patients, and society as a whole taints its citizens. This is the grand strategy of discrimination, invalidation, and scapegoating. Man searches for, creates, and imputes differences, the better to alienate the Other. By casting out the Other, Just Man aggrandizes himself and vents his frustrated anger in a manner approved by his fellows.[8]

Armitage's poem presents the loner in the anorak as just this kind of outcast, and the speaker's troubled fascination emerges out of his awareness of the exclusionary mechanisms of society – Armitage's work as a probation officer has no doubt sensitised him to these processes and their victims.

What is interesting about the poem in relation to gender and sexuality is the way in which it invokes the scene of gay sexual attraction but overturns it in order to present a version of masculinity which is not often seen – a man's almost physical, intimate sense of empathy and concern for another, unknown man. Such a sense of concern is usually only acknowledged in terms of men's familial or sexual relationships. This could be seen as an instance of Butler's 'reconfiguration and redeployment' of existing and familiar ways of being male. The poem does reflect the clash of different 'injunctions' in the sense that men are expected to have such capacity for nurturing and empathy at home, as fathers and lovers, but are required to separate this off from their public performance of masculinity in the work context and outside the home. The imagery of a gay encounter between strangers is at once familiar and, still, a little subversive, and for this reason it is useful in signaling the difficulty and danger involved in challenging cultural norms of masculine behaviour.

But while the poem itself might be seen as a successful 'reconfiguration or redeployment' of existing discourses, the man who is the focus of the poem actually effects, through his behaviour, a rather different mode of subversion. The corporeality of the encounter between the two men is important because it indicates a basic level of human vulnerability – reminding us, in the case of the urine stain, of childhood and of the way in which the scripts of adult behaviour involve the policing of the body. But I think it would be wrong to see the body here as antagonistic to the discursive; instead the poem shows how the body itself can tell a story. 'Script' seems the wrong word for this narrative, and Butler's notions of redeployment and reconfiguration also seem inappropriate, because the poem shows how an individual can use the body to tell a story which *is not* part of the acceptable range of roles or behaviours, but explicitly tells of (one might say *performs*) their breakdown or failure. In this case, paradoxically, the man who is in one sense both failure and outcast uses his body to communicate powerfully and effectively. This notion of the body as storyteller, as conveyor of meaning, is perhaps useful as a way of moving towards a breaking down of the troublesome opposition of body and mind, the material and the discursive.

I have focused on *Zoom!* because as a collection it presents such an interesting collocation of 'masculine' voices; there are many more examples besides those I have chosen. Armitage's subsequent collections continue and develop his interest in masculinity, though no collection has quite as much importance as *Zoom!* in this respect. *Kid* (1992) contains several poems that meditate on adolescence and the search for an adult male sexual and personal identity, with the title poem portraying Robin asserting his independence: 'I'm not playing ball boy any longer, Batman'.[9] The collection also contains several poems voiced for or about a character called Robinson, whom Armitage has adopted from the work of mysteriously disappeared American poet Weldon Kees, and reinvented. *Kid* thus mediates on poetic influence and independence (Gregson has suggested a punning link between 'Robinson' and Robin, son of Batman[10]) but at the same time Robinson provides an alter ego figure for Armitage, as he did for Kees.[11] For Armitage, in a collection containing several lyrical and celebratory poems about relationships that could be voiced for a 'Simon Armitage' figure ('In Our Tenth Year', for example), Robinson provides a means to explore the breakdown of relationship and of social ties. The cumulative effect of the Robinson poems is the portrayal of a character for whom the roles and tasks proffered by society proved impossible. Many of these tasks have to do with his role as a man – his wife apparently kicks him out or worse (and later he perhaps murders her) and in a work context he rejects male friendship: 'I couldn't give / a weeping fig for those so-called brothers / who are all voltage, no current' (*K*, 87). The 'Robinson' poems continue Armitage's focus on the loner and, since Kees and Robinson blur, they evoke an image of the poet as recluse or exile that is at odds with Armitage's very open and engaged self-presentation in public readings and appearances.

The struggle to find a kind of self-definition that will survive within society is explored in the title sequence of the *Book of Matches* (1993). This sequence consists of thirty sonnets that are dominated by the need for self-definition, linked by the motif of telling one's life story while a match burns down. At the beginning of the sequence many of the poems are over-strenuous in their attempts to claim identity, but by the end the subject has loosened into a kind of mesmeric fascination with his own, ever more wide-ranging narratives. Gregson suggests that the speakers are different people,[12] but the references to age in the poems suggest that the poems are efforts by 'one' speaker to create different versions of the self over time, some of them earnest, some self-parodying. Some of the early poems come across as strained attempts to define and claim a kind of 'masculine' strength, autonomy and decisiveness ('People talk nonsense and I put them straight', 'People never push me into doing things / I don't want to do', 'A safe rule in life is: trust nobody', 'Mice and snakes don't give me the shivers'[13]), but these are juxtaposed with poems which reveal more openness and insecurity. One of the poems presents as beautiful the memory of a boyhood glimpse of 'the parish spinsters' making love: 'Like water, to carry not to spill, / I went with it, out of the rain, the woods, / the instance of that new, unlikely love' (*BM*, 8). Overall the sequence seems to search for a way to negotiate a male identity that allows such experiences their place and significance.

Armitage's subsequent major poetry collections, *The Dead Sea Poems* (1995), *CloudCuckooLand* (1999) and *The Universal Home Doctor* (2002), are all much *less* concerned with the issues of gender and sexuality – and in particular, with the issues of masculinity and maleness. Armitage's focus shifts towards the metaphysical (perhaps prodded by the millennium, for which he wrote the long poem *Killing Time* (1999)), and although there are still many poems about intimate relationships, they do not manifest the same interest in the performance of gender. Nevertheless, I will end this discussion of Armitage by mentioning a poem from *The Universal Home Doctor* that, in common with quite a few of his more recent poems, presents relationship in terms of a rather unproblematic 'we', rather than probing the specifically gendered experiences of individuals. But 'The Strid' does explore the ambivalence of the 'we' in question towards the institution of marriage, as the couple find themselves making for 'the Strid' (a dangerous 'crossing point / on the River Wharfe') after their wedding, in a dramatic, romantic impulse which, the poem muses retrospectively, could easily be interpreted as a kind of death-wish.

The poem emphasises the sense of role playing which the wedding provokes – 'you in your dress of double-cream / me done up like a tailor's dummy'[14] – and, in the final imagined drowning scene, suggests the fear that marriage might bring entrapment and the death of the self:

> exhibits X and Y,
> matching rings on swollen fingers,
>
> and proof beyond doubt
> of married life –
>
> the coroner's voice, proclaiming us
> dead to the world, husband and wife. (*UHD*, 15–16)

The poem's most striking image for relationship is the 'two back-to-back rocks // hydraulically split / by the incompressible sap of the spine', after which the speaker notes 'let it be known / that between two bodies made one // there's more going on / than they'd have us believe' (14). The poem evokes the difficulty of negotiating the conflict between the complexity of personal experience and the reductiveness of social rituals, and conveys a sense of the couple's desire to make their performance of gender – for marriage is historically the most public performance of gendered roles – their own through some kind of 'reconfiguration' or 'redeployment'. The ending, however, with its irony that is at once flippant and morose, and its mockingly conventional life/wife rhyme, suggests that they have not achieved this.

Carol Ann Duffy

Carol Ann Duffy, who was born in Scotland in 1955 but grew up in England, is one of the most popular and beloved of contemporary poets. Many have compared her public profile with Philip Larkin's in a previous generation, and although Duffy is politically poles apart from Larkin, Justin Quinn has argued convincingly that in tone and technique the two poets have much in common.[15] This is particularly true of the early collections: *Standing Female Nude* (1985), *Selling Manhattan* (1987), *The Other Country* (1990), and *Meantime* (1993). It was with the comic brio of *The World's Wife* (1999) that Duffy broke through into truly large-scale popularity, though, and she has followed this up most recently with the appealing yet hard-hitting *Feminine Gospels* (2002). Duffy and Armitage have much in common, most obviously their fondness for the dramatic monologue and fascination with cliché and idiom. For both poets, these characteristics relate closely to their determination to explore the way in which discourses and cultural norms are 'performed' by speaking and acting subjects – and for Duffy even more than for Armitage, the central focus of interest is gender and sexuality. We can see the influence of Sylvia Plath in Duffy's use of the dramatic monologue and mythologisation to explore the experience and performance of gender.

Critics have demonstrated the way in which Duffy's poems interrogate 'the way in which language "speaks" the individual and the implications of this process for women whose subjectivity and social existence is negatively constructed in this way'.[16] Rather than retrace the steps of critics like Thomas who have explored the performative effects of Duffy's poetry, I will concentrate in this chapter on Duffy's portrayal of the body. The issue of bodily experience is often avoided in contemporary theoretical discussion because it represents a crux in the debate over social construction. While we might be happy to accept that our conscious thought life is in some sense a product of pre-existing social systems, it is less easy to accept that the body – or even bodily experience – can be categorised entirely in this way. Even if we accept that our adult experience of embodiment is necessarily always mediated by symbolic systems, is this equally the case for a foetus, for example?

Such issues are raised by Carol Ann Duffy's poem 'Homesick', from the 1987 collection *Selling Manhattan*, which seems to evoke a state of embodied experience prior to language:

> When we love, when we tell ourselves we do,
> we are pining for first love, somewhen,
> before we thought of wanting it. When we rearrange
> the rooms we end up living in, we are looking
> for first light, the arrangement of light,
> that time, before we knew to call it light.[17]

Such 'nostalgia' tends to be frowned on as dangerous self-delusion today, but I think this is wrong; poems like this one point us towards important questions, contentious and unresolved in contemporary theory, about the relationship between the body and consciousness. These issues relate closely to the gender/sex debate, as gender has historically been linked to consciousness and sex to the body. This dualism, deriving ultimately from Descartes, is becoming less and less persuasive, both for theorists like Butler who argue that 'sex' as a material, non-linguistic reality does not exist, and for other theorists who argue that such dualism, which assumes a neat split between mind and body, is radically inadequate as a way of describing our holistic experience of sexed embodiment.

Carol Ann Duffy is always attentive to the ways in which the experience of embodiment shapes our selfhood. The dramatic monologue is of particular interest in this respect, because as a genre it has always thrived on a sense of division or dialogism, often, but by no means always, produced by the reader's sense of a difference of opinion or perspective between speaker and author. One of the easiest ways of indicating difference is making the gender of the speaker different from that of the poet. It is interesting that while in Duffy's early poetry there are many poems which use this device (such as 'You Jane' and 'Psychopath'), there are none in the last two collections. *The World's Wife* contains only monologues voiced for women, while *Feminine Gospels* is made up mostly of poems narrated in the third person, with a few lyrics interspersed. I want to concentrate mostly on Duffy's two most recent collections, but will begin by looking briefly at some of the early cross-gendered monologues.

'You Jane', from *Standing Female Nude*, is interesting as an early example of a male-voiced monologue that draws attention to sexual difference. The poem paints a glaring picture of male brutality; as David Kennedy notes, 'each assertion of male prowess is placed with a statement that either displays contempt for or enacts domination of women.'[18] The ideological distance between poet and subject is of course obvious given what we know of Duffy from her other poems, but this is also indicated within the poem by the mocking title. There is another suggestion of the poet's perspective, as Deryn Rees-Jones has noted, in the final lines:

> I wake half-conscious with a hard-on, shove it in.
> She don't complain. When I feel, I feel here
> where the purple vein in my neck throbs.[19]

Whether the final line is an 'unexpected return to the poetic', as Rees-Jones suggests,[20] or simply an image which implies an external rather than an internal perspective, the image certainly reminds us of the poet's presence (as might the ironically perfect iambic hexameter of 'I wake ...'). We are reminded of the poet's construction of the subjectivity depicted in the poem, and, more than this, of the poem as a woman's fantasy of a particular kind of male subjectivity. The poem's focus on the *body* and on the man's sexual relationship with his wife emphasises the otherness of the subjectivity that Duffy is trying to give us access to. Or is she? Poems like 'You Jane' might make us a little uncomfortable not because of the effort to represent the experience and subjectivity of a person very different from the author (most literature is based on this imaginative empathy), but because the difficulty and risk of this leap of imagination is not made obvious in the poem, apart from the slight self-consciousness of that last line. This might be behind Duffy's fascinating comment in 2002 that 'I now probably wouldn't write a poem like "You Jane", because although it was based on a real person it might come across as a stereotype. I doubt I would now write a poem in the male voice.'[21]

The relationship between the two sentences of Duffy's comment is enigmatic, but if there is a problem with 'You Jane', it must be that the poem (aided by its title) comes across as having prejudged its subject – and judged him very negatively – and in this sense does not *really* attempt to see the world from the subject's perspective. 'Psychopath', from *Selling Manhattan*, is different in this regard; it also signals the 'outsideness' of its perspective through the title,[22] but throughout the poem we get a sense of the historical causes of the speaker's behaviour – sexual abuse as a child, anger and hurt at his mother's affair with 'the Rent Man' and his father's disappearance – and also of the complex and confused processes of his mind, in which Dirty Alice (the childhood abuser) and the girl he is about to rape become blurred into one. There is a distinctive quality to the speaker's language and imagery, as he reworks cliché and idiom slightly oddly, that conveys a sense of interiority – 'Let me make myself crystal', 'A right-well knackered outragement'; 'Bang in the centre of my skull, / there's a strange coolness' (*SM*, 28–9) – even as Duffy through allusions to Eliot ('down by the dull canal', 'The barman calls Time' (29)), alliterative phrases ('my shoes scud sparks against the night' (28)), and references to reflection, image and representation reminds us of the poet's outside – and necessarily partial – perspective, as Gregson and Rees-Jones have shown.[23]

The poem shows how the subject's violent version of 'masculinity' is formed from a collocation of available cultural norms and icons; as Rees-Jones notes, 'The psychopath sees himself in terms of the heroes of Hollywood films – James Dean, Marlon Brando, Elvis, Humphrey Bogart. His projection of self is itself a masquerade of masculinity.'[24] As well as reminding the reader of the poet's presence, the speaker's references to image and reflection ('My reflection sucks a sour Woodbine and buys me a drink' (29)) also suggest a self-consciousness on his part about the way he has gone about constructing a self-image from the culture's icons of masculinity. We might compare him with Armitage's speaker in 'All Beer and Skittles'; while both poems rely on the reproduction of idiom to accentuate the repetitive performance of cultural scripts of masculinity, Duffy's speaker seems more self-conscious of this process, more bitter, more playful, and more able to tweak the script. Nevertheless, he has no real capacity for change. The depressing predictability of the transition from abused child to rapist may be blamed partly on the way in which the stories our culture tells – or told in the 1950s – about masculinity leave no way for men to understand their experience as victims of sexual abuse. The abuser shows a contempt for the child's body ('Dirty Alice flicked my dick out when I was twelve. / She jeered' (28)) which is then reproduced by the man as he juxtaposes the image of a dog crapping by a lamp post with his own seduction attempt and rape.

'Psychopath', as an attempt by Duffy to imagine a 'masculine' subjectivity of the most disturbed and disturbing kind, is effective, and if Duffy does ever return to male-voiced monologues, it will be interesting to see how her approach has changed. Recently, though, she has used monologues by women to comment upon masculinity as well as femininity. *The World's Wife* has been enormously popular; even in New Zealand, where I am writing, a home-grown stage version toured the country. Because the collection is 'themed' – nearly every speaker is a woman involved in some way with a man famous from history, mythology, or fiction, while a few are women famous in their own right, like Pope Joan – some critics have seen it as a populist step for Duffy. But although the collection provides entertainment, it explores very complex issues, and although the dominant note is humour, many of the poems are like brightly lit rooms with dark, shadowy corners. The poem from *The World's Wife* that cries out for consideration in relation to the gender/sex debate is *'from Mrs Tiresias'*.[25]

This poem from *The World's Wife* is comical, flippant, and provocative. Tiresias is turned into a woman, and, after splitting up with his wife, goes out into the world, 'entering glitzy restaurants / on the arms of powerful men', or 'on TV / telling the women out there / how, as a woman himself, / he knew how we felt' (*WW*, 16). According to his wife, however, his performance of femininity was never quite convincing:

> The one thing he never got right
> was the voice.
> A cling peach slithering out from its tin.
>
> I gritted my teeth. (*WW*, 17)

This poem in a sense rejects the idea that people can simply pick and choose their gender identity – 'one day I'll "do" masculinity, the next femininity' – since Tiresias is unable to perform femininity convincingly (at least from his wife's perspective) even with the useful aid of a body labeled as female by society. At the same time, however, it rejects the idea that gender derives simply from the body – that if you have a female body femininity will come 'naturally'. Instead, it suggests that being 'feminine' is a complex state that is the result of a long process of social enculturation *and* a long experience of particular kind of sexed physical embodiment.

Interestingly, Mrs Tiresias turns from her radically altered husband to another woman, raising the fascinating possibility that Tiresias's transformation could represent, on a symbolic level, an attempt to please his wife by becoming what she really wanted – a female lover. He does so only to find that his performance of femininity is inadequate. Of course, in the actual myth, Tiresias is turned into a woman because he struck two snakes when they were copulating, and becomes famous for his claim (for which he was punished by Hera) that women gain more enjoyment from sex than men. Here, Duffy's Tiresias flirts with powerful men but it is suggested that he cannot adjust to sex with men: 'I knew for sure / there'd be nothing of *that* / going on / if he had his way' (16). Jeffrey Wainwright suggests that whereas in the Greek myth, Hera is angry with Tiresias for revealing the secret of women's pleasure in sex with men, in Duffy's version the secret that women do not want men to know 'is a lesbian one', and Tiresias catches a glimpse of a different way of being feminine when he sees his wife's lover and imagines the two women together.[26] There is a sense that sex between 'women' might allow Tiresias to find a way of being which slips between the dominant cultural norms of 'masculine' and 'feminine' and find an alternative way of being a 'woman', although it is not altogether clear that his wife will welcome him into this world.

'Pope Joan', quoted at the opening of this chapter, also explores the significance of the sexed body. The poem does not suggest that Joan somehow fails to pull off the performance of masculinity which her role requires (until the final dénouement, of course) or that she feels guilty for her deceit and embraces her 'womanly' identity out of guilt; instead, Joan looks with a cold eye on the system of privilege and power which constitutes the church, and dismisses it as a sham, finding the miraculous instead in the body and in the specifically female activity of giving birth. Pope Joan's experience of the body in childbirth is of it taking her somewhere different, somewhere she hadn't been before – this new and strange sense of the body's energy she figures as 'the power of God' (*WW*, 68). She is not able, then, to talk of this 'new' bodily experience in an utterly new way – she is reliant on reworking existing ways of talking – but the poem still reminds us that the experience of *being a body* is crucial in shaping – and sometimes shaking up and entirely reforming – our sense of selfhood and being.

While at times Duffy does emphasise a sense of being trapped within the dominant discourses of gender, many of the poems in *The World's Wife* are actually notable for celebrating women's capacity to achieve a kind of agency over their sexual relationships and their gender identity, in the face of efforts to subdue and control them. For example, in 'Little Red Cap', the opening poem, the speaker self-consciously adopts the role of 'sweet sixteen, never been, babe, waif' in order to attract the wolf, who is a successful and very 'masculine' poet, reading poetry in a clearing with 'red wine staining his bearded jaw' (*WW*, 3). Her seduction of the wolf is all in aid of poetry; she finds that in his lair 'Words, words were truly alive on the tongue, in the head, / warm, beating, frantic, winged; music and blood' (4). But at the end of ten years in the woods the wolf's song comes to seem deathly, repetitive, drained of life, so 'Little Red Cap' takes her axe to the wolf and sees

> the glistening, virgin white of my grandmother's bones.
> I filled his old belly with stones. I stitched him up.
> Out of the forest I come with my flowers, singing, all
>   alone. (4)

If the wolf represents the male literary tradition,[27] then the grandmother's bones symbolise the silencing of past generations of women writers. The bones provide a symbolic resource for 'Little Red Cap' to start a new life – and write a new kind of poetry – on her own. Even in consciously adopting the apparently subordinate role of the young, adoring, vulnerable girl, she is able to achieve a kind of agency that enables her to gather resources to emerge out of that role. Any new gender identity she adopts will not be entirely self-created – the 'grandmother's bones' suggest that she draws on the past – but there is a strong sense that it is possible to make real choices about what kind of gendered identity one wants to have or live.

The picture of women's autonomy which emerges from *The World's Wife* suggests a broader concept of agency than is allowed for, for instance, by Butler's notions of parody and the clash of multiple injunctions. It has to be said, however, that in *The World's Wife* women are most successful at achieving some kind of agency by getting rid of their menfolk in some way (see 'Eurydice', 'Mrs Rip Van Winkle'), or else their achievement of agency scares their men off ('Pygmalion's Bride'). There are very few poems which suggest the achievement of agency by women within an equal relationship with a man; 'Mrs Beast', for example, declares the necessity of inequality within the relationship and asserts her dominance: 'Let the less-loving one be me' (75). The only poem (apart from the sonnet 'Anne Hathaway', which is something of an anomaly in the book) that envisages a mutually satisfying relationship can only do so by making the woman in question, 'Queen Kong', so much bigger than the man that gender roles are forcibly overturned.

Duffy's reluctance to envisage women achieving a sense of self-creation and self-determination within heterosexual relationships leads, perhaps, to her decision to leave men behind altogether in *Feminine Gospels*, where most of the poems are stories told in the third person about women characters. The collection is a curious and vibrant mixture of styles, moving from fantastical yet sombre allegories, through the tour de force of the long narrative poem 'The Laughter at Stafford Girls' High', to the meditative lyrics and elegies that close the book. The book is marked by a consciousness of the international crises of 2001 and 2002, and several of the poems seem to imagine forms of embodiment that are a response to the desperation seen around the world. For instance, in 'Tall' the woman grows taller and taller, at first being seen as an oddity and a freak, but growing steadily until she

> was taller than Jupiter, Saturn, the Milky Way. Nothing
> to see. She looked back and howled.
>
> > She stooped low
> and caught their souls in her hands as they fell
> from the burning towers.[28]

The following poem, 'Loud', also seems to emerge out of a feeling of impotence or inadequacy in relation to current events. The woman, enraged by 'the News', becomes louder and louder, until finally, her voice, bawling, hollering and howling, expresses and contains all the terror, sorrow and violence of the world (*FG*, 26). These two poems obviously work to counter traditional notions of the female body as weak, small and vulnerable, but, more than this, they emphasise the desire to respond to the world not just by talking, disapproving, discussing, but as an embodied human being – to make the body act powerfully, or at the very least, express emotions forcefully and dramatically.

'The Laughter at Stafford Girls' High School' in a sense continues this theme because the laughter that infects the school uncontrollably, and sets off a chain of events leading to most of the staff resigning to pursue their secret dreams and the school closing down, is precisely so threatening to the school's sense of propriety and decorum because laughter involves the whole embodied person, and, in this case at least, isn't under conscious control. The chaos is not strictly carnivalesque because order is never regained; it is an exuberant vision of the collapse of the pompous, earnest, prudent and decorous, and of the victory of mirth and clear-sightedness. There is not a man in sight, apart from Mrs Mackie's husband, whom she leaves, and in this sense the poem epitomises the woman-centred vision of *Feminine Gospels*. Does this, along with the choice of exclusively female speakers in *The World's Wife*, mean that Duffy is comfortable thinking about 'women' as a collective, that she is comfortable with the idea that there is a clear binary division between the sexes? In a sense this is true – she does not really disrupt the category of 'woman' or 'women' as referring to a sex within the binary male/female (Tiresias's sex-change still operates around the binary), and she assumes some commonality of experience in the way in which, historically, women have struggled with restrictive sex/gender roles and an imbalance of power in relation to men. However, the meaning and lived experience of that femaleness – and one's experience of one's body – is presented as negotiable and varying within historical and cultural contexts. Certain aspects of female embodiment are held in common in some very basic sense – for example, menstruation, which Tiresias finds particularly challenging – but the subjective experience of this embodied reality is not fixed or determined or in any sense 'natural'.

The first poem from *Feminine Gospels* provides an ambiguous commentary on this very point. 'The Long Queen' envisages a figure who has something of the quality of Elizabeth I (she rejects all her suitors and takes Time for a husband, she sends 'her explorers away in their creaking ships' (1)) and is the queen of all girls and women, ruling them unseen from a mysterious place. The Long Queen is an ambivalent figure, as the section on the law on 'childbirth' suggests:

> *Childbirth*: most to lie on the birthing beds,
> push till the room screamed scarlet and children
> bawled and slithered into their arms, sore flowers;
> some to be godmother, aunt, teacher, teller of tall tales,
> but all who were there to swear that the pain was worth it.
> No mother bore daughter not named to honour the
> Queen. (2)

This stanza suggests that all women, whether they actually give birth or not, have some commonality in their relationship to children – or at least, this is what the Long Queen's law envisages or enforces. The poem is marvellously ambiguous on this point, for while it frequently seems to be celebrating the common experiences shared by women, there is an undertone of compulsion suggested by the references to colonialism (explorers are sent out to ensure that she is 'queen of more') and the insistence that women should be happy with their lot – the pain of menstruation should be 'insignificant, no cause for complaint' (2), and childbirth should always be considered worth the pain. Reminiscent again of historical exploitation by monarchies, the tears of women are turned into jewels 'for the Long Queen's fingers to weigh as she counted their sorrow' (2), an ambiguous image since it also suggests empathy. The final stanza seems to present the Long Queen positively as gaining pleasure from the stories of women, 'her ear tuned / to the light music of girls, the drums of women, the faint strings / of the old' (2). Overall, the poem is a very effective symbolic representation of the ambivalence which women feel towards the categories 'woman' and 'women'. Cleverly and subtly, it protests against the 'imperialism' of those who want to dictate how women *should* feel about their female embodiment, but at the same time it celebrates – in a qualified way – the possibilities of empathy and community which commonality *can* facilitate.

Grace Nichols

Grace Nichols was born in Guyana in 1950 and lived there until 1977, when she moved to Britain. She has published four major collections of poetry for adults, as well as novels and poetry for children. Nichols's first collection, *i is a long memoried woman*, published in 1984, evokes moments in the lives of the black women who collectively and individually experienced slavery and the forced shift from Africa to the Caribbean. The collection is one long sequence, divided into five sections, and the poems vary greatly in their style, moving between standard English and creole, and between conventional free verse and poetry which in its rhythms and use of repetition evokes oral literature. The sequence reveals a sense of solidarity on the part of the poet with women of past generations, whether in Africa or the Caribbean, and it also manifests a strong focus on the female body, both as an image for strength, resistance and continuity, and as the object of violence and exploitation by white people. Many of the poems explore the struggles, agonies and precarious pleasures of being a mother in the desperate context of slavery.

The first poem, 'One continent / to another', merges at the beginning mother and child, so that the 'she' in the poem is at once giving birth and being born:

Child of the middle passage womb
push

daughter of a vengeful Chi
she came
   into the new world
birth aching her pain
from one continent/to another[29]

The middle passage is imagined as a traumatic and painful birth,
from which the 'new world' woman emerges in pain and humili-
ation ('the metals dragged her down'). But (setting the tone for the
whole sequence, which emphasises women's capacity to endure,
to create and to begin again) the woman 'moved again' and sets
out to start a new life, grieving for the fact that her children will be
'walking beadless / in another land' and shocked by the 'loss of
deep man pride' in the men's eyes (*lmw*, 6–8). In the very next
poem, though, Nichols makes sure that we are not assigning her
poetry to the cult of women's maternal suffering. Her speaker
(this poem is in the first person, whereas the first one is in the
third) rejects the embracing of suffering, the view that 'mother is
supreme burden' (9), instead seeing her own role as that of the
spreader of joy and pleasure, the teller of tales, the healer.

The following poem, however, shows the difficulty of main-
taining such a stance under such physical and mental oppression.
'Days that Fell', in its repetition of the first four stanzas after an
intervening section of determination and hope, traces the endless
cyclical movement from depression to resolve to depression:

And yet ……
And yet ……

the cutlass in her hand
could not cut through
the days that fell
like bramble (11)

The whole sequence plays out the struggle to survive and emerge
through 'the days that fell / like bramble', to hold on to hope
despite the memory of past trauma and the humiliations of the
present.

One of the most shocking poems tells the story of a woman
who suffers a terribly painful death in punishment for having
killed her own newborn baby to save it from a life of slavery. 'Ala'
takes its title from the name of the Ibo mother-goddess of fertility

and death, and the end of the poem turns into a prayer to Ala:

> O Ala,
> Uzo is due to return to you
> to return to the pocket
> of your womb
>
> Permit her remains to be
> laid to rest – for she has
> died a painful death (24)

There is considerable emphasis placed on a dynamic of female support and spiritual nourishment, whether it be in relation to a female deity (as in 'Ala' and 'Yemanjoi'), to the speaker's mother (as in 'Sacred Flame' or '...... Your Blessing'), or to the sense of women as a collective (as in 'We the women'). References to women's biology reinforce the sense of a commonality between women, but this is in no sense simplistically celebratory, as this example from 'Among the Canes' reinforces with its comparison between menstrual flow and the loss of faith:

> Like the cyclic blood
> that snaps within her
> so too her faith
> flowing
>   in darkness   across the fields
> now she's over-run
> by the mice of despair (27)

The emphasis on women's shared experience, along with the centrality of the body in the sequence, has led several critics to view it in terms of that problematic concept, *écriture féminine*, which tends to be associated with French feminist theorists like Cixous, Irigaray and Kristeva. Gabrielle Griffin, for example, links Nichols's *i is a long memoried woman* with *écriture féminine* and with Kristeva's concept of the semiotic.[30] Loosely, *écriture féminine* suggests a kind of writing which is distinctively feminine. Insomuch as *écriture féminine* refers to a kind of writing that subverts the linear, logical order of the symbolic, and is associated with an openness to bodily drives, rhythms and desires, it can be compared to Kristeva's concept of the semiotic, but complex differences emerge between Cixous, Irigaray and Kristeva over the extent to which *écriture féminine* (or a writing open to the semiotic) is specifically linked to the female body, as opposed to being associated with femininity as a marginalised position within the patriarchal symbolic order. Denise deCaires Narain notes that

> the thematic focus on the body in Nichols' work parallels many French feminist concerns: the frequent emphasis on woman's body as signifying plenitude and possibility, rather than limitation and despair; the celebration, rather than shame, attendant upon menstruation, childbirth, and other 'messy' female bodily functions and fluids; the characterization of patriarchy as rigidly rational and uncreative; the irreverent tone and playful mockery of canonical, patriarchal texts and the deployment of the erotic as a counter-discourse; and suggestions of autoeroticism in the image of the fecund black woman enjoying her sensuality for and of itself.[31]

At times, Nichols's exploration of the symbolic dimensions of bodily experience is more complex than is implied by the word 'celebration', as her use of the image of menstruation in 'Among the Canes' demonstrates, but it is true that much of her work is energised by a desire to reclaim the black female body and to explore repressed dimensions of female sexuality and eroticism.

However, Narain goes on to question the extent to which Nichols can be stylistically (as opposed to thematically) associated with *écriture féminine*, arguing that 'Nichols' emphasis on presenting positive images of black women signals a belief in the power to shift the resonances of words and images without a radical challenge to the symbolic system which generates such images and words.'[32] We should also note that while Nichols does, within the sequence, alternate between standard English and various kinds of creole usage, within each poem her usage of register is relatively consistent, meaning that the categories remain stable. Rather than celebrating Nichols's writing as radically, anarchically disruptive of the dominant symbolic order, perhaps we can view it more in terms of Kristeva's therapeutically informed perspective on the healthiness of a balance between the symbolic and the semiotic. Nichols's speaking subjects welcome the body and the energies and drives that it brings (the semiotic), and they incorporate it to some extent through the emphasis on oral rhythms, but they do not enact a radical rejection of the communicative and representational power of the symbolic order of language.

We do see in Nichols's poetry an effort to reclaim ownership and enjoyment of the body in the face of slavery's physical appropriation of the black female body and Western culture's disparagement of it. Like Kristeva, she emphasises the way in which childbirth can generate distinctive and intensely significant experiences of embodiment for women. At the same time, these experiences are experienced in and through culture, so that the woman in *i is a long memoried woman* who becomes pregnant with the white man's baby is torn by the conflicting dynamics generated by her cultural and historical position; between guilt and self-hate, on the one hand, and forgiveness and healing on the other. But the specificity of the sexed body seems to provide particular kinds of potential; in this case, Nichols sees pregnancy and motherhood as providing an opportunity for a specific kind of nurturing and openness to the other. It provides a means of transforming the violent and ugly into the loved and beautiful:

> my tainted
>
> perfect child
>
>> my bastard fruit
>> my seedling
>> my sea grape
>> my strange mulatto
>> my little bloodling (56)

Nichols's second collection, *The Fat Black Woman's Poems*, published in 1984, emphasises the way in which black women must struggle to achieve a positive and healthy sense of embodiment in the face of negative stereotypes. The first half of the collection is entitled 'The Fat Black Woman's Poems', and, like *i is a long memoried woman*, it moves freely between first-person and third-person accounts of, quite simply, being a fat black woman. The fat black woman is intensely aware of the way in which society views her body: the 'white robed chiefs' of Asanti tribal power who sit 'resigned' as she asserts her power by refusing to leave the golden stool, the symbol of the Asanti nation;[33] the white slave-owning family who employ her mother as a 'Jovial Jemima' whose body must work for the white children before her own (*FBW*, 9); the 'pretty face sales girls' in London who 'exchange thinning glances' as she shops for clothes (11); the men who 'only see / a spring of children / in her thighs' (14); the history of racist fascination with the black woman's body which is alluded to by the repeated use of the word 'steatopygous' in 'Thoughts drifting through the fat black woman's head while having a full bubble bath' (15);[34] the assumptions which underpin phenomena like 'Miss World' (20).

The sequence's overt ambition is to put forward a manifesto which counters all these discourses: a manifesto which celebrates the body of a fat black woman as erotic, powerful, sensual, confident, and comfortable in itself. The poems take a humorous approach; the fat black woman is not only confident enough to take on the world, but takes it on laughing. 'The Fat Black Woman Remembers', however, suggests that laughter can sometimes be a cover for darker emotions, as the woman pictures her mother, 'playing / the Jovial Jemima', 'tossing pancakes / to heaven / in smokes of happy hearty / murderous blue laughter' (9). When the fat black woman takes on a first-person voice, as in 'Invitation', the prejudices of her interlocutors are always implied:

If my fat
was too much for me
I would have told you
I would have lost a stone
or two (12)

The most effective poem in the sequence is perhaps 'The Fat Black Woman Composes a Black Poem', which addresses Nichols's interest in the way in which 'black' needs to be reimagined to counter the associations embedded in Western literature and mythology.[35] The poem is overtly about blackness rather than gender, but even here the experiences of black women as sexual objects are suggested: 'Black as the intrusion / of a rude wet tongue' (16). The poem seeks both to evoke the trauma and suffering which is associated with being black, and to rediscover beautiful blackness: 'Black as the sweetness / of black orchid milk'.

Towards the end of the sequence the tone becomes less humorous and more earnest, and the final two poems envisage a kind of apocalypse in which humanity is wiped out through its own foolishness (shrapnel, wasted shells, toxic shoals of fish blight the landscape (23)), leaving the fat black woman in 'Afterword' to emerge from the forest 'flaunting waterpearls / in the bush of her thighs / blushing wet in the morning sunlight' (24). Interestingly, the focus is on vision: 'there will be an immense joy / in the full of her eye / as she beholds' and this is enabled because the wind has pushed 'back the last curtain / of male white blindness'.

In a critique of Gabrielle Griffin, Denise deCaires Narain notes that we must be wary of slipping into the trap of assuming that 'black women's texts are *especially* corporeal' because 'black women are somehow more in touch with their bodies and more "natural" ',[36] as such a view relies on a limiting stereotype. Nevertheless, we should not let our caution about this prevent us from seeing the occasions upon which Nichols herself seems to suggest this very thing. Does 'Afterword', the final poem, present the black woman as intrinsically more 'natural' than either men or white people ('male white blindness' seems to implicate both), needing only to free herself from false ideology in order to experience her true natural self? Certainly there is a 'blindness' around in the world which is blamed on white men, or white people and men; does this blindness prevent *everyone*, white men included, from living naturally, in a way which nurtures rather than destroys the earth, or is this naturalness only truly possible for black women? The poem is ambiguous on this, but it certainly views the black woman as having a special capacity (whether by nature or because of historical oppression is unclear) to envisage a better and, it is implied, a more natural future way of life. This future is not entirely utopian, though; the potential for conflicts of power still remains, as is suggested by the final line. The fat black woman needs to 'stake her claim again', asserting a new and different role in history, this time one of empowerment rather than oppression.

'In Spite of Ourselves', the second half of the collection, with its diverse portraits of individuals, both English and Caribbean, and its meditations on memory and childhood, links us into *Lazy Thoughts of a Lazy Woman and other poems*, published in 1989, which is more loosely structured than either 'The Fat Black Woman's Poems' or *i is a long memoried woman*. In *Lazy Thoughts* we encounter a view of being a woman that clearly links the experience of femininity with the body. A poem like 'Ode to My Bleed' declares the capacity of the biological cycle of menstruation to 'tell me who I am / reclaiming me', reminding her of the moon, the tides, the seasons, birth and death.[37] The sense of being connected with ancient and eternal natural cycles is, for Nichols, a powerful aspect of her experience of being an embodied woman. In terms of Kristeva's scheme of three 'generations' or phases,[38] this is second-generation feminism, determined to celebrate woman's difference rather than simply claim power within the patriarchal system. In line with Cixous and Irigaray in particular, Nichols sees female sexuality as a subversive erotic force – 'my black triangle / has spread beyond his story / beyond the dry fears of parch-ri-archy' (*LT*, 25) – and as fundamental to the origins and process of writing, 'For poems are born / in the bubbling soul of the crotch' (16).

In this collection Nichols sets out to transform disempowering representations of women; so in 'Configurations' the familiar erotic subtext of colonisation, white man as conquerer and seducer, black woman as land to be seduced and conquered, is reworked so that the black woman is pleasured and empowered:

> She delivers up the whole Indies again
> But this time her wide legs close in
>   slowly
> Making a golden stool of the empire
> of his head. (31)

We remember the golden stool of the Asanti of Ghana from 'The Assertion'; the transformation of the white man's head into such a stool suggests that the black woman is not only in a position of power in the relationship, but is achieving power through the reclamation and reinterpretation of her own African heritage and customs. Another limiting representation of black women is referred to in 'Of Course When They Ask for Poems About the "Realities" of Black Women', in which Nichols explores the pressure to produce depictions of black women which feed particular agendas. In particular it is the liberal agenda that is critiqued here, as Nichols suggests that the apparently altruistic desire to hear about the difficulties experienced by black women actually emerges out of a need to keep black women in their place as victims, people for whom the white intelligentsia can feel sorry.

In *Sunris*, Nichols's 1996 collection, the most interesting section is the long title sequence which celebrates carnival as a joyous amalgamation of influences and histories; a place in which all of the Caribbean's cultural and religious strands come together. So the French influence is manifested in 'Papa Bois', the Pan-figure of Caribbean folktales, while native American history is strongly present in the dialogue with Montezumi, the Aztec emperor who welcomed Cortes because he thought he was a god. 'Africa' herself appears as a 'woman in a shroud of grey',[39] and African gods like Yemanja and Kali dance alongside the Virgin Mary:

> And you too Virgin Mary gyal
> shaking up like celebration
> I see dih Pope casting doubts
> bout your immaculate conception (73)

The tone shifts from humour like this to the incantatory rhythms of the refrain:

> *And is dih whole island*
> *Awash in a deep seasound*
> *Is hummingbird possession*
> *Taking flight from dih ground*
> *Is blood beating*
> *And spirit moving free*
> *Is promiscuous wine*
> *Is sanctity.* (54)

Although the sequence (and the collection generally) is less focused on gender and sexuality than Nichols's previous writing, carnival is, in Nichols's introduction, clearly set up as a temporary escape from restrictive gender roles: 'Who can keep their daughters forever from the "forbidden" or more "rowdy-side" of life?' (*S*, 1). The beginning of the poem asserts that this is a specifically female interpretation and experience of carnival:

> Symbol of the emancipated woman I come
> I don't care which one frown
> From the depths of the unconscious I come
> I come out to play – Mas Woman.
>
> This mas I put on is not to hide me
> This mas I put on is visionary – (52)

The 'mas' or costume she puts on seems to combine the symbols of Isis, the sun-goddess, and Iris, the goddess of the rainbow. The 'deep dance mystery' that is carnival allows her to envisage a different reality in which the goddesses and gods of myriad mythologies come to life in the dancers; it also represents a sensual and erotic generosity and openness. The energy of carnival is not linked specifically to the female but it is an erotic energy, an energy that can be harnessed if it is chosen but oppressive if it is not:

> It was me of my own free will
> Who choose to be embraced by this river.
> To enter freely into this sweat-of-arms
> Wrapped like innocent electrical eels about me (64)

Like 'The Fat Black Woman's Poems', this poem also ends with the evocation of a new dawn:

> With the Gods as my judge
> And dih people my witness,
> Heritage just reach out
> And give me one kiss.
> From dih depths of dih unconscious
> I hear dih snake hiss,
> I just done christen myself, SUNRIS. (74)

Self-assertion is enabled through mythologisation; as 'Mas-Woman' the speaker is able to claim a prophetic and visionary role, speaking to and for a hybrid and various community from a perspective that is highly conscious of its femininity.

For Nichols, being a woman is intrinsically linked to the specificity of the experience of the female body. Whether this makes her 'essentialist', a word which I have deliberately avoided throughout this chapter because it has become tedious in current debate, is another question. It is possible to believe that the specificity of female embodiment provides particular potentialities for certain distinctive kinds of experience, without asserting that the exact nature of these experiences remains the same through history and across cultures. However, Nichols does often emphasise continuity and commonality over difference, for example in her suggestion in 'Ode to my Bleed' that her experience of menstruation connects her with 'The first primeval fire / lit in the forest temple // Where I watched / O so long ago' (*LT*, 24). This would be labeled 'essentialism' by many theorists as it seems to imply there is something stable and universal about 'woman'. Whether this is something to be rejected or not must be decided by individual readers, not all of whom will be postmodernist in their views on the matter. But such a label seems to risk minimising the degree to which Nichols is also interested in achieving change – changing how black women are seen, changing how black women see their own bodies and their sexuality, changing the entire cultural vista, both in the Caribbean and in England – by claiming a voice. And while Nichols draws on African mythology and other strands of Caribbean tradition, she is not interested in simply recreating a lost past; her poems set in England show clearly that she embraces the way in which cultures and individuals can change and hybridise. This change inevitably applies to gender and sexuality as well, as, for instance, in 'Winter Thoughts', where the Caribbean speaker finds images for her sexuality, 'reduced' but still intense, in England's winter:

> I've reduced the little
> fleshy tongues of the vagina
> to the pimpled grate
> and the reddening licking flames (*FBW*, 32)

Conclusion

This chapter has sought to draw out points of comparison and difference between three poets who have never before been brought together in a discussion of gender and sexuality. Armitage and Duffy have in common their skilled use of the dramatic monologue in order to reveal the process of the construction of self-image, including sex/gender identity, something that Nichols also experiments with in some of 'The Fat Black Woman's Poems'. All of the poets are in different ways concerned with the manner in which society enforces particular versions of masculinity and femininity – and for Nichols, of course, the discourses of femininity cannot be separated from those of race. All proffer alternatives to the dominant versions – Armitage in a muted fashion, Duffy and Nichols much more flamboyantly. Interestingly, when one places Armitage's poetry alongside Nichols's and Duffy's, one notices that the body is much less prominent in his poetry (despite its interesting role in 'A Painted Bird for Thomas Szasz'), even

though masculinity is such a prominent issue. This is, I think,
reflective of a wider imbalance in men's and women's awareness
of – or at least interest in – embodiment and its contested
significance.

Notes

1 Carol Ann Duffy, *The World's Wife* (London: Macmillan, 1999), p. 68.
  Henceforth referred to as *WW*.
2 Judith Butler, *Bodies that Matter: On the Discursive Limits of Sex* (New York:
  Routledge, 1993), p. 7.
3 Judith Butler, *Gender Trouble: Feminism and the Subversion of Identity*
  (New York: Routledge, 1990), p. 140.
4 Butler, *Gender Trouble*, p. 145.
5 Ibid., p. 146.
6 Simon Armitage, *Zoom!* (Newcastle upon Tyne: Bloodaxe, 1989), p. 11.
  Henceforth referred to as *Z*.
7 Ian Gregson comments that Armitage's poems achieve a 'detachment that
  arises from the sense of distance that arises between the colloquial idioms
  and the poetic form in which they are placed, Armitage's symmetrical
  stanzaic patterns'. *Contemporary Poetry and Postmodernism: Dialogue and
  Estrangement* (Basingstoke: Macmillan (now Palgrave Macmillan), 1996),
  p. 118.
8 Thomas S. Szasz, *The Manufacture of Madness: A Comparative Study of the
  Inquisition and the Mental Health Movement* (London: Routledge and Kegan
  Paul, 1971), p. 292.
9 Simon Armitage, *Kid* (London: Faber, 1992), p. 37. Henceforth referred
  to as *K*.
10 Gregson, *Contemporary Poetry and Postmodernism*, p. 119.
11 See David Kennedy's *New Relations* for a discussion of the influence of
  Weldon Kees (and Robert Lowell) on Armitage. *New Relations: The
  Refashioning of British Poetry 1980–1994* (Bridgend: Seren, 1996), pp. 203–7.
12 Gregson, *Contemporary Poetry and Postmodernism*, pp. 251–3.
13 Simon Armitage, *Book of Matches* (London: Faber, 1993), pp. 9, 10, 14, 15.
  Henceforth referred to as *BM*.
14 Simon Armitage, *The Universal Home Doctor* (London: Faber, 2002), p. 14.
  Henceforth referred to as *UHD*.
15 Justin Quinn, 'The Larkin-Duffy Line', *Poetry Review*, vol. 90, no. 3 (2000),
  pp. 4–8.
16 Jane Thomas, ' "The chant of magic words repeatedly": gender as linguistic
  act in the poetry of Carol Ann Duffy', in *The Poetry of Carol Ann Duffy:
  'Choosing Tough Words'*, eds Angelica Michelis and Antony Rowland
  (Manchester: Manchester University Press, 2003), pp. 121–42 (p. 121).
17 Carol Ann Duffy, *Selling Manhattan* (London: Anvil, 1987), p. 19.
  Henceforth referred to as *SM*.
18 Kennedy, *New Relations*, p. 227.

19 Carol Ann Duffy, *Standing Female Nude* (London: Anvil, 1985), p. 34.

20 Deryn Rees-Jones, *Carol Ann Duffy* (Plymouth: Northcote House, 1998), p. 21.

21 Peter Forbes, 'Profile: Carol Ann Duffy', *Guardian Review*, 31 August 2002, pp. 20–4 (p. 20).

22 Neil Roberts has argued that 'outsideness' is a key motif for Duffy. Of 'Psychopath' he argues that 'Of all titles, this one most brashly appears to claim a privileged interiority. At the same time the word is a "label", attached from the outside and appropriating the ability of the subject to speak from the inside.' *Narrative and Voice in Postwar Poetry* (Harlow: Addison-Wesley Longman, 1999), p. 188. For myself the second of these qualities is most prominent; the title only signals 'interiority' in the sense that the medical profession claims to have privileged access to the minds of the mentally ill; this is not a true sense of subjective interiority.

23 Rees-Jones, *Carol Ann Duffy*, pp. 21–2; Gregson, *Contemporary Poetry and Postmodernism*, pp. 96–7. Gregson writes: 'The language of Duffy's poem suggests the poet's voice as much as the psychopath's – "my shoes scud sparks against the night" is imagist in rhythm and in the way it juxtaposes light and dark, and sounds like something that would be more comfortable in the third person rather than the first' (p. 97).

24 Rees-Jones, *Carol Ann Duffy*, p. 21.

25 The 'from' was added to the title after a pedantic audience member at a reading felt it necessary to remind Duffy that there was more to the story of Tiresias than what was included in the poem.

26 Jeffrey Wainwright, 'Female metamorphoses', in *The Poetry of Carol Ann Duffy: 'Choosing Tough Words'*, eds Angelica Michelis and Antony Rowland (Manchester: Manchester University Press, 2003), pp. 47–55 (p. 49).

27 Rees-Jones, *Carol Ann Duffy*, p. 27.

28 Carol Ann Duffy, *Feminine Gospels* (Basingstoke: Picador, 2002), p. 24. Henceforth referred to as *FG*.

29 Grace Nichols, *i is a long memoried woman* (London: Caribbean Cultural International, 1983), p. 6. Henceforth referred to as *lmw*.

30 Gabrielle Griffin, 'Writing the body: Reading Joan Riley, Grace Nichols and Ntozake Shange', in *Black Women's Writing*, ed. Gina Wisker (Basingstoke: Macmillan (now Palgrave Macmillan), 1993), pp. 19–42 (p. 26). According to Kristeva, the semiotic is experienced by infants in the presymbolic *chora* (the rhythmic, expressive space of oneness with the mother which exists prior to the development of representational language and a sense of self). The semiotic is continually present to varying degrees within the symbolic order, for example in the rhythms and tones through which bodily energy and affect are discharged in language. See 'The semiotic and the symbolic', in *The Portable Kristeva*, ed. Kelly Oliver (New York: Columbia University Press, 1997), pp. 32–70.

31 Denise deCaires Narain, *Contemporary Caribbean Women's Poetry: Making Style* (London: Routledge, 2002), p. 194.

32 Ibid., p. 195.

33 Grace Nichols, *The Fat Black Woman's Poems* (London: Virago, 1984), p. 8. Henceforth referred to as *FBW*.

34 See Denise deCaires Narain's discussion of this poem in *Contemporary Caribbean Women's Poetry*, pp. 187–8. Narain notes how Saartjie Bartmann,

the 'Hottentot Venus', became a focus for European 'fetishizing of the black woman's buttocks'. She quotes Sander L. Gilman, who says that 'Sarah' Bartmann was exhibited in Europe 'not to show her genitalia but rather to present another anomaly which the European audience ... found riveting. This was the steatopygia, or protruding buttocks, the other physical characteristic of the Hottentot female which captured the eye of early European travellers.' Sander L. Gilman, 'Black bodies, white bodies: Toward an iconography of female sexuality in late nineteenth-century art, medicine, and literature', in '*Race*', *Writing, and Difference*, ed. Henry Louis Gates Jr (Chicago: University of Chicago Press, 1985), pp. 223–62 (p. 232). Quoted in Narain, p. 187.

35 See Nichols's comments on this in 'The battle with language', in *Caribbean Women Writers: Essays from the First International Conference*, ed. Selwyn R. Cudjoe (Wellesley, MA: Calaloux, 1990), pp. 283–9 (p. 287).

36 Narain, *Contemporary Caribbean Women's Poetry*, p. 194.

37 Grace Nichols, *Lazy Thoughts of a Lazy Woman and Other Poems* (London: Virago, 1989), p. 24. Henceforth referred to as *LT*.

38 See Julia Kristeva, 'Women's time', trans. Alice Jardine and Harry Blake, *Signs*, vol. 7, no. 1 (1981), pp. 13–35.

39 Grace Nichols, *Sunris* (London: Virago, 1996), p. 65. Henceforth referred to as *S*.

4

'Widdershins round the kirk-yaird': Gender, Sexuality and Nation

Eavan Boland, Gillian Clarke, Kathleen Jamie, David Kinloch

In a poem called 'Cailleach', the Irish-language poet Nuala Ní Dhomhnaill tackles that image which has been the focus of so much feminist criticism in recent years: woman as land. The poem is translated by John Montague as 'Hag':

> Once I dreamt I was the earth,
> the parish of Ventry its length and breadth,
> east and west, as far as it runs,
> that the brow of the Maoileann
> was my forehead, Mount Eagle
> the swell of my flank,
> the side of the mountain
> my shanks and backbone,
> that the sea was lapping
> the twin rocks of my feet,
> the twin rocks of Parkmore
> from the old Fenian tales.

The dream is forgotten until one day on the beach the narrator's daughter comes running to her frightened:

> 'What's wrong?' 'O, Mam, I'm scared stiff,
> I thought I saw the mountains heaving

like a giantess, with her breasts swaying,
about to loom over, and gobble me up.'[1]

'Hag' does not renarrate a specific legend or myth, but takes its impetus from the many stories and poems in which Ireland is imaged as a woman. Rather than woman as land waiting to be occupied, raped, reclaimed, named, fertilised, cultivated, and so on, the identification with the land is for the narrator in 'Hag' a fantasy of power. The primary sensation of the description of the dream is above all of hugeness, while the figure whom the daughter sees on the beach is gigantic, threatening, and in motion. The symbolic significance of what is narrated in this poem is psychologically complex in terms of the mother–daughter relationship, given that the mother identifies herself with the giantess figure but is at the same time the figure to whom the daughter runs in order to be saved from the threat of the giantess. The poem can be read as encoding the ambivalence of maternal power for the daughter who is attempting to achieve individuation and separation. In Ireland, traditional images of woman as land have used the figure of 'woman' to represent the relationship between man and nation; Ní Dhomhnaill's poem recuperates the image of woman as land to express the complexities of the relationship between mother and daughter, and to explore the sensation of material and physical power.

This kind of revisionist myth-making has been particularly necessary in Ireland. When, in 1943, De Valera, president of the Irish Free State, pronounced his vision of the new Catholic society that he envisaged for his country, it was strongly based on conservative values of rural piety. It would be, he says,

A land whose countryside would be bright with cosy home-steads, whose fields and villages would be joyous with the sounds of industry, with the romping of sturdy children, the contests of athletic youths and the laughter of comely maidens, whose firesides would be forums for the wisdom of serene old age. It would, in a word, be the home of a people living the kind of life that God desires that man should live.[2]

The origins of the Republic of Ireland are strongly rooted in such visions of unchanging values, traditional ways of life, and clearly demarcated gender roles. Even in the present day gender and sexuality remain central to the image of the nation, with issues such as divorce and abortion generating raging controversies in which the nature and very existence of the Irish nation is claimed to be at risk. These debates are subtly energised by a tradition of nationalist rhetoric that has relied upon feminine images to represent the Irish nation: Kathleen Ní Houlihan, the Shan Van Vocht. The Irish context provides a particularly clear example of a pattern that recurs, with differences, in other cultural contexts. The concepts of nation and gender are often intricately intertwined, each participating in the construction of the other. Feminism has often seen this intersection – and particularly the common identification of women and land – as deeply problematic, and nationalism itself is frequently viewed by feminists as being a regressive, exclusionary and homogenising ideology. However, an alternative perspective is put forward by Marilyn Reizbaum:

> The feminist call in Scotland and Ireland for the reformulation of the canon of Scottish and Irish works parallels the challenge to the mainstream Anglo-American establishment presented by Scotland, Ireland, and other countries in cultures like them – former colonies who retain a marginalized standing in relation to the former colonizer.[3]

Here nationalism and feminism are aligned as valid and necessary struggles for recognition and autonomy by oppressed groups or cultures. Reizbaum recognises, however, the tendency of nationalist ideologies to become oppressive, and argues that this is a danger faced also by feminism:

> Nationalism and feminism encounter many of the same vexing questions: that is, does an assertion of positive identity necessarily move toward unanimity, homogeneity, essentialism, fixity, to an ironic betrayal of the principles by which the movement is guided?[4]

Reizbaum argues that the conjunction of nationalism and feminism will produce a 'dynamic relation of movements' which can be 'more revolutionary in its resistance to a reductive and/or idealized type'.[5] The idea behind this is simply that individuals or groups with multiple investments or agendas will have to face conflicts and contradictions which will force them to modify overly simplistic notions and to allow ideas from one arena to feed into and alter the ideas in another.

The relationship between discourses of femininity and discourses of nation naturally alters when women become more involved in the actual institutions of the nation, and as social norms change. Recent years have seen major political changes in this regard. The nineties saw the rise of the Northern Ireland Women's Coalition, which has played a key role at crucial moments in the shaky history of the Northern Irish Assembly, and in 2000 the Centre for the Advancement of Women in Politics was set up at Queen's University, Belfast. From 1990 to 1997 Mary Robinson was the first female President of the Republic of Ireland, in 1993 the Republic legalised homosexuality under pressure from the EU, and in 1995 the Irish voted to allow divorce. Abortion is still banned in the Irish Republic. Some 39.5 per cent of the SMPs elected to the Scottish Parliament in 2003 are women, and 50 per cent of members of the Welsh Assembly elected in 2003, compared to only 16.7 per cent of the Northern Irish Assembly (despite the efforts of the Women's Coalition), 18.1 per cent of members of the House of Commons (2001) and 13.3 per cent of members of the Daíl (2002). So the new institutions, discounting the Northern Irish Assembly, have considerably more female politicians.

The relevance of the issue of nation and gender is not, however, limited to women. Nationalist movements frequently draw on a very limited palette in their portrayal of masculine roles as well, valorising militaristic or macho qualities in men and excluding homosexual male identities from the range of acceptable roles. In this chapter I would like to discuss the poetry and prose of three women and one man: Eavan Boland from the Republic of Ireland, Gillian Clarke from Wales, and Kathleen Jamie and David Kinloch from Scotland. It is important not to minimise the differences between these contexts. For example, although the image of the 'Celtic' sovereignty-goddess, which is important in my discussion of Eavan Boland, can be found in myths and tales written in Welsh, Scots Gaelic and Irish, this figure – and her various transformations in nationalist literature – is much more prominent in the Irish tradition than in the others. The idea of the 'nation' clearly has a different history in each of these contexts, and this chapter seeks not to smooth over these differences but to tease out some interesting parallels, connections and contrasts between poets writing in Ireland, Wales and Scotland today.

Eavan Boland

While other Irish writers may grow impatient with the pressure to write on 'the matter of Ireland', Boland (b. 1944) has been committed from very early on to exploring the relationship between writing and nation. The Irish Republic has always been characterised by an awkward disjunction between its ideal self-image and its face in the mirror of everyday life; the most obvious example, for a long time, was the official constitutional claim to the six counties of Ulster, which Irish voters relinquished in 1998 as part of the Good Friday Agreement. Eavan Boland's poetry and prose suggests that other disjunctions have been more invisible or unacknowledged. She argues that the image of the nation that has propelled and underpinned Irish Republicanism is an oppressive, reductive and false image that ignores the realities of women's historical experience:

> Irish poems simplified women most at the point of intersection between womanhood and Irishness. The further the Irish poem drew away from the idea of Ireland, the more real and persuasive became the images of women. Once the pendulum swung back, the simplifications started again. The idea of the defeated nation's being reborn as a triumphant woman was central to a certain kind of Irish poem. Dark Rosaleen. Cathleen ni Houlihan. The nation as woman; the woman as national muse.[6]

Boland also suggests that nationalist ideology has excluded women from the role of writer by fostering and celebrating the image of the romantic nationalist male poet who draws on the feminised nation for his subject matter and inspiration.

In *Object Lessons* Boland describes her slow journey towards the development of a distinctively female poetic voice in a literary context dominated by men. She herself sees her early poetry as derivative, modeled on a late Romantic formalism and a Yeatsian cadence. There is certainly a radical divide between her first two books, *New Territory* (1967) and *The War Horse* (1975), and the Plath-influenced *In Her Own Image* (1980), with its intense, dark, sometimes satirical contemplations of women's experience of their bodies. After *Night Feed* (1982), which evoked the details of everyday domestic experience and motherhood, we can see Boland becoming more and more concerned with writing a poetry which would not simply reject the idea of the nation but engage with it in a new way, recuperating women's experience. *The Journey and Other Poems* (1987), *Outside History* (1990), *In a Time of Violence* (1994), *The Lost Land* (1998) and *Code* (2001) all reflect this concern. Instead of the woman as muse or regenerative principle, Boland seeks to uncover the connections between 'the defeats of womanhood and the suffering of a nation'.[7] She aims to uncover a more complex version of the nation by revealing women's stories and the way in which they have been repressed by the 'mythologies' of Irish nationalism.

Frequently Boland represents this process in terms of an opposition between myth and history. History is usually identified as 'what really happened', a reality which is often painful. Myth is presented as the product of an urge to escape from reality, a desire for false comfort, an inability to face and remember the truth, an unwillingness to confront the real suffering of powerless groups like women, and a desire to make reality conform to an aesthetic pattern:

> O consolations of the craft.
> How we put
> the old poultices on the old sores,
> the same mirrors to the old magic.[8]

Myth is seen as 'the songs / that bandage up the history, / the words / that make a rhythm of the crime' ('Mise Eire', *JOP*, 10). In 'Outside History' the stars represent distance, abstraction, inhumanity; they are 'outside history' and are implicitly associated with myth, as the narrator decides to move 'out of myth into history':

> I have chosen:
>
> out of myth into history I move to be
> part of that ordeal
> whose darkness is
>
> only now reaching me from those fields,
> those rivers, those roads clotted as
> firmaments with the dead.[9]

History, then, is generally associated with human suffering and loss, and also with action and event. Myth is the product of the trajectory 'from action to image', '[f]rom event to invention'.[10] In particular, Boland is interested in the way women's lives have been smoothed over and elided by art and myth-making. So 'Self-Portrait on a Summer Evening' watches Chardin 'painting a woman / in the last summer light': 'Before your eyes / the ordinary life / is being glazed over' (*JOP*, 12).

'Mise Eire', one of Boland's most well-known poems, situates this process within Irish nationalism. 'Mise Eire' means 'I am Ireland', and the poem attacks the tradition of nationalist rhetoric that personified Ireland as an idealised female figure. The poem is a response to a famous Irish-language poem also called 'Mise Eire', by Patrick Pearse, one of the leaders of the 1916 Easter Rising. The English version of Pearse's poem is as follows:

> I am Ireland:
> I am older than the Old Woman of Beare.
>
> Great my glory:
> I that bore Cuchulainn the valiant.
>
> Great my shame:
> My own children that sold their mother.
>
> I am Ireland:
> I am lonelier than the Old Woman of Beare.[11]

The Old Woman or Hag of Beare (Cailleach Bhéarra) derives from the sovereignty-goddess figure and was often used in politicised literature to personify Ireland.[12] In Irish mythology, the right king had to be found to sleep with the sovereignty-goddess before the land (and the goddess) could be regenerated; from Pearse's perspective, the right young men had to be found to fight for Ireland and restore her to herself. As Clair Wills notes, 'Mise Eire' was also 'the normal response of the beautiful and radiant maidens of the eighteenth and nineteenth-century Aisling ("Vision") poems on interrogation concerning their identity'. The maiden would reply 'I am Ireland and I am sick because I have no true and manly husband.'[13] Boland's poem seeks to oppose individual women's histories to this appropriation of the feminine to evoke the nation. The speaker, who might be thought of as a representative modern Irish woman or as a figure representing the 'real' Irish woman, says

'I won't go back to it – // my nation displaced / into old dactyls' (*JOP*, 10) – dactyls perhaps indicating a somewhat strained and artificial verse in English, and the heroic metre of the classical epics – and follows this with images of the masculine tradition of rural nationalist agitation. Instead of 'the songs / that bandage up the history, / the words / that make a rhythm of the crime', the speaker turns to an alternative and more disturbing history: 'My roots are brutal' (10). The speaker then locates her history or true roots in the experiences of an Irish prostitute in the English garrison, and an impoverished mother emigrating to America.

Many feminist critics have felt uncomfortable with this poem, concerned that Boland has in fact reproduced the kind of simplifying strategies that she is trying to subvert. Clair Wills comments that although Boland seeks to provide instances of women's 'personal' experience to counter the public appropriation of femininity, the poem itself reveals that there is no sphere of experience which can be designated 'personal': 'what the poem in fact stresses is that [the woman's] sexuality is publically owned (through prostitution), her personal story *is* a public narrative.'[14] Gerardine Meaney comments that the 'versions of femininity presented in the poem are once again shocking in their stereotyping … . The feminine "I" speaks from either side of the madonna–whore dichotomy, instanced as the garrison prostitute and the emigrant mother.'[15] Both of these critiques are valid, and Meaney's in particular draws attention to the fact that Boland's attempts at revisionism sometimes fail because the images which she presents as alternative are themselves rather stereotyped and one-dimensional.

While Boland often operates around a dichotomy between 'myth' and 'history', there is also a consistent alternative conception of 'myth' to be found in her work – a version of myth that is not opposed to history but expressive of its truths. Boland has, in fact, a conception of oral narratives as the 'real myths', as opposed to those myths that have been accepted and developed by the literary and political establishment. In *Object Lessons* she describes the story of her great-great-grandfather's Jacob and Leah style marriage to the wrong girl as a 'real' myth, as opposed to those of the Celtic Revival:

> While hayricks burned and gunfire could be heard at night after evictions, Germanic scholars worked over the old Irish stories and resurrected them in a new European timeframe.

In all this some of the real myths were ignored: those down-to-earth and hand-to-mouth yarns which start in fear and short-circuit into a pure and elaborate invention. Which bind a community together not by what they explain but by the very fact that they were forced to explain it.[16]

The old Irish myths are seen primarily as the tools of romantic Irish nationalism, while the oral narratives are seen as spontaneously generated stories reflecting true experience. In Chapter 7 of *Object Lessons* this sense of 'positive myth' is extended; we are told that poetry 'enters at the point where myth touches history'.[17] Boland goes on to suggest that 'myth' is the profundity in everyday things, associated with ritual, continuity with the past, and a sense of cyclical time.

It is this positive version of myth that Boland seeks to recover in poems exploring oral narratives shared by women. In 'The Oral Tradition', the speaker, who has been leading a poetry workshop or reading, overhears a woman telling another woman the story of someone who had to give birth alone in a meadow. She is waylaid by the story, and identifies this narrative with the 'oral song' which is 'layered like an amber in / the wreck of language / and the remnants of a nation'. Travelling home, the wheels of the train take up the rhythm of the story: 'singing innuendos, hints, / outlines underneath / the surface, a sense / suddenly of truth, / its resonance' (*JOP*, 16). Here we have the qualities of orality, rhythm, continuity with the past. This oral tradition is, however, perceived by Boland to be endangered if not irrecoverable. 'What we lost' imagines the speaker's mother as a child being told a story by her mother, and claims, 'Believe it, what we lost is here in this room / on this veiled evening' (*OH*, 43):

The fields are dark already.
The frail connections have been made and are broken.
The dumb-show of legend has become language,
is becoming silence … . (44)

Boland's poetry is characterised by a persistent sense of loss – loss of the Irish language, loss of the fullness of the oral tradition, the loss or elision of individual women's histories. Her poetry does at times veer too strongly towards sentimental nostalgia or regret; lines like 'we are too late. We are always too late' (*OH*, 45) suggest that the speaker has already come to terms with the loss she is mourning, that she is at a stage of almost self-indulgent grief, rather than at the point of crisis. There is a sense, sometimes, that the elegiac position has been too complacently and too easily established.

At other times – for example, in the long poem 'Anna Liffey' from *In a Time of Violence* – Boland's work is powerful in its exposure of the difficulties encountered by women seeking to build a sense of self which takes full account of – and engages positively with – their historical, cultural and geographical contexts. 'Anna Liffey' 'usurps' the 'name and theme'[18] most famously used by Joyce in *Finnegans Wake*, and probes both the limits and the potential of the symbolic feminisation of the Liffey river in Dublin. Boland is wary of the dangers of too-rigid symbolism, wanting to use language lightly and leave 'signs' or 'marks' rather than archetypes: 'A river is not a woman' 'any more than / A woman is a river', although its patience, its powerlessness, 'the history it makes and suffers', 'the names it finds' are all 'signs' of a connection (*ITV*, 43). The river is a teller of stories, a creator rather than a silent witness, a symbol of the constant flow of narratives. As in all of Boland's poetry, there is a struggle to come to terms with a sense of fragmentation, and a longing for unification and constancy:

> Maker of
> Places, remembrances,
> Narrate such fragments for me:
>
> One body. One spirit.
> One place. One name.
> The city where I was born.
> The river that runs through it.
> The nation which eludes me.
>
> Fractions of a life
> It has taken me a lifetime
> To claim. (42)

Although the speaker at the beginning seems to long for wholeness, stability, and unity of language and experience, as the poem progresses mutability and instability become more prominent. The mutability of water, from sea, river and rain to a single tear, becomes an image for the way in which the relationship between language and experience is continually shifting and unstable. In particular, Boland explores the way in which subjective experience of the body can alter our relationship to the linguistic structures we inhabit, and in particular, the way in which a woman's experience of ageing seems to find no easy expression in language:

> An ageing woman
> Finds no shelter in language.
> She finds instead
> Single words she once loved
> Such as 'summer' and 'yellow'
> And 'sexual' and 'ready'
> Have suddenly become dwellings
> For someone else –
> Rooms and a roof under which someone else
> Is welcome, not her. (44–5)

'Anna Liffey' clearly reflects a desire on Boland's part to face the mutability of language and of home, and to create an image of woman that will encode this instability. This is successful on several levels: the Liffey is central to Dublin's identity and its narratives of identity, is truly located, and yet it flows out and into the sea, allowing that identity to dissolve and be dispersed; it is continually in movement. The end of the poem is perplexing, however, as instead of continuing to hold the troubling and productive tension between self, place, and language, it opts for resolution through dissolution; as the Liffey flows into the sea so the individual will flow into 'nothingness'. Intriguingly, Boland implies that her femininity, which is experienced as the greater part of '[e]verything that burdened and distinguished me' (46), is identical with the body and will disappear when her body disappears. What *will* endure will be a 'voice', but this voice, according to the metaphor of the poem, will be dissolved into the 'phrases of the ocean', just as the Liffey flows towards its own 'nothingness' (46). Although the conclusion achieves a kind of grandeur, it may disappoint in its decision to opt for a rather rhetorical dissolution rather than ending with a sense of commitment to the difficult, ongoing process of expressing an embodied, located existence in language.

Boland's next collection, *The Lost Land*, is dedicated to Mary Robinson, 'who found it'.[19] The president had quoted Boland in her inaugural address, bestowing on Boland, as Clair Wills says, a kind of unofficial poet laureateship in the Republic of the Robinson years.[20] The collection is dominated by the same preoccupations as earlier collections: the sense of scarring or woundedness in Irish identity and language, the longing for a true sense of home, and the importance of remythologising, of 'changing the story' (*TLL*, 57). Gender is still very prominent here, as in 'Daughters of Colony', where the speaker asserts a common sense of 'broken speech' and 'other-whereness' with the daughters of colonial families who were never quite at home anywhere. Most obviously, however, 'Mother Ireland' engages explicitly with the myth of woman as land, imagining the moment in which the mythologised figure learns her name and rises up from the land to tell a different story. The interesting part of this poem is the ending, in which the newly independent 'Mother Ireland' – or, perhaps, the collective of Irish women through history – looks 'with so much love / at every field' that 'they' misunderstand her:

> *Come back to us*
> they said.
> *Trust me* I whispered (39)

It is tempting to read 'Mother Ireland' in this case as representing Boland herself, and the poem as being about the pressure from the literary and political establishment to stop being oppositional. In any case, it clearly implies the need for an ongoing, stubborn and scrupulous examination of the stories that are being told about women and the nation.

Code, Boland's latest collection (published, with a few differences, as *Against Love Poetry* in the USA), has a sense of freshness about it, partly due, perhaps, to the influence of Boland's American experiences, and partly due to the decision to write a nuanced and complex sequence on 'Marriage'. This sequence, which is the record and celebration of the poet's thirty-year marriage, views the personal experience of marriage in the wider context of feminism and the dominant literary and mythological narratives of love and eros. But the book's second sequence, 'Code', returns us more fully to Boland's preoccupation with history, and, particularly, with women's role in it. As Clair Wills notes, several poems in the sequence suggest that '[i]f only we know where to look, there are means of deciphering the hidden, fragmentary messages from the past, of recovering lives from history's enigmatic scramblings.'[21]

In a poem like 'How the Earth and all the Planets were Created', however, the poet-speaker searches without success for any 'codes' to illuminate her grandmother's life:

> I went to find the grave of my grandmother
> who died before my time. And hers.
>
> I searched among marsh grass and granite
> and single headstones
> and smashed lettering
> and archangel wings and found none.[22]

In the absence of any information whatsoever about her grand-mother, the speaker decides to erase all known history from the landscape, to view it as her grandmother was looked upon, 'Unloved because unknown. / Unknown because un-named' (C, 44). As the famous scene of the battle of the Boyne becomes sim-ply 'willow-trees and distances' the speaker drives home looking at the night sky and sees the constellations,

> some of them twisted into women:
>
> pinioned and winged
> and single-handedly holding high the dome
> and curve and horizon of today and tomorrow.
>
> All the ships looking up to them.
> All the compasses made true by them.
> All the night skies named for their sorrow. (44)

The poem seems to suggest that we must begin again with our naming of the world if we are to do justice to the role of women within it, a narrative that has been elided. Historical retrieval is one strategy; another is to look afresh and create new and differ-ent narratives and images to mediate our experience of the world.

In another poem in this collection, 'Is it Still the Same', Boland considers the young generation of Irish women writers who are beginning to undertake these tasks, and who are now starting to combine writing and parenting:

> I wrote like that once.
> But this is different:
> This time, when she looks up, I will be there. (47)

Wills asks (but does not answer) the question, 'Is this overweening pride, or an accurate sense of her own importance?'.[23] While we may be somewhat uncomfortable with Boland's rather solemn presentation of her own status within Irish literature, there is no doubt that, in many ways, that final line is simply, indubitably true. Boland *has* had a remarkable impact on Irish poetry, by bringing a feminist consciousness into a literary scene that was overbearingly male, and pointing out the oppressiveness of the convergences of discourses of gender and nationalism. Whether young Irish women poets view their poetry as aligned with or opposed to Boland's aesthetic, her presence is always intensely felt.

Gillian Clarke

The Welsh poet Gillian Clarke is one of many women poets from other national contexts who have referred to Boland as a strong influence. Boland was born in 1944, Clarke in 1937. They are both part of the generation of women who fought for a radical change in women's role in society in the 1960s and 1970s. Their poetry has a great deal in common; both poets seek to represent women's experiences of domesticity and motherhood and to explore the possible tensions but also the possible energies generated by the conjunction of domestic life and poetry. In both cases, their work of the 1970s was new simply in its decision to confront poetry with the ordinary life of women. Clarke and Boland seek to explore the limitations and restrictions of traditional feminine roles but also to retrieve and valorise some traditionally 'feminine' activities that have been denigrated in the past.

Whereas Boland in volumes like *Night Feed* seeks to represent the life of a suburban mother, Clarke's framework is predominantly rural, particularly in her earlier work. In its approach to nature and to place, Clarke's poetry works in a tradition shared with R.S. Thomas, Ted Hughes, Seamus Heaney and Michael Longley, but differs in its attentiveness to the processes and relationships associated with the female: pregnancy, childbirth, mothering. Her poetry about rural life is often distinctively Welsh in its place-names and other references, and Clarke, like Boland, links the situation of individual women with the ideologies that shape Wales as a nation. Welsh nationalism in the twentieth century has struggled to gain momentum, in the face of rapid social changes including large-scale movements of English people into Wales.

Nigel Jenkins compares Wales's 'sprawling belly of a frontier' to Scotland's 'neat little waist of a border', suggesting that Welsh defensiveness about or overprotectiveness of Welsh culture can be traced to the insecurity of a people 'on the edge' who are always in danger of being pushed off.[24]

This overprotectiveness and anxiety can be clearly seen in Welsh critics' responses to Gillian Clarke's poetry. Several male critics have been anxious to assert that feminism takes a secondary place in Clarke's work because she does not wish to undermine Welsh solidarity. M. Wynn Thomas, for example, asserts that

> Solidarity is a feature of the Welsh past which is more than ever a necessity in the Welsh present if there is to be a Welsh future. Under such socio-cultural circumstances, the issue of gender-conflict takes on a very different complexion. Clarke's poetry consistently tries to redress the balance – of the historical record, in social arrangements, of cultural life – in favour of previously slighted female experience. But it attempts to do so *without* destroying the fragile integrity of her people by setting male against female.[25]

This is an astonishingly naïve comment, for a book published in 1999, and the astonishment is intensified when one reads in the next paragraph a reference to Marilyn Reizbaum's article. Wynn Thomas enacts another instance of the ideology of nationalism and national solidarity repressing very real tensions and differences within the communities that make up the nation. He fails to appreciate the homogenising and exclusionary tendencies of this kind of drive for solidarity. Wynn Thomas's readings of Clarke's poems persistently seek to show that gender differences are, for Clarke, ultimately subsumed within 'the overriding, primary category of the undifferentiatedly "human" '.[26] This is a kind of wilful misreading of Clarke; in fact, Clarke's poems repeatedly emphasise the way in which gender is a disruptive factor within traditional conceptions of Welshness.

Clarke's poem 'Llyr', from her second full collection *Letter from a Far Country* (the first was *The Sundial*, 1978), is one of those Wynn Thomas cites as finally subsuming gender differences to the universalities of the 'human condition'.[27] In fact, this poem is one of the most penetrating in its critique of the patriarchal character of Welsh culture. The speaker remembers the experience of visiting her first Stratford play, which happens to be *King Lear*. The Welsh origins of the name Lear, which occurs as Llyr in a number of Welsh myths, trigger a sudden perception of doubleness and the complexity of the relationship between language and meaning, and this is merged with a sense of the oppressive but also vulnerable character of the patriarchal culture represented by Lear, Llyr, and the old men who seem to dominate the Welsh landscape:

> The landscape's marked with figures of old men:
> The bearded sea; thin-boned, wind-bent trees;
> Shepherd and labourer and night-fisherman.
> Here and there among the crumbling farms
> Are lit kitchen windows on distant hills,
> And guilty daughters longing to be gone.[28]

This reverses the familiar Celtic motif of woman as land, and instead participates in a characteristic Clarke pattern of the outdoors being associated with men and the woman or girl feeling contained and trapped inside the house. The 'Old Celtic kings' are associated with all 'forefathers' and 'the more recent dead':

> Those we are still guilty about, flowers
> Fade in jam jars on their graves; renewed
> Refusals are heavy on our minds. (*LFC*, 27)

Cordelia's refusal here becomes a symbol for all the times a woman has refused to conform to the expectations of a significant father-figure; the guilt and anxiety that goes with it, but the necessity of that refusal. The father-figures here are specifically associated with Welshness, from Lear to the 'figures of old men' marking the Llyn landscape. Far from subsuming gender difference into an evocation of universal human sadness, the poem's ending dwells on the instability of meaning and the implicit context for this is the failure of Lear and Cordelia to understand the same things from the same words – a failure this poem links overtly to gender difference.

Clarke's long poem 'Letter from a Far Country', in the same collection, has also been classified as diluted feminism. Jeremy Hooker argues that the fact that the poem shows love for the traditional way of life prevents the poem from expressing real rage; he sees this as 'a compromise as far as feminist convictions are concerned' but suggests that this duality 'greatly enriches it as a work of art and increases its psychological authenticity'.[29] This kind of argument is obviously motivated by a desire to deny the potential complexity of feminist perspectives, as if only rage can be classified as truly feminist. In fact, a key aspect of the feminist agendas of both Boland and Clarke is the recovery of the dignity and worth of women's historical experience. Clarke portrays a woman fulfilling a traditional homebound role and experiencing this both positively and negatively. The aestheticising of the daily household tasks which we find in the first sections of 'Letter from a Far Country' is similar to Boland's description of traditional female roles in 'What we lost', where the careful crafts of country-women are linked to the crafting of stories for children (*OH*, 43–4), while the ambivalence in 'Letter from a Far Country' mirrors Boland's darker ambivalence about ritualised domesticity in *Night Feed*: 'am I / at these altars, / warm shrines, / washing machines, dryers // with their incense / of men and infants / priestess / or sacrifice?'.[30]

Jeremy Hooker is right in saying that the 'duality' of 'Letter from a Far Country' is central to its effect; it surprises the reader because it holds contrary impulses so close together: the desire to be gone, to reject the lifestyle which is offered, and the affection for the rhythms and beauties of the known life. What makes the poem complex is the uncertainty which the reader is left with as to how this affection functions for the speaker: is it produced simply by a seductive ideology of being indispensable, having a place – a sense of importance which in fact masks the real powerlessness of the woman concerned? Does the comfort of familiarity actually function as a powerful constraint, preventing the woman from leaving, or is it a desperate effort to compensate for the perceived impossibility of escape? All of these possibilities are present; the poem is shaped by the counterpointing of the desire to celebrate the loveliness of traditional tasks and routines with a persistent anxiety about the psychological and ideological roots of this desire.

In the version of 'Letter' which is included in the *Collected Poems*, this is emphasised by an added final poem, which is printed in italics, and asks *'If we launch the boat and sail away / Who will rock the cradle? Who will stay?'*.[31] This poem is not present in the original 1982 version. On her website notes for students,

Clarke gives the following account of the new ending:

> A-level students have challenged me that the verses are a
> cop-out, letting the side down, giving in to male domination.
> That's not what I intended. This separate 'poem' was written as
> a nursery rhyme, like something that plays in our heads
> whether we like it or no, a bit like 'Stand by your man'. It's a
> song (it has a tune, as you'll know if you heard my cassette)
> and was written to be sung or hummed during the radio
> broadcast, like a subliminal message that's hard to escape.[32]

The poem clearly has a different effect when it is read aloud in the
way Clarke describes, and the ideological pressure exerted by the
song is much clearer in this context. Even reading the published
text, though, the familiar, nursery rhyme melodies of this section
suggest its role as a deeply engrained, persistent ideology.

'Letter from a Far Country' involves Wales deeply in its
meditation on gender roles. The 'Far Country' of the title is not
merely metaphorical – Wales as a nation is implicated in the main-
tenance of restrictive social structures. Welsh patriarchs and
matriarchs are critiqued for their efforts to make the younger
generation comply with tradition:

> I hear the dead grandmothers,
> Mamgu from Ceredigion,
> Nain from the North, all calling
> their daughters down from the fields,
> calling me in from the road.
> They haul at the taut silk cords;
> set us fetching eggs, feeding hens,
> mixing rage with the family bread,
> lock us to the elbows in soap suds. (17)

The Plathian image of the cord tying mother-figure and daughter
together hints at the intensity of the ambivalence in the relationship. The Welsh names set the context firmly within Welsh social
and familial norms. The male side of this control follows:

> On the graves of my grandfathers
> the stones, in their lichens and mosses,
> record each one's importance.

Diaconydd. Trysorydd.
Pillars of their society.
Three times at chapel on Sundays.
They are in league with the moon
but as silently stony
as the simple names of their women. (17–18)

'Diaconydd' means deacon and 'Trysorydd' means treasurer: these men hold the power within the community, a community that centres around churchgoing. 'They are in league with the moon' suggests, along with the following stanza exploring the physical experience of childbirth and motherhood, the sense of a dual restriction by biology and culture:

We are hawks trained to return
to the lure from the circle's
far circumference. Children sing
that note that only we can hear.
...
Nightly in white moonlight I wake
from sleep one whole slow minute
before the hungry child
wondering what woke me. (18)

This might seem to imply that women's role in mothering is instinctive and therefore unchangeable, but the first image of hawks *trained* to return to the lure complicates this. Clarke's description of the values of traditional Welsh society exposes an ideological link between woman and home, woman and farm, woman and place, which acts to create a pressure on women to remain the stable connector between people and the land in a context where movement away from the family land for the purposes of employment, as well as actual emigration, are experienced as a threat to Welsh nationhood. Clarke's evocation of this ideology is relatively straightforward; what makes her poem more complex is the self-conscious probing of the extent to which the speaking woman's construction of self is imbricated with these kinds of ideas. However, the poem might ultimately disappoint, or seem rather dated, in that it remains stuck in the dialectic of 'leave or stay' without managing to affirm the possibility of change in domestic roles which might actually allow both partners their share of freedom and responsibility for nurture.

In *Letting in the Rumour* (1989), Clarke returns to family relationships in 'Cofiant', a long sequence based on the Welsh genre of biographies written mostly about preachers. Clarke refers to and quotes from the *cofiant* written by her great-grandfather about his father, but her own *cofiant* is very different. Although the meeting point of all the narratives is the author herself, the story is really one of a collective rather than an individual. The genealogy of the poem is based on the male line, and the final genealogical list begins tellingly with Clarke's own position as 'daughter' before it moves on to the long incantation of patrilineal descent, drawing attention to the erasure of women from Welsh family histories. Clarke redresses this by giving prominence to women's stories, and the sequence also includes the stories of some men who are peripheral to the direct line of descent. The poem seems to seek to explore a variety of ways of remembering, from the traditional narration of the first part of the 'Gruffydd' section ('And then about seven-score men / of Gruffydd's tribe / died through the treachery / of the men of Ystrad Tywi'[33]), to the relatively formal evocations of men of earlier generations like the two Rowland Jones, to remembrances with a more personal tone, which are for the most part about women but also include a powerful poem in memory of Clarke's father. Beginning in the present and moving back in time, the sequence shows that despite the fact that Welsh narratives of history and biography have been overwhelmingly male in style and focus, it is possible to create a hybridised model which does not reject these narratives but intertwines them with alternative perspectives, manipulates and moulds them to form a new feminised narrative which is able to incorporate and elucidate history, drawing on traditional forms and transforming them.

The King of Britain's Daughter, published in 1993, also ends with a long sequence that dominates the collection. 'The King of Britain's Daughter' shows that Clarke, like Boland in the case of Ireland, is fascinated by Welsh mythology. However, her approach in this sequence (written for an oratorio) is certainly less revisionist than Boland's tends to be; in this case this is influenced by the fact that the sequence is in effect an elegy for Clarke's father, who died when she was twenty. Clarke's sequence connects memories of her father, who by recounting myths of place made the landscape come alive for her, with the story of Branwen, daughter of Llyr, and her brother Bendigeidfran (also known as Bran).

The mythical brother Bendigeidfran, who rescues his sister from a marriage which has turned into servitude in Ireland, only to be killed in the process, is for Clarke symbolically identified with her father, and, as she comments in a prose piece on the poem, with 'the brother I never had'.[34] Bendigeidfran, the 'king of Britain' after the death of his father Llyr, is presented as powerful, enraged, protective, passionate and huge:

Oh, my face is salt,
my anger the flung sea.
Under my fist the waves are wild swans
beating out of black mountain lakes.
The spume flies up before my thighs
serpents and burning flags and tattered sails.[35]

Branwen's grief at his death, along with the poet-speaker's sense of loss at the death of her father, is the emotional core of the poem.

Clarke does not overtly challenge (as Boland surely would) the clear opposition in the myth between male power and activeness and female passivity, which could be read as implying a male role to reclaim the sovereignty of the feminised nation (Britain, in this case, although in her headnote Clarke emphasises Wales [36]) from outsiders. Instead, any sense of an alternative perspective rests simply in the poem's profound sense of the final *absence* of the imposing male presence and of the poet-speaker's capacity to fill, alone, the role of teller of tales that her father modeled for her. Whereas Branwen dies of grief after the death of her brother, 'Her memory erased / from the stones / by the wind and the rain, / her name / on the tongue of a bird' (*KBD*, 17), the poet-speaker, while grieving, goes on to live with an absence which is in itself generative of poetry – the stone that rocked for four thousand years, Bendigeidfran's stone, has fallen 'some winter night / between here and childhood' (1), and his giant stone footprint is drowned by the rising tide. These symbols of male potency and mythic scale have been swamped by the sea, which seems to model an alternative kind of narration, provisional and adaptive:

The sea writes on the sand
in a scribble of weed and gullbones,
binder twine, coke cans, torn nets,
fish-hooks, broken glass, bladderwrack,

a freehand of mermaid hair and sea-ribbon,
polystyrene chip-trays, spatulas, flip-flops
and sometimes the drowned.
It discards, draft after draft,
each high tide a deadline. (19)

The poem also interacts with the earlier poem 'Llyr' to suggest, through the King Lear–Cordelia relationship, the daughter's ambivalence towards the father's authority and the idea of the independent daughter finally inheriting the land.

Clarke's latest two collections, *Five Fields* (1998) and *Making the Beds for the Dead* (2004), both published after the *Collected Poems*, do not emphasise the intersections of gender and nation. Containing a number of commissioned and occasional poems, these collections show Clarke's skill at moving between Wales and other contexts – Manchester after the bombing, Bosnia, Iraq. In *Making the Beds for the Dead*, Clarke's rootedness in the rural community in Wales gives her the intimacy of knowledge necessary to write a powerful sequence on the 2001 Foot and Mouth epidemic. The sense of apocalyptic terror generated in rural dwellers by the piles of burning carcasses is linked to the global sense of horror at the events of 11 September 2001. Throughout these two collections, with their widening interests, Clarke nevertheless continues to evoke the particular skills of rural women, in particular in her memories of her mother in the sequence 'Glass', from *Five Fields*, and in her descriptions of animal midwifery in poems like 'A Difficult Birth, Easter 1998', from the same collection.

Both Boland and Clarke come from a generation of women for whom the predominant mode, when exploring issues of gender and nation, was argument and protest, mourning and regret, or a kind of lyrical reclamation and celebration. Lost histories, oppressive and restricting nationalist ideologies, the apparent elision of the female voice in the literature of the nation – all these things provoked a response (in some writers at least) that was overwhelmingly earnest in tone. It might be argued that this kind of tone does not speak so well to the current generation. After all, women *are* (thanks in no small part to Boland) now being represented in the narratives of Irish nationhood; after a media row the *Field Day Anthology of Irish Literature* was forced to add two further fat volumes of writing by women to its comparatively slender first three volumes that scandalously underrepresented

women's writing. Political representation, as I noted in the introduction, has increased for women in Scotland, Ireland, Northern
Ireland and Wales, and this naturally has an effect on the experienced relationship between gender and nation. In fact, when we
look at some of the younger writers who concern themselves with
the intersection of gender, sexuality and nation, there is a sense
of a rather positive, playful tone. There are two features of this
work which I would like to concentrate on in the rest of this chapter:
firstly, the tendency to treat issues of gender and nation with a
humorous, subversive confidence, and, secondly, the growing
interest in issues of gender, sexuality and nation on the part of
male poets.

Kathleen Jamie

Firstly I'd like to look at Kathleen Jamie, a Scottish poet born in
1962 whose mastery of the dramatic monologue and interest in
gender reflects affinities with both Carol Ann Duffy and Liz
Lochhead. Jamie's 1994 collection, *The Queen of Sheba*, was the first
in which she took the 'matter of Scotland' as her subject, after several collections heavily influenced by her travels in Tibet, Pakistan
and elsewhere.[37] The epigraph to the collection is 'This one's for the
folks at home.' The collection is full of poems that address issues of
gender and sexuality in a very Scottish context. 'Arraheids', which
is written in Scots, cleverly responds to the image of woman as
land, and specifically to the Celtic image of the withered old
woman who has a special symbolic relationship to the land.[38] The
flint arrowheads displayed in cases in Scottish museums are
revealed as being the subversive, muttering tongues of grannies,
which have been lying 'fur generations in the land'.[39] Against or
underneath the militancy and solemnity of the official and
masculine narrative of Scottish history, the grannies' tongues are
outwardly conformist (they 'lee / aa douce in the glessy cases in
the gloom / o oor museums, an / they arenae lettin oan' (*QS*, 40))
but in fact grumpily irrepressible. They are as permanent and
scratchy as flint or chert, and although they do not deign to present *their* version of Scottish history within the poem, it is clear that
they are compulsive talkers and would not take long to begin if
given the right kind of attention. Where Boland mourns the loss of
the female oral tradition, Jamie is more likely to see evidence of its

secret and powerful continuance within a masculine society. Witchcraft is one image for this secret culture or resistance; in 'Arraheids' the grannies' tongues are compared to 'Wicked cherms', while in 'Bairns of Suzie: a hex' the wild 'Bairns of the witch of this hill', 'loose limbed and laughing', send out 'fast / invisible arrows, hexed' for the town's dour establishment figures (*QS*, 25–6).

'The Queen of Sheba', one of Jamie's most well-known and popular poems, attacks with great gusto the limitations of the roles, values and aspirations which are offered to girls in contemporary Scottish society. In response to the conventional put-down 'Whae do you think y'ur? – the Queen of Sheba?', Jamie envisages that exotic personage descending on small-town Scotland with its Presbyterian living rooms, its 'mutton-shanks / boiled for broth', its 'chlorine stink' at the swimming pool, its Wimpey housing scheme, and its various patriarchs (*QS*, 9–11). It is hinted that this last group is hypocritical in its authoritarianism, as 'Currie Liz' on the gala float is careful to lift 'her hands from the neat wheel / to tinkle her fingers / at her tricks / among the Masons and the elders and the police' (10). The religious framework for the determination to police the boundaries of Scottishness is suggested in the biblical idiom of 'She's heard, yea / even unto heathenish Arabia / your vixen's bark of poverty' (9), and the Queen of Sheba deliberately flouts religious authority by leading her camels 'widdershins round the kirk-yaird' (10). In opposition to the repression, dourness, drabness and poverty of aspiration in the lives of Scottish girls, the Queen of Sheba represents exoticism, sensuality, freedom, humour, rebellion, self-confidence and love of knowledge for its own sake ('we want to take / PhDs in Persian' (11)). This image of freedom is a particularly feminine one, and the repression within Scottish society is seen as particularly exerted upon women; girls should 'Stick in / with the homework and you'll be / cliver like yer faither. / but no too cliver, / no *above yersel*' (10). The worst thing for a girl to be is 'above yersel', and this is what the Queen of Sheba most emphatically is, by Scottish standards.

The poem's use of Scots is crucial in the positioning it achieves in relation to Scottish culture. The poem is very critical of the values of the society it represents, but the use of Scots words and phrases situates the poem itself (and implicitly the author) within the community it critiques. Much of the Scots phrasing and vocabulary is found in sections of the poem clearly intended to be direct speech, such as the advice about being 'no too cliver'. Importantly, however, the narrative voice also uses Scots vocabulary; the 'vixen's bark of poverty' has 'come down / the family like a lang neb, a thrawn streak, / a wally dug you never liked / but can't get shot of' (9).[40] While the poem starts off addressing Scotland as 'you', by the end the narrator is one of the 'thousand laughing girls' who

> draw our hot breath
>   and shout:
> THE QUEEN OF SHEBA! (11).

The poem also betrays a certain frustrated affection for the frumpier side of life, in its attention to the details of Vi-next-door's wardrobe, for example. 'The Queen of Sheba' is a critique of Scottish life from the inside, which envisages the possibility of a radical upheaval and transformation simply through a deliberate reclamation of joy, sensuality and energy.

'Mr and Mrs Scotland are Dead' is less exuberant and more meditative, even melancholy. Instead of viewing the stereotypical, representative figures of 'Mr and Mrs Scotland', with their rigidly defined gender roles, as oppressive, the poem presents them as past, powerless and representative of a vanishing ideology. The link between ideologies of gender and national identity is symbolised by Mr Scotland's tools, which have 'SCOTLAND, SCOTLAND, stamped on their tired handles' (*QS*, 37). The anxiety which underlies these structures is perhaps hinted at in the beginning of the entry for 'M' in the *Dictionary for Mothers*: 'M:– Milk, *the woman who worries* …;' (37). The cherished objects of these average, cautious, polite lives are now detritus in a landfill, to be sifted through and identified as at once foreign and familiar – above all, 'old-fashioned' – and finally to be bulldozed. The narrator's urge to take the items home is tied up with self-consciousness about the impermanence of the cultural norms with which he or she identifies – they also will also be looked at with a stranger's eye and discarded. Implicitly, therefore, the poem asks us to look critically at contemporary ideas about gender and nationhood, even those we consider to be modern and liberal, since these ideas themselves will necessarily be critiqued by a later generation.

The significance of the new Scottish Parliament for Jamie is revealed by the interaction of the final two poems in *Jizzen*, her 1999 collection.[41] The penultimate poem is entitled 'On the Design Chosen for the New Scottish Parliament Building by Architect Enric Miralles', and is only two short lines long:

> An upturned boat
>   – a watershed.[42]

Significantly, the final poem, following this, describes the rebirth of a female poet. It is entitled 'Meadowsweet' and is accompanied by the note 'Tradition suggests that certain of the Gaelic women poets were buried face down' (*J*, 49). Here the advent of the new national institution is clearly associated with a sense of possible literary regeneration. We can also see the Gaelic woman poet's rebirth as a metaphor for the rebirth of Scotland as a nation; Jamie has taken the traditional trope of the woman as land and nation and reinvented it so that the rebirth is initiated by the woman herself – who digs herself out, unlike Seamus Heaney's nationally symbolic female bog bodies who are dug out by men. Moreover, the reborn woman is a speaking subject – a poet, no less. The names of the seeds which show her the way to dig herself out are interesting – bastard balm and tokens of honesty being perhaps suggestions for the qualities necessary for the development of a fertile cultural and literary discourse in the new Scotland. This poem captures the sense of confidence concerning the relationship between women and Scottish nationhood that is present in Jamie's poetry generally. Jamie's poems that deal with the issue of the relationship between women and the nation or nationalism are very aware of the injustices and oppressions of the past, but they are buoyant – sometimes even exultant – about the possibilities of the present and the future.

David Kinloch

Critical and theoretical discussions about the intersections of gender, sexuality and nation often only consider writing by women and representations of femininity by male writers. However, there is a growing awareness on the part of male writers of the importance of the relationship between masculinity and nationhood.

Clearly nationalist ideologies construct and shape discourses of masculinity as well as discourses of femininity, and certain sexual orientations and behaviours are reinforced and others repressed by the dynamics of nationalism. Christopher Whyte notes that Scottish cultural nationalism frequently figures the 'process of assimilation to England' as a 'dilution' of a 'pre-existing core of Scottishness', a dilution which 'is envisioned in gender terms as an emasculation'.[43] At the same time, Helen Kidd argues that although 'there is a Scottish Mac/hismo', 'it covers a subtext of topographical bisexuality and cultural codes at odds with those of English constructions of gender. Plumage and kilts are feared battle dress and indexes of Scottishness.'[44] The subtext of alternative masculinities and sexualities within Scottish literature and culture is only starting to be explored.[45]

David Kinloch, a gay Scottish poet born in 1959, has been exploring these issues in his recent work. He has so far published three collections, *Dustie-fute* (1992), *Paris-Forfar* (1994), and *Un Tour d'Ecosse* (2001), and his work shows the influence of Edwin Morgan, whose playfulness and openness to experimentation he shares. *Un Tour d'Ecosse* is very conscious of the political moment in Scottish history, and addresses its significance through a focus on sexuality; as Lorca is made to say in 'Little Glasgow Ceilidh':

> You play these games
> With tartan names
> And defunct patois
> But what will a Parliament do
> For Scottish poofs?[46]

Kinloch's work is thoroughly internationalist, embracing influences from continental and American literature, and the title sequence of *Un Tour d'Ecosse* takes us on a mad *Tour de France*-style cycle tour of Scotland with Lorca and Whitman as the declaiming, manic cyclists.

One poem in this sequence, entitled 'Braveheart' and spoken, or rather exclaimed, by Walt Whitman, comically satirises the image of nationalism which Mel Gibson personified in his role as William Wallace in *Braveheart*. Whitman's homoerotic paean to Mel and Will merges in true Whitman fashion into a paean to himself, as all three blur:

> O Mel, I
> Confuse you, mix you in my mind with Wallace.
> And who could blame me? For you and Wallace
> Commingle in my scented breast, you
> Two and I, comrades all (*TE*, 74)

Whitman views Mel from afar at a Hollywood premiere of *Braveheart*, saluting his 'Peach of a biceps – your musk white thighs – muncher of power-breakfasts, Braveheart!' (75). The poem satirises the militant, stereotypically masculine version of romantic nationalism by subjecting its icon to a homosexual gaze, but at the same time the mad energy which drives Whitman and Lorca in their pursuit around Scotland, and the democratic, liberatory potential of Whitman's poetry, are seen as genuinely having something in common with the Scottish struggle for political independence, so that the revolutionary fervour of *Braveheart* is mocked yet reinvented.

The specifically homophobic character of *Braveheart* (which provoked protests by gay groups) is alluded to in a prose poem called 'Whacky Races' in the same sequence, in which Kinloch opposes the macho Mel to various other cinematic characters whom he *does* want to claim for Scotland. Mel's 'sweet saltired face and mesomorphic buns', his 'slowmotionbagpipehorses' and his 'gratuitous splattering over the castle courtyard of an utterly dishy royal bumboy and paramour' (*TE*, 78) are rejected in favour of images of gay cinematic icons or significant moments in cinema, such as the first use in cinema (by Cary Grant) of the word 'gay' in its modern sense. The sequence as a whole proposes a Scotland that is radically open to influence and the interaction of cultures, that is international in its enthusiasms and is in turn the focus of others' enthusiasms and energies. The openness to other cultures and languages (Kinloch is a lecturer in French and many of his poems make surprising connections between French, English, and Scots) is insistently linked to openness regarding gender norms and sexual identities.

Another poem in *Un Tour d'Ecosse*, called 'Saltires', enters even more explicitly into current politics by commenting on those 'Petitioners of our Parliament / Who wish to regulate / The Saltire's shade of blue' (50). The poem runs through the possible

fetishistic nationalist associations of the blue which the petitioners are seeking to purify, some of them somewhat disturbing (blue
grapeshot from the Field of Culloden and a blue box made of the
pulley of the Scottish Maiden). In response to this drive for symbolic purity the poem first posits the possible foreignness of blue –
'we live in a whole / Geography of colour: / Antwerp blue, Mars
violet' – but then suggests why not 'no blue at all, / But the
colours that hide / In our Colours' (51), asking

> What rainbows bend
> Through the prisms that tip
> From blue furls
> Before they re-jink into white,
> The grooves of our national straits? (52)

There is a clear criticism of the narrowness and drive to
homogeneity and regimented existence that is symbolised by the
concern about the flag. In contrast, Kinloch posits a multiplicity
and openness to difference that is finally put in terms of sexuality –
no prizes for guessing the colour the poem turns to as an
alternative to blue. The blues of Flowerdale Bay are waters

> That simply purr
> Around an evening pier
> Before the pastel pink
> Flag of The Bruce
> Sashays the sky to Skye. (52)

The darker implications of such concern with cultural purity,
and its link with sexual politics, are powerfully exposed in a poem
from Kinloch's earlier 1994 collection, *Paris-Forfar*. 'Warmer Bruder'
takes its title, as a note explains, from the German phrase 'hot
brothers', which was 'used viciously of homosexuals in the death
camps of Sachsenhausen and Flossenburg'.[47] The poem draws a
symbolic parallel between the snow being shoveled by homosexual prisoners in the concentration camps, and the snow falling in
Grangemouth (Scotland) outside the hospice where AIDS patients
are dying. In both places 'Smoke, the ghost of blood, / Fills up the
melting sky' (*PF*, 53). The poem is an elegy for both groups of men,
and suggests a link between the Nazi hate for homosexuality and
contemporary attitudes towards homosexual AIDS sufferers.

Kinloch draws our attention to the yoking within Nazi ideology of racial purity and sexual purity, in order to suggest that the same dangerous tendency might exist, albeit in a less malign form, in Scottish culture.

Conclusion

Could we say that any of these four writers seek to contribute to the formation of a 'nationalist' discourse or literature? Certainly all four are concerned with the issue of national identity and locate much of their work firmly in a 'Welsh', 'Scottish' or 'Irish' context. All seek to create new images of 'Welshness', 'Scottishness' or 'Irishness' – images which challenge traditional delineations of these categories. Their work, however, can only be called 'nationalist' in the sense that it is generally positive about furthering political and cultural independence (in the case of the Welsh and Scottish writers) and is passionate about exploring – and shaping – the contours of 'Welsh', 'Scottish' and 'Irish' culture and identity today. Kathleen Jamie and David Kinloch demonstrate a marked *internationalism* in their work, and any Scottish identity they envisage is unreservedly open to the flow of ideas and inspiration from other cultures and places. In the case of all four writers, a profound and personal awareness of the way in which restricting discourses of gender are codependent with restrictive discourses of nationhood has been a key enabler of their ability to offer new perspectives on both issues; thus the work of all four poets supports Reizbaum's hope that a 'dynamic relation of movements' can be productive in a special way. Boland and Clarke were in a sense lone campaigners, pioneers of a poetry which addressed the issues of gender and nation, and their poetry reflects the intensity and difficulty of this territory. Jamie and Kinloch come from a later generation which has the achievements of the sexual and social liberation of the sixties and seventies well behind it, and are writing at a time of great optimism for the Scottish sense of nation, and their poetry reflects this in its confidence and vivacity.

Notes

1 Nuala Ní Dhomhnaill, *Pharoah's Daughter*, with translations by thirteen poets (Oldcastle: Gallery, 1990), p. 135.

2 Seamus Deane (ed.), *The Field Day Anthology of Irish Literature*, vol. 3 (Derry: Field Day, 1991), p. 748.

3 Marilyn Reizbaum, 'Canonical double cross: Scottish and Irish women's writing', in *Decolonizing Tradition: New Views of Twentieth-Century 'British' Literary Canons*, ed. Karen R. Lawrence (Urbana, IL: University of Illinois Press, 1992), pp. 165–90 (p. 166).

4 Reizbaum, 'Canonical double cross' pp. 166–7.

5 Ibid., p. 168.

6 Eavan Boland, *Object Lessons: The Life of the Woman and the Poet in our Time* (London: Vintage, 1996), p. 136.

7 Boland, *Object Lessons*, p. 148.

8 Eavan Boland, 'Listen. This is the noise of myth', *The Journey and Other Poems* (Manchester: Carcanet, 1987), p. 49. Henceforth referred to as *JOP*.

9 Eavan Boland, *Outside History* (Manchester: Carcanet, 1990), p. 45. Henceforth referred to as *OH*.

10 Boland, *Object Lessons*, p. 60.

11 Patrick Pearse, 'I am Ireland', in Deane, *Field Day Anthology*, vol. 2, p. 558.

12 Gerardine Meaney, 'Myth, history and the politics of subjectivity: Eavan Boland and Irish women's writing', *Women: A Cultural Review*, vol. 4, no. 2 (1993), pp. 136–53 (p. 146).

13 Clair Wills, 'Contemporary Irish women poets: The privatisation of myth', in *Diverse Voices: Essays on Twentieth-Century Women Writers in English*, ed. Harriet Devine Jump (Hemel Hempstead: Harvester Wheatsheaf, 1991), pp. 248–72 (p. 256).

14 Ibid., p. 258.

15 Meaney, 'Myth, history', p. 146.

16 Boland, *Object Lessons*, pp. 12–13.

17 Ibid., p. 166.

18 Eavan Boland, *In a Time of Violence* (Manchester: Carcanet, 1994), p. 43. Henceforth referred to as *ITV*.

19 Eavan Boland, *The Lost Land* (Manchester: Carcanet, 1998). Henceforth referred to as *TLL*.

20 Clair Wills, 'No longer islanded', *Times Literary Supplement*, no. 5157, 1 February 2002, p. 12.

21 Ibid., p. 12.

22 Eavan Boland, *Code* (Manchester: Carcanet, 2001), p. 44. Henceforth referred to as *C*.

23 Wills, 'No longer islanded', p. 12.

24 Nigel Jenkins, *Footsore on the Frontier: Selected Essays and Articles* (Llandysul: Gomer Press, 2001), pp. 22–3.

25 M. Wynn Thomas, *Corresponding Cultures: The Two Literatures of Wales* (Cardiff: University of Wales Press, 1999), p. 200.

26 Ibid., p. 190.

27 Ibid., pp. 192–3.

28 Gillian Clarke, *Letter from a Far Country* (Manchester: Carcanet, 1982), p. 27. Henceforth referred to as *LFC*.

29 Jeremy Hooker, *The Presence of the Past: Essays on Modern British and American Poetry* (Bridgend: Poetry Wales Press, 1987), p. 154.

30 Eavan Boland, *Night Feed* (Dublin: Arlen House, 1982), p. 26.

31 Gillian Clarke, *Collected Poems* (Manchester: Carcanet, 1997), p. 55.
32 www.gillianclarke.co.uk/pages/for Students/notesLetterFromAFar.htm, accessed 6 October 2004.
33 Gillian Clarke, *Letting in the Rumour* (Manchester: Carcanet, 1989), p. 124.
34 Gillian Clarke, 'The King of Britain's daughter', in *How Poets Work*, ed. Tony Curtis (Bridgend: Seren, 1996), pp. 122–36 (p. 125).
35 Gillian Clarke, *The King of Britain's Daughter* (Manchester: Carcanet, 1993), p. 13. Henceforth referred to as *KBD*.
36 Clarke is clearly keen to make this a specifically Welsh story. John Kerrigan notes that she does not include the whole narrative: 'Actually, in *The Mabinogion*, the story does not stop there. Wounded by a poisoned spear, Brân urges his followers to decapitate him and bury his head in London. When they do this, they secure Britonnic rule of the island. But it is typical of Gillian Clarke – who considers herself Welsh and European, but not British – to cut London out of her account.' 'Divided kingdoms and the local epic: *Mercian Hymns to The King of Britain's Daughter*', *Yale Journal of Criticism*, vol. 13, no. 1 (2000), pp. 3–21 (p. 14).
37 *Black Spiders* (Edinburgh: Salamander Press, 1982) and *The Way We Live* (Newcastle upon Tyne: Bloodaxe, 1987) were the two regular poetry collections before *The Queen of Sheba*; Jamie also published books of travel writing and collaborated on a narrative poem.
38 Although this sovereignty-figure is not as common in the Scottish context as in the Irish, Juliet Wood notes that the 'Cailleach Bhearra still exists in Irish and Scots-Gaelic folklore as an extremely complex entity whose appearances cannot easily be reduced to one source, mythological or otherwise.' 'Celtic goddesses: myths and mythology', *The Feminist Companion to Mythology*, ed. Carolyne Larrington (London: Pandora, 1992), pp. 118–36 (p. 131).
39 Kathleen Jamie, *The Queen of Sheba* (Newcastle upon Tyne: Bloodaxe, 1994), p. 40. Henceforth referred to as *QS*.
40 'Lang neb' means a long nose, 'thrawn' when applied to people means 'perverse, obstinate, intractable', and a 'wally dug' is an ornamental porcelain dog.
41 I have not been able to include discussion of Jamie's 2004 collection, *The Tree House*, as it came out just as this book was being completed.
42 Kathleen Jamie, *Jizzen* (London: Picador, 1999), p. 48. Henceforth referred to as *J*.
43 Christopher Whyte (ed.), *Gendering the Nation: Studies in Modern Scottish Literature* (Edinburgh: Edinburgh University Press, 1995), p. xii.
44 Helen Kidd, 'Writing near the fault line', in *Kicking Daffodils: Twentieth-Century Women Poets*, ed. Vicki Bertram (Edinburgh: Edinburgh University Press, 1997), pp. 95–109 (p. 97).
45 See, for example, Edwin Morgan's essay 'A Scottish trawl', in *Gendering the Nation*, ed. Whyte, pp. 205–22.
46 David Kinloch, *Un Tour d'Ecosse* (Manchester: Carcanet, 2001), p. 72. Henceforth referred to as *TE*.
47 David Kinloch, *Paris-Forfar* (Edinburgh: Polygon, 1994), p. 52. Henceforth referred to as *PF*.

5

'A fusillade of question marks': Poetry and the Troubles in Northern Ireland

Seamus Heaney, Michael Longley, Ciaran Carson

Poetry in Northern Ireland over the last few decades has shown remarkable vibrancy and diversity. The troubled political situation has certainly contributed to the energy and urgency of this poetry, as writers have struggled with the difficult task of finding a voice that speaks to and through the conflict. Poets are exposed to intense external pressure to comment on 'the situation', but once they do, they open themselves up to accusations of easy exploitation of violence for literary effect, as well as keen moral scrutiny of every aspect of their 'position'. Seamus Heaney's poetry, in particular, has, over the years, been the subject of fierce debate and has served as the substratum for the development of a fascinating critical discourse on the relationship between poetry and politics in the Northern Irish context. This criticism is, of course, only a part of a larger debate concerning Irish literature generally. Since W.B. Yeats's troubled question, 'Did that play of mine send out / Certain men the English shot?',[1] Irish writers in the twentieth century have turned over and over the complex issues surrounding the political efficacy and responsibility of the artist.

The literary scene in Northern Ireland naturally cannot be adequately represented by my difficult choice of just three poets

142

(Muldoon, of course, is covered in Chapter 6). Among those I was not able to discuss in detail, Medbh McGuckian, Derek Mahon and Tom Paulin stand out as both brilliant and exemplary. McGuckian's beautiful, perplexing poetry has long sought to explore the conditions of division in Northern Ireland, often alongside and through the desires and conflicts of familial relationships, all the time using a style characterised by complex metaphorical jumps and associative logic. Derek Mahon writes an austerely philosophical poetry, full of intensity and rigorous self-questioning, and some of his poems, like 'Rage for Order', 'Ecclesiastes' and 'A Disused Shed in Co. Wexford', have become landmarks in the Northern Irish poetry of the Troubles. Tom Paulin explores the legacy of Ulster Protestantism with fierce ambivalence, linking it to broader Dissenting traditions. A passionate liberal, Paulin frequently takes the failed 1798 uprising of the United Irishmen as his touchstone, emphasising the way in which Protestants and Catholics fought together in the republican cause and elevated the principles of political independence and self-determination above religious affiliation. It is worth noting that out of those mentioned here, only Carson, Longley and McGuckian continue to live in Northern Ireland; Heaney, Mahon, Paulin and Muldoon live variously in the Republic of Ireland, America and England. Nevertheless, the strong links which all of these poets feel towards the North of Ireland have ensured that it is possible to continue to talk of them as part of a Northern Irish literary community, even as they become part of other communities as well. Of course these writers are all part of a very established generation now, and a new generation of poets who live in the North is emerging; among the people to watch are Leontia Flynn, John Hughes, Martin Mooney, Colette Bryce, Paula Cunningham and Gearóid MacLochlainn.

Seamus Heaney

Seamus Heaney was born in 1939 in rural Co. Derry. His first full-length collection, *Death of a Naturalist*, was published by Faber and Faber in 1966, and *Door into the Dark* followed in 1969. Heaney's first two volumes attracted much praise for their sensuous evocation of rural life and childhood memories, and their densely alliterative and onomatopoeic language. Patrick Kavanagh was a crucial presence for Heaney, because he demonstrated that it was possible to make poetry out of the everyday details of an Irish rural life, and Hopkins, Hughes and Anglo-Saxon poetry were strong influences on Heaney's wielding of sound in this early work. But it was not until the publication of *Wintering Out* in 1972 and (in particular) *North* in 1975 that readers and critics began to see Heaney's poetry as providing what many longed for: a representative poetic 'response' to the escalating Troubles in Northern Ireland, which had led in 1972 to the reinstatement of direct rule from London after the events of Bloody Sunday. In reviewing *North*, Conor Cruise O'Brien wrote: 'I had the uncanny feeling, reading these poems, of listening to the thing itself, the actual substance of historical agony and dissolution, the tragedy of a people in a place: the Catholics of Northern Ireland.'[2] The scope of *North* was the result of the radical development of a motif which had in fact been present throughout all of Heaney's books: the land as the memory or collective unconscious of the nation or culture.

In the very first poem of *Death of a Naturalist* we find Heaney comparing his writing to the activity of digging and looking to what the earth holds. In *Door into the Dark*, published in 1969, the bogland is claimed as a metaphor for Ireland:

> Our pioneers keep striking
> Inwards and downwards,
>
> Every layer they strip
> Seems camped on before.
> The bogholes might be Atlantic seepage.
> The wet centre is bottomless.[3]

Heaney was immediately aware of the potential which 'Bogland' opened up for him; he commented that it 'was the first poem of mine that I felt had the status of symbol in some way; it wasn't trapped in its own anecdote, or its own closing-off: it seemed to have some kind of wind blowing through it that could carry on'.[4] But it was not until Heaney read a book by P.V. Glob entitled *The Bog People* that his symbolic use of the bog image was dramatically extended. His own description of the impact which Glob's book made on him is worth quoting:

> It was chiefly concerned with preserved bodies of men and women found in the bogs of Jutland, naked, strangled or with

their throats cut, disposed under the peat since early Iron Age times. The author, P.V. Glob, argues convincingly that a number of these, and in particular the Tollund Man, whose head is now preserved near Aarhus in the museum at Silkeburg, were ritual sacrifices to the Mother Goddess, the goddess of the ground who needed new bridegrooms each winter to bed with her in her sacred place, in her bog, to ensure the renewal and fertility of the territory in the spring. Taken in relation to the tradition of Irish political martyrdom for that cause whose icon is Kathleen Ni Houlihan, this is more than an archaic barbarous rite: it is an archetypal pattern. And the unforgettable photographs of these victims blended in my mind with photographs of atrocities, past and present, in the long rites of Irish political and religious struggles.[5]

The first poem in which Heaney draws on this sense of connection is 'The Tollund Man' in *Wintering Out*, and in *North* the analogy is developed further in a group of poems about bog bodies discovered in both Jutland and Ireland. But this linking of the ritual sacrifices of Iron Age cultures with Irish political martyrdom is not the only major analogy in *North*; the Viking invasions of Ireland in the tenth century are also brought in as parallels for the violence of contemporary Northern Ireland. Such broad comparisons were bound to invite some questioning, and one of the accusations critics have leveled at Heaney is that he elides the very real differences between the historical and cultural contexts that he compares. Edna Longley asks,

> does the idea of the North really provide an umbrella for the not very Nordic north of Ireland, fertility rites and capital punishment in prehistoric Denmark, and the conquests of the Vikings in Ireland – coming to or from the north? Although all these different places, time-zones and moral worlds clearly strike genuine imaginative chords in Heaney, why attempt to unify them into a mythic confederation?[6]

Ciaran Carson also expresses concern that Heaney's tendency to see the same patterns repeated in different times and places implies that history will repeat endlessly and inevitably, removing the need for human responsibility:

> It is as if he is saying, suffering like this is natural; these things have always happened; they happened then, they happen now,

and that is sufficient ground for understanding and absolution. It is as if there never were and never will be any political consequences of such acts; they have been removed to the realm of sex, death and inevitability.[7]

In order to consider the implications of Heaney's controversial 'mythic confederation', I would like to look closely at two poems, 'The Tollund Man' and 'Punishment'. In 'The Tollund Man' the speaker imagines going to Aarhus in Denmark to see the preserved head of the Iron Age man. The poem's language consistently sacralises the Tollund Man, linking him into the Christian tradition with words like 'mild', 'saint' and 'stained face'. The motif of sacrifice and regeneration is explicitly linked to twentieth-century Irish violence in the second section, where Heaney refers to two incidents from the troubled days of the 1920s:[8]

I could risk blasphemy,
Consecrate the cauldron bog
Our holy ground and pray
Him to make germinate

The scattered, ambushed
Flesh of labourers,
Stockinged corpses
Laid out in the farmyards,

Tell-tale skin and teeth
Flecking the sleepers
Of four young brothers, trailed
For miles along the lines.[9]

Edna Longley comments that 'Heaney does not distinguish between voluntary and involuntary "martyrdom" ';[10] this is true, as the references here are vague and decontextualised enough to suggest a generalised image of victims of the Troubles, many of whom clearly had no desire for martyrdom of any kind. The question of voluntariness, however, also points us towards the broader issue of what kind of choice the Tollund Man is seen to have made. Heaney draws here on a paradox inherent in Christian theology: the idea that divine will and individual human choice can coexist. The drama, for the Tollund Man, is the process of coming to choose that which is already planned or willed, and thus attaining a 'sad freedom' (*WO*, 37); the opposition between 'voluntary' and 'involuntary' is in fact dissolved. Instead of the Christian divinity Heaney implies the presence of a national or tribal ideal that may command a similar obedience and facilitate a similar 'true' freedom and selfhood. The allusions to Iron Age rites suggest that this 'goddess' is one whose service – and regeneration – requires periodic deaths. The idea of sacrificial martyrdom is of course a motif which has a long history in Irish nationalism, exemplified most famously by Pearse's invocation of the imagery of Christian martyrdom in his staging of the 1916 Easter Rising.

The second section of 'The Tollund Man' remains in a conditional tense ('I could risk blasphemy') and the last section of the poem indicates a definite unease with the motif of sacrifice: 'Out there in Jutland / In the old man-killing parishes / I will feel lost, / Unhappy and at home' (*WO*, 37). 'Punishment' takes up this feeling of disturbance much more sharply. In 'Punishment' the speaker makes a connection between a girl killed for adultery in the Iron Age and Catholic girls in Northern Ireland who were tarred and feathered for going out with British soldiers in the early 1970s. The speaker frames himself as the 'artful voyeur' and says to the dead girl 'I almost love you / but would have cast, I know, / the stones of silence'.[11] Like 'The Tollund Man', this poem also sites itself in a Christian context, but the various Biblical allusions do not sit comfortably together. An allusion to the woman caught in adultery and forgiven by Jesus draws attention to the responsibility of the individual to intervene and prevent violence. But other phrases which connect the *girl* with Jesus (for example, 'all your numbered bones') create just the hint of the idea that this death, after all, might be purposeful – although we can *also* read them as implicating Christianity very negatively in a paradigm of violent, sacrificial religions.[12]

This conflict of interpretation is only intensified by the final stanzas, where the speaker says,

> I who have stood dumb
> when your betraying sisters,
> cauled in tar,
> wept by the railings,
>
> who would connive
> in civilised outrage
> yet understand the exact
> and tribal, intimate revenge. (*N*, 38)

There has been much debate over how to interpret these lines – the poem seems to devalue 'outrage' through the word 'connive' and to validate 'revenge' through the use of the word 'exact'. (In an important discussion, David Lloyd argues that 'the supposedly irrational is endowed ... with the features of enlightenment – exactitude, intimacy of knowledge.'[13]) The narrator seems to be attracted to the idea of collective action, to the assimilation of the individual will into the will of the 'tribe'. The word 'understand' is crucial – it suggests that an emotional understanding of violence puts the speaker in a position where to object to it is hypocritical, to act against it impossible. Yet while to act against or reject one's own 'understanding' might *feel* hypocritical or impossible, another face of 'Punishment' urges that very thing. The effect of presenting all the contradictions implicit in the speaker's attitude to the girl (identification with the victim and identification with the killers; love and failure to defend; outrage and understanding) is to suggest that, after all, identifying one's own apparently 'natural' response is not enough: 'natural' responses themselves are conflicted and contradictory, and instead, a decision must be taken through a self-conscious process of evaluation.

Debate over the poem's stance on the issue of individual responsibility has been matched by controversy over Heaney's tendency to eroticise death and violence.[14] Certainly the eroticisation of the girl's body in 'Punishment' is the most disturbing aspect of the poem. It reveals the sexual dynamics involved in violence – including communal violence – and draws us away from the imagined perspective of the girl as subject towards the subjectivity of the observer-poet, reconstituting her as object. We certainly cannot see Heaney as completely unconscious in this; the phrase 'artful voyeur' is far too pointed. Yet the unease of some critics and readers stems from a sense that Heaney holds back from a clear exposure – and condemnation – of the potentially eroticised nature of violence, and of the violence of certain sexual stances. The issue is present in the poem as a pressurising undercurrent but is not directly confronted.

In 'Punishment', despite the religious references, the paralleled incidents do retain a sense of historicity and are not completely softened into symbol; attention is drawn to the girl as an individual with a particular history: 'you were flaxen-haired, / undernourished' (*N*, 38). In other examples of the bog poems, this is less clear: 'Come to the Bower', for example, eroticises and universalises a female bog body as 'the dark-bowered queen' (*N*, 31). But while such romanticisation and aestheticisation of a violent death is problematic, it must be recognised that *North* incorporates a self-consciousness of this. This is apparent in 'Punishment', and is made even clearer in 'Strange Fruit', where the speaker allows the empty gaze of a dead girl to rebuke him for his tendency to romanticisation:

> Murdered, forgotten, nameless, terrible
> Beheaded girl, outstaring axe
> And beatification, outstaring
> What had begun to feel like reverence. (*N*, 39)

Heaney's bog poems are difficult and disturbing because they are themselves conflicted, marked by fault lines that should not be smoothed over but instead carefully charted. They reflect an internal struggle with issues that were highly pertinent in the radicalised political climate of the 1960s and 1970s and continue to be so today, in the broader international context as well as in Ireland. The most significant of these issues is the tendency of nationalist (and fundamentalist) discourses to romanticise martyrdom and violent death.

North represents a staging post in Heaney's writing career and his next volume, *Field Work* (1979), is markedly different in tone and style. Heaney moves away from the broad historical or mythical sweep and concentrates on the relationships of everyday life. The 'Glanmore Sonnets', which form the centrepiece of the book, evoke the pastoral mood of the Heaneys' new residence in Co. Wicklow, where they had been living since their much-publicised move to the Republic in 1972. But the everyday life evoked by *Field Work* is one still deeply affected by the continuing conflict in Northern Ireland, and it is *Field Work* which contains some of Heaney's most moving elegies for victims of the Troubles. These elegies also reflect the continuation of some of the anxieties and struggles which were pivotal to *North*. In 'Casualty', for example, we see the same tension between group or 'tribe' and individual that we saw in 'Punishment'. 'Casualty' relates the story of a Catholic fisherman who was killed by a bomb while drinking in a Protestant pub during an IRA curfew imposed after Bloody Sunday. Echoing Yeats's poem 'The Fisherman', 'Casualty' creates a picture of a loner, someone who operates by his own rules. The speaker then remembers the funeral service for the victims of Bloody Sunday and the sense of close-knit community it created:

> The common funeral
> Unrolled its swaddling band,
> Lapping, tightening
> Till we were braced and bound
> Like brothers in a ring.[15]

But the dark side of this 'binding' is highlighted by the next stanzas which describe the fisherman's death after he had 'gone miles away' to find a drink '[f]or he drank like a fish / Nightly, naturally'. The poet asks,

> How culpable was he
> That last night when he broke
> Our tribe's complicity? (*FW*, 23)

The poem ends with an evocation of a fishing trip on which a sense of freedom and personal, natural rhythm is found in isolation and a retreat from the pressures of the social and communal, but of course the fact that this is an elegy reminds us that such an escape can only ever be partial and temporary.

In Heaney's next two volumes this sense of tension between the individual and the community is explored further. *Sweeney Astray* and *Station Island* are closely interlinked. *Sweeney Astray* is Heaney's translation of the medieval Irish poem *Buile Suibhne*, the tale of an Irish king who rebels against the growing presence of Christianity in Ireland. Cursed by Ronan the cleric, he is turned into a bird-man, and goes wandering Ireland, alternately praising the beauties of the wild landscape and cursing the church, and lamenting his lonely plight and longing for the comforts of home and community. Mad Sweeney's journeying is paralleled in *Station Island* by the title sequence, in which a speaker closely related to Heaney's biographical self embarks on the annual Lough Derg pilgrimage. The pilgrimage involves movement from station to station, and Heaney uses this progressive (and circular) structure to establish a parallel with Dante's *Divine Comedy*. Like Dante, the Heaney figure encounters various ghosts from the past. The dialogues with these figures centre on the questions of responsibility and activity; throughout the sequence the poet is trying to rid himself of a passivity he links with religion:

> I hate how quick I was to know my place
> I hate where I was born, hate everything
> That made me biddable and unforthcoming.[16]

The final encounter is with James Joyce, who bids the poet to

> ... Keep at a tangent.
> When they make the circle wide, it's time to swim
>
> out on your own and fill the element
> with signatures on your own frequency,
> echo soundings, searches, probes, allurements,
>
> elver-gleams in the dark of the whole sea. (*SI*, 93–4)

But throughout both *Station Island* and *Sweeney Astray* what is repeatedly demonstrated is the way in which the individual subject is always embedded in the social, the way in which individual direction is always chosen within the parameters of culture. The figure of mad Sweeney, the bird-man whose lyrical outbursts are always directed towards the society which he has simultaneously rejected and been expelled by, destabilises oppositions between nature and culture, freedom and compulsion, individual and community. So when in 'Sweeney Redivivus', the third part of *Station Island*, the voice of the pilgrim alighting from the Lough Derg boat is merged with the voice of Sweeney the vagrant, this new speaker is conscious of the way in which his subjectivity is shaped by the community and communal values. He searches for places of marginal location and identity which will nurture an inner distancing, a self-consciousness and a suspicion of coercive cultural structures. He settles in

> My hidebound boundary tree. My tree of knowledge.
> My thick-tapped, soft-fledged, airy listening post. (*SI*, 100)

The Haw Lantern (1987) sees Heaney searching for a more distanced and ironic political voice after the intensities of *Wintering Out* and *North* and the personal travails of *Station Island*, while also clearing space for the expression of personal and familial loss. It features a beautiful elegiac sequence called 'Clearances' and a group of allegorical poems commenting ironically on politics and the writer's role. Both *The Haw Lantern* and

Seeing Things (1991) are concerned with ideas of boundaries and borders. The 'Squarings' sequences in *Seeing Things* are dominated by an acute sense of the possibility of sudden movement into another state of being, and are intrigued by moments of stillness or balance between two states or spheres. There is a sense of flow and lightness in these poems which contrasts strongly with Heaney's earlier obsession with earth and depth, something which the poet notes in 'Fosterling': 'So long for air to brighten, / Time to be dazzled and the heart to lighten'.[17]

However, in *The Spirit Level* (1996) Heaney makes an emphatic return to many of the issues he wrestled with in *North*. This is most evident in the sequence 'Mycenae Lookout', which is based on the events of Aeschylus's *Agamemnon*. The sequence contains a poem called 'Cassandra' which alludes to 'Punishment' in theme, imagery and form, and which centres on the repeated lines 'No such thing / as innocent / bystanding'.[18] With regard to both individual responsibility and the eroticisation of violence, 'Mycenae Lookout' is explicit and hard-hitting where 'Punishment' was reticent and ambivalent. While there is an overwhelming sense of the difficulty (even impossibility) of assessing the rightness or wrongness of choices, a consciousness of the degree to which circumstances, in their capriciousness, resist human attempts to direct events, and a pessimism about the human capacity for violence, 'Mycenae Lookout' nevertheless strongly reclaims a belief in the capacity of the individual for agency and the necessity of individual moral responsibility. It also clearly rejects the aestheticisation of violence that the earlier work ambivalently explores.

Heaney's latest collection, *Electric Light* (2001), published after his acclaimed translation of *Beowulf*, has something of the lightness of *Seeing Things*, but is much more focused on memory. The mood of *Electric Light* is tranquil and leisurely; where *Seeing Things* revealed Heaney making a determined effort to move away from 'heaviness of being', the celebration of pleasure, ease and beauty seems to come naturally to the poet of *Electric Light*. The collection was of course the first of Heaney's to be written after the Good Friday Agreement, the IRA ceasefire and the establishment of the Northern Irish Assembly, and it was finished before the Assembly ran into its current difficulties. The mood of optimism in Northern Ireland is reflected in the feeling of freedom which characterises this collection, as Heaney moves between memories of his Derry childhood, elegies for friends (many of them famous writers), wry meditations on his current status as celebrity writer, genteel classical Eclogues, and benedictions laid upon a new generation. Reviewers have had their reservations about the volume; Harry Clifton in *Poetry Review*, for instance, voices anxiety over the way in which Heaney rather too glibly 'steal[s] a piece of East European political relevance' in 'Known Worlds', and he critiques the heavy-handedness of the collection's 'classicising agenda'.[19] Clifton also remarks that the volume is characterised by 'a chatty, colloquial line that stays squarely in the middle range of feeling and reminiscence, and works by accumulation rather than short-winded intensity, an ingathering of apparently casual matter that adds up to more than the sum of its parts'.[20]

The collection *does* risk seeming too comfortable and self-indulgent, and the poems which avoid this entirely tend to be some of those which excavate strange moments in the poet's childhood (like 'Electric Light' and the compelling 'Out of the Bag') or those which bring us back yet again to the Troubles. 'The Augean Stables', one of the 'Sonnets from Hellas', contrasts starkly with 'Known World'. In 'Known World', part of which is drawn from the poet's apparent 'notes' from his trip to Belgrade in 1978, the poet-speaker's comfortable socialising with the literati – lunches that end in 'siesta and woozy wake-ups / Just before sunset'[21] – is set ironically beside the divisions of both Northern Ireland and the Balkans, but the poem never moves beyond that wry, ironic juxtaposition. In contrast, 'The Augean Stables' enacts the fracturing of the poet's meditative tour of Greece by news from home:

> And it was there in Olympia, down among green willows,
> The lustral wash and run of river shallows,
> That we heard of Sean Brown's murder in the grounds
> Of Bellaghy GAA Club. And imagined
> Hose-water smashing hard back off the asphalt
> In the car park where his athlete's blood ran cold. (*EL*, 41)

It is the reinvigoration of the cliché 'blood ran cold', along with the collapse of the rhyme scheme in the last four lines and the transition from the lilting evocation of Greece to the hard sounds of the conclusion, which gives this poem its capacity to jolt the reader. The use of the classical analogy (the cleansing of the

Augean stables by Heracles), which is developed in the first part of the poem, is also disturbing, as the image of the 'reeking yard and stables' suggests the clogged-up mire of the politics of Northern Ireland but also contrasts the excessive, larger-than-life, saturated quality of the Greek mythological world with the stark, minimalist and chilling contemporary image of blood being hosed in a car park. The urge, then, to draw on ancient templates in viewing Northern Ireland has not diminished for Heaney, and we shall see that he is not alone in this – indeed, the Eclogues and the 'Sonnets from Hellas' in *Electric Light* were perhaps influenced by Michael Longley's precise, measured and gentle versions of the classics.

Electric Light is also marked (in poems like 'The Border Campaign') by Heaney's recent translation of *Beowulf*, a project which in itself must be read as a significant part of Heaney's engagement with the violence of Northern Ireland's recent past. Fate and human agency, blood feuds and fear, the destructive side of human passion; these are the deep obsessions of the Anglo-Saxon epic poem and, as Heaney himself comments in his introduction,

> Putting a bawn into *Beowulf* seems one way for an Irish poet to come to terms with that complex history of conquest and colony, absorption and resistance, integrity and antagonism, a history that needs to be clearly acknowledged by all concerned in order to render it ever more 'willable forward / again and again and again'.[22]

Michael Longley

In *Tuppenny Stung* Michael Longley describes himself as a child as a 'withdrawn watcher', in contrast to his twin brother who was a 'rebel'. He goes on to describe his response to his brother's hurts:

> If he was chastised, I would shed tears of sympathy. When he was ten Wendy and I visited Peter in hospital where he was recovering from an eye-operation. Bandages covered both his eyes, but I knew he was crying as we prepared to leave. No surge of passion or compassion in later life has quite equalled the wracking of my whole being that I experienced then.[23]

This anecdote highlights some of Longley's most valuable qualities as a poet: his capacity for empathy and identification, and his acuity as an observer. Longley's focused energy has gone, like Heaney's, into finding 'images and symbols adequate to our predicament',[24] but 'our predicament' for Longley is less the conflicting energies, desires, angers, guilts and sorrows which perpetuate and shape the violence, and more the grief and loss experienced as a result of the violence. This grief belongs sometimes to perpetrators as well as victims, as 'Wounds' demonstrates:

> He collapsed beside his carpet-slippers
> Without a murmur, shot through the head
> By a shivering boy who wandered in
> Before they could turn the television down
> Or tidy away the supper dishes.
> To the children, to a bewildered wife,
> I think 'Sorry Missus' was what he said.[25]

Michael Longley was born in Belfast in 1939, to English parents who had recently moved to Northern Ireland. His first collection, *No Continuing City*, was published in 1969, and was followed by *An Exploded View* (1973), *Man Lying on a Wall* (1976) and *The Echo Gate* (1979). These collections were all well-received, but Longley was somewhat marginalised within the critical and publicity machine which had grown up around the poetry of the Troubles, as his poetry was often hard to incorporate into the critical arguments over identity and nationalism.[26] Nevertheless, as Peter McDonald remarks, the poetry of these collections 'couldn't have been written in any other environment than that of Northern Ireland',[27] and it includes some very powerful elegies for victims of sectarian violence, including the well-known poem 'The Linen Workers', which adopts the characteristic Longley strategy of merging a private with a public grief, linking the death of his father with that of the ten linen workers.

The first four collections contain many elegies, and not only for victims of the Troubles; the First World War is a central emotional crux for Longley. But it is in *Gorse Fires*, with which he broke a ten-year silence in 1991, that we see Longley really come into his own as elegist. *Gorse Fires* was followed by *The Ghost Orchid* in 1995, *The Weather in Japan* in 2000, and *Snow Water* in 2004, and it is these four collections which I want to concentrate on here, since they represent Longley's mature voice and his strongest poetry. *Gorse Fires* and *The Ghost Orchid* are also particularly interesting in the way in which they utilise the resources of classical literature, often as a lens through which to obtain a new perspective on current events in Northern Ireland.[28] Longley's poetry is markedly internationalist in scope, and moves easily between the Irish and English cultural contexts, as did that of Louis MacNeice in an earlier generation. Longley's work is deeply influenced by MacNeice and Yeats, but also by poets writing out of a thoroughly English tradition: George Herbert, Edward Thomas, Philip Larkin, Geoffrey Hill, Ted Hughes.

Longley is extremely attentive to the details of his personal, familial and cultural past, and is eager to conserve and preserve the legacy of that past. This may be seen in his identification with his father's war experiences, his fascination with his parents' childhoods and familial heritages, and his determination to identify with both British and Irish historical experiences. His poems reflect an acute sense of the preciousness of things that have been lost and a tendency to take on the role of the poet as the one who remembers and thus conserves. However, while Longley is often acutely disturbed by loss and mutability, his poetry does not reflect an effort to stave off or defend against these experiences. In fact, his use of lists and inventories often acts to intensify and heighten a sense of disruption, uncertainty and loss. For example, in the first poem of the 'Ghetto' sequence, a sequence about the victims of the Holocaust, the list of familiar, comforting, ordinary objects serves to create an agonising sense of rupture as the futility of the effort to retain a vestige of identity and normality is recognised:

> Because you will suffer soon and die, your choices
> Are neither right nor wrong: a spoon will feed you,
> A flannel keep you clean, a toothbrush bring you back
> To your bathroom's view of chimney pots and gardens.
> With so little time for inventory or leavetaking,
> You are packing now for the rest of your life
> Photographs, medicines, a change of underwear, a book,
> A candlestick, a loaf, sardines, needle and thread.
> These are your heirlooms, perishables, worldly goods.
> What you bring is the same as what you leave behind,
> Your last belonging a list of your belongings.[29]

Similarly, in poem VIII of the same sequence, the list of familiar things which are drawn by children in the concentration camps ('drawings of kitchens / And farms, farm animals, butterflies, mothers, fathers') only serves to accentuate the surreal and horrific nature of their present environment, as the pictures turn 'into guards at executions and funerals / Torturing and hanging even these stick figures' (*GF*, 43).

In poem V of the 'Ghetto' sequence, however, there *is* a sense that the list of the names of different kinds of potatoes can offer some kind of 'resistance' to suffering. Again, the poem does not seek to stave off the recognition of suffering, but allusions to the Irish famine indicate that the list is proffered with a sense that the names emerge from a cultural history of emotional resilience:

> My delivery of Irish Peace, Beauty of Hebron, Home
> Guard, Arran Banners, Kerr's Pinks, resistant to eelworm,
> Resignation, common scab, terror, frost, potato-blight. (*GF*, 42)

This kind of offering-up of a list of nouns in response to suffering is most famously seen in 'The Ice-Cream Man', a poem which remembers when '[t]hey murdered the ice-cream man on the Lisburn Road' (*GF*, 49). Here the list of ice-cream flavours represents the delight of the familiar, of the known, of continuity. The list of plants is more complex. Critics have been anxious to assert that the list does not try to 'console',[30] and certainly the litany of flowers is not invested with any explanatory or compensatory significance. However, the poem is as much about the relationship between father and daughter as it is about the murder of the ice-cream man. Certainly the poem *as a whole* does not aim to console; on the contrary, it highlights the child's grief in a way that points to the harrowing and devastating effect of violence on children's lives. *Within* the poem, however, the list of flower names is offered by the father in the context of the relationship as providing a measured space within which the child can experience and express her grief; at the same time, its calmness and gentleness are surely part of an effort to soothe and console. The voice seeking to limit and modulate the emotional damage done to a child should be distinguished from the impact of the poem as an artistic object on the reader. Longley does deeply value continuity, familiarity and belonging. At the same time, however, his poems consistently address and seek out experiences that are founded on disruption and transience, on homes that are places of conflict and uncertainty, on isolation and *not* belonging. This last is reflected particularly in Longley's poems about the west of Ireland, which dwell on a paradoxical feeling of belonging and exclusion.

Michael Longley's decision to utilise the *Odyssey* and the *Iliad* as material through which to explore his experience of the conflict in Northern Ireland raises several difficult issues, including the fact that Homer's retrospective storytelling was characterised by a romanticisation of the past heroic era and, at times, a glorification of violence. The stories were set in a semi-mythical past even for Homer's audience; the Greeks of that era looked back on the Mycenaean culture as representing a time when things were fundamentally different: heroes were semi-divine, the gods were close to humanity, the division between mortality and immortality was indefinite and permeable, and there was a sense of unity, order and energy in the world. Nostalgia for the heroic era of the *Odyssey* and the *Iliad* has persisted throughout European history up till the present day.

'The Butchers' is based on a passage in Book XXII of the *Odyssey* that approaches an Iliadic tone in its frenzy for blood and honour. Longley, however, thoroughly undermines any potential for heroism in Odysseus's return to Ithaca and his slaughtering of the suitors and the disloyal servants. Through parallels with violence in Northern Ireland and Europe (established through the title[31] and the poem's placement after 'The Ice-Cream Man', 'Tradewinds' and other poems dealing with contemporary conflict), 'The Butchers' drags the events out of a remote and 'different' past into a present-day context. A passage from *Tuppenny Stung* reveals a possible connection for Longley between his experience of the Troubles and his response to this Homeric passage. When, at age nine, Longley's Protestant friends found him uncertain of his politics, they provided him 'to secure the conversion' with

> pamphlets which purported to describe Catholic atrocities from the twenties and thirties. Every page carried blurred photographs of victims who, it was claimed, had been tortured and mutilated, their brains or hearts cut out, their genitals chopped off. Forgeries? Adaptations of photographs of road accidents from forensic files? Or real victims? This vitriolic propaganda burned deep into my mind.[32]

This seems to find echoes in Longley's account of Odysseus's killing of Melanthios:

> And when they had dragged Melanthios's corpse into the
>   haggard
> And cut off his nose and ears and cock and balls, a dog's
>   dinner,
> Odysseus, seeing the need for whitewash and disinfectant,
> Fumigated the house and the outhouses ... (*GF*, 51)

Longley highlights the surreal, absurd quality of Homer's account of Odysseus's cleaning operations, providing a heavily ironic perspective on the original. The most vivid and resonant part of the poem is the last eleven lines,[33] in which Longley imaginatively transforms the journey of the suitors' ghosts to Hades, leaving us to wonder at the end in what ways our political present may resemble 'a bog-meadow full of bog-asphodels / Where the residents are ghosts or images of the dead'.

'The Butchers' exploits the brutality of some moments in Homer, but some of Longley's adaptations gain much of their effect from his re-creation of Homer's sense of a time which was more vivid, beautiful and ordered than the present. 'Homecoming', 'A Bed of Leaves', 'The Oar' and 'The Camp-Fires' are among these. There is a quality of longing or nostalgia in the deliberate, enchanted, lingering tone of these poems. But when the subject-matter includes violence, Longley is careful to complicate this tone. In 'The Camp-Fires' he alludes to contemporary events, thus darkening the sense of imminent tragedy which in the original is softened by the heroic context. The mention in the second line of 'no-man's land' and 'the killing fields' taps into our sense of the horror of twentieth-century war, while the comparison with the Co. Mayo landscape draws the poem into the Irish context. Lines like 'where salmon run from the sea, / Where the shepherd smiles on his luminous townland'[34] create a striking pastoral effect, a sense of an idyllic landscape, and the relatively regular hexameters create a sense of achieved balance, but the placement of the parentheses (which enclose all but the first two and last two lines) accentuates the effect of the second, troubling line on the last two lines of the poem, so that the approaching sunrise is sensed as overwhelmingly ominous. The contemporary allusions do not, however, disallow or negate the beauty of the scene; there is instead a sense that the horror of real and tangible suffering is even greater precisely *because* of the human tendency to go through life continually envisaging an alternative reality, or interpreting experience in terms of ideas of the infinite, perfect and divine.

'Ceasefire', in *The Ghost Orchid*, has been seen as Longley's most politically engaged poem; it was published in the *Irish Times* two days after the IRA announced a ceasefire in 1994. Its scene is the encounter between Priam and Achilles in the *Iliad*, when Priam comes to plead with Achilles for the body of his son Hector. Steven Matthews has argued that

> the sonnet form provides a salutary model for the balances and loving-harmonies which might be attainable in the North of Ireland should the moment of ceasefire be carried to its next logical stages of forgiveness, sitting down together, admiring the graceful strengths of the other side and talking.[35]

While this is an attractive reading, there are limits to the extent to which we can view this poem as a model for a political process. Firstly, we might wonder whether, by imagining the parties in Northern Ireland in the roles of Priam and Achilles, the poem comes too close to distancing and heroicising what urgently needs to be a very realistic, down-to-earth and accessible process. But secondly, and more importantly, the poem's complex meditation on fate and human agency prevents it from being viewed as a simple model for political change. Readers familiar with the *Iliad* will know that in Homer's poem the meeting of Priam and Achilles and their mutual bonding in grief is seen as a ritualised, scripted interlude in the war which must inevitably go on, rather than as an opportunity for either of the two men to radically change the course of events. Although the *Iliad* ends with the return of Hector's body, we know that the war goes on, that Troy falls, and that Achilles will soon die as well; Achilles' own earlier 'ceasefire' is broken in order that he might fulfil the prophecy of his own death. However, the gods have only ordained that Achilles must return Hector's body to Priam. Within the space of time when Priam and Achilles are together, nothing is ordained and nothing is excluded. The bond between them (in both poem and original text) is highly charged and deeply ambivalent, and the fact that they manage to weep together in a grief which is simultaneously shared and separate engenders a hope in the possibility of change through relationship: 'Priam curled up at his feet and / Wept with him until their sadness filled the building' (*GO*, 39). But the encounter between Priam and Achilles gains its potency because its placement at the end of the *Iliad* necessitates a doubleness in our thinking of it. At one moment we can envisage its symmetry and harmony as permanent, final and conclusive, but at the next we are compelled to imagine it breaking apart hopelessly into the very chaos of war that went before. The scene is in a special way both timeless and static, miraculously wrested from the tumult of events.

Longley exaggerates this effect by breaking the sonnet up into smaller frames. The exchange as Longley describes it has a sense of ritual action, of fulfilling a scripted pattern, and this is reflected in the poem's form as it moves towards the final, retrospective alexandrine couplet, spoken by Priam, 'who earlier had sighed',

> 'I get down on my knees and do what must be done
> And kiss Achilles' hand, the killer of my son.' (*GO*, 39)

This final couplet emphasises the role of fate and necessity over human choice rather *more* than recent translations of the *Iliad* do in the equivalent passage;[36] Longley's emphasis allows him to dramatise the tension between fate and agency. The moment of connection between Priam and Achilles is both fated and chosen; it begins as fated, with Priam's sense of his actions being compelled, but turns into something chosen as the men weep together. The numbered stanzas invite us to envisage change and progress but through the retrospective final couplet Longley reminds us of the fated nature of the encounter, and closes off the possibility of this relationship moving into narrative; it remains as portraiture. We can only imagine two possibilities: a freezing of the moment, or a collapse back into chaos. In its emphasis on the suspended moment 'Ceasefire' provides no model for a political process that must take place in and through the chaos and turbulence of ordinary life and daily conflicts. But it does very effectively capture the fear that the scope for agency released by the moment of ceasefire may be engulfed again by deterministic narratives. At the same time, the seductiveness of these narratives, of the concepts of fate and destiny, is recognised; and, implicitly, the difficulty of imagining anything other than a renewed surrender to them.[37]

Should Michael Longley have been subjected to the same criticisms that Heaney was in regard to his tendency to unify disparate historical contexts into a 'mythic confederation' (in the words of Edna Longley)? Perhaps, but as my discussion of Heaney showed, the most interesting criticism of Heaney's poetry does not concern the simple fact that he sees similarities between disparate historical contexts, but that in doing so he seems to exhibit a kind of attraction to the idea of cyclical repetition of sacralised violence. In other words, comparing the present to the past or to some mythological context is not in itself problematic; what matters is how this is done. The classical texts that Longley draws on certainly have their dangers when they are linked to the contemporary context, given the nostalgia, the glorification of violence and heroism, and the attraction to ideas of fate and determinism that characterise many of these narratives in the original. Longley for the most part avoids these dangers; 'Ceasefire' perhaps comes closest to vulnerability, but it can be read as a profound and complex meditation on the tension between agency and determinism. In other poems, Longley is perhaps protected by his characteristic stance as elegist; in comparison to Heaney he is less often concerned to probe the difficult and controversial question of *why* violence occurs in human societies, and more likely to concentrate on the task of expressing grief and loss.

The Homeric adaptations include quite a few elegiac moments, as in 'Anticleia', where the poet's love and grief for his own mother speaks through the Homeric story. *The Weather in Japan* and *Snow Water*, Longley's two most recent collections, are very much a consolidation of Longley's chosen role as elegist. These two collections are characterised by a similar mixture of elegies, poems about aging and the poet's own approaching death, poems about war, and Longley's signature nature lyrics. Perhaps *The Weather in Japan* is more absorbed and agonised by death and the process of dying than *Snow Water;* in *Snow Water* the elegies seem more accepting, the focus more on the quality of the friendships celebrated than on the experience of absence and loss.[38] *The Weather in Japan* is oriented around the image of quilt-making, which for Longley evokes the care, complexity and compassion of the individual life. It is intriguing to see a male poet investigating an image so firmly associated with poetry and criticism by women. 'The Design' is one of Longley's most precise and haunting short poems:

> Sometimes the quilts were white for weddings, the design
> Made up of stitches and the shadows cast by stitches.
> And the quilts for funerals? How do you sew the night?[39]

The Weather in Japan (which, as suggested by the title, shows the continued influence of minimalist Japanese poetry on Longley's work) does not frequently refer to Northern Irish politics or conflict. One exception is 'All of these People', which, in common with several of the poems in *The Weather in Japan*, refers back to motifs included in earlier poems; in this case we hear again of the murdered ice-cream man, this time in company with an assassinated greengrocer. Together with other community figures like the butcher and the cobbler they represent hospitality, decency and openness; they stand for 'the opposite of war', which is 'not so much peace as civilisation' (*WJ*, 16). This contrast between the blessed regularity of everyday communal life and the violent dislocation of war is also the theme of *Snow Water*'s 'War and Peace', another of Longley's classically inspired pieces, in which Achilles' hunting down of Hector, 'like a sparrowhawk / Screeching after a horror-struck collared-dove' is set against the bright, tranquil sensuality of the Trojan women rinsing, in the warm and cold water of the Scamander river, 'glistening clothes in the good old days, / On washdays before the Greek soldiers came to Troy'.[40]

In both *The Weather in Japan* and *Snow Water*, then, we see a movement away from overt reference to the Troubles in Northern Ireland, but a strengthening of Longley's status as elegist and mourner of war. At the same time the collections together, with their emphasis on the domestic as an alternative value system, are doing something rather new. Quilt-making, tea-brewing (in 'Snow Water'), cooking (in 'Yellow Bungalow'), grocery-shopping (in 'Praxilla') – all these domestic activities are owned and valued highly in Longley's poetry. The revision of traditional (and even current) conceptions of poetic masculinity that this entails is considerable. As noted by Michael Murphy in his review of *The Weather in Japan*,[41] the small poem 'In the Iliad' is likewise radical in its questioning of masculinity. Men's nipples here come to symbolise firstly their sense of inadequacy in child-rearing ('She turned in the small hours her hungry face / To my diddy and tried to suck that button' (*WJ*, 14)) and at the same time their vulnerable desire to succeed in the battlefield:

> We wear them like medals for our children
> And even in nakedness look overdressed.
> In the *Iliad* spears go through them and,
> Later, one's ripped from Agamemnon's chest. (14)

Suggesting, perhaps, a connection between male aggression and a sense of inadequacy in personal relationships and nurturing, the poem also evokes the socially enforced split between men's private roles and public personae. Longley's capacity to breach this divide between the personal and familial and the public and political is part of what makes him such an important figure within the context of Northern Irish writing, along with his skill as an elegist. As Ruth Ling comments, 'At their best, Longley's elegies are so full of paradox that ... the very words of consolation simultaneously shoulder the full weight of the loss.'[42] In other words, any opposition between consolation and the full confrontation of loss becomes irrelevant in poems that ask 'what type of art might best heal yet best stay true to the pain'.[43] In his capacity as a poet of grief and of healing Michael Longley has come to fill a profound and valuable role in Northern Irish poetry. There has been little major change, only consolidation, in Longley's poetic in his last two volumes, but it may be that a reorientation is imminent, as the last poem in *Snow Water* seems to suggest:

> Is this my final phase? Some of the poems depend
> Peaceably like the brown leaves on a sheltered branch.
> Others are hanging on through the equinoctial gales
> To catch the westering sun's red declension.
> I'm thinking of the huge beech tree in our garden.
> I can imagine foliage on fire like that. (62)

Ciaran Carson

Michael Longley has remarked that he finds it hard to write about Belfast, where he has lived nearly all his life.[44] In contrast, the poetry of Ciaran Carson is almost obsessively urban, and takes the streets of Belfast as its unstable territory. Where Heaney and

Longley both retain some affinity with the Romantic notion of the 'nature poet', Carson deliberately sets his poetry up in opposition to such notions. Carson, born in 1948, is a decade younger than Heaney and Longley, and represents a generation of poets who entered into adulthood in a context of extreme political turbulence. Carson's first collection, *The New Estate*, was published in 1976, and a pamphlet, *The Lost Explorer*, in 1978, but although these were well-received, Carson's next collection, *The Irish for No*, did not appear until 1988. Carson's own comments illuminate the significance of this long break and the difference between the early poems and those of *The Irish for No*. He says that his job as the traditional arts officer for the Arts Council of Northern Ireland had pulled him away from the written word towards oral forms:

> The idea of art being on the page was one thing, and the idea of art being a form that can expand itself, involve a lot of things, like conversation, dancing, singing, playing music was another. In that it was of the world and in the world. The stuff I had been doing up until then, in terms of writing seemed a bit thin, pale, contained, too aesthetic. So, I just went off the whole idea of being a 'poet'.

However, his reading of C.K. Williams's *Tar* brought him back to poetry:

> It gave me the idea that you could do something, with the extended poem, the long line. In that it could give you a story, a narrative, include the real world in a sense. It wasn't the kind of poem that was about art, or form, but the world. I mean, the kind of poetry he was doing, C.K. Williams, wasn't too far removed from storytelling that you heard in bars. So I embarked on it, playing with the apparently sprawling line, which to my mind, had a shape in terms of the line of the song.[45]

Except for his most recent collection, *Breaking News*, which enacts a radical shift in style, Carson's work from *The Irish for No* onwards has been characterised by his use of the long line, which often sprawls well beyond the limits set for it by the conventional lay-out of poetry publishers, and by his appropriation of other features of the ballad and oral storytelling traditions: long, convoluted narratives and an orientation towards aural effect. Carson's poetry is always open to surprise, to distraction, to digression, and it glories in the unexpectedness of language and memory at the same time as it uses their instability to probe the insecurities and traumas of a place and a culture devastated by years of violent conflict.

The title poem of *The Irish for No* takes its starting point from the fact that in Irish there are no words for 'yes' and 'no' (affirmation is achieved through a repetition of the verb and a negative qualifier). Carson's positioning of this concept at the centre of the collection is important; it implies a valuing of ambiguity and ambivalence, an avoidance of absolutes and certainty. This is given a literary context in 'The Irish for No', where allusions to Keats's 'Ode to a Nightingale' are juxtaposed with references to Seamus Heaney's early poetry. In 1975, in his famous review of Heaney's *North* (quoted earlier), Carson took a phrase from Heaney's poem 'Exposure', turned it into a question, and used it as his title: 'Escaped from the Massacre?'. He answers the question himself: 'No one really escapes from the massacre, of course; the only way you can do that is by falsifying issues, by applying wrong notions of history, instead of seeing what's before your eyes.'[46] Earlier in the piece he argues that Heaney has become 'the laureate of violence – a mythmaker, an anthropologist of ritual killing, an apologist for "the situation", in the last resort, a mystifier'.[47] It is in the context of these trenchant criticisms that we must read Carson's allusions to Heaney in his later poetry. In 'The Irish for No' Carson alludes to Heaney's early poetry from *Death of a Naturalist* and *Door into the Dark*, implying that the romantic desire for release through death that is found in Keats's poem is paralleled in Heaney's poetry by a fascination with death and with the possibility of catharsis and aesthetic closure. Carson's own poetry rejects this tendency as 'Mish-mash. Hotch-potch' (essentially, 'mystification'), and opts instead for the disturbance of the ordinary and the uncertain, 'what's before your eyes':

> Staples hyphenate a wet cardboard box as the upturned can
>   of oil still spills
> And the unfed cat toys with the yin-yang of a tennis-ball,
>   debating whether *yes* is *no*.[48]

In *The Irish for No* and *Belfast Confetti* (1989) this resistance to closure and finality is demonstrated repeatedly: the fracturing of narrative evokes a city which is incessantly disrupted, its workings exposed and efforts to create smoothness, coherence and pattern incessantly undermined:

> But the whole Victorian creamy façade has been tossed off
> To show the inner-city tubing: cables, sewers, a snarl of
>   Portakabins,
> Soft-porn shops and carry-outs. A Telstar Taxis depot that is a
>   hole
> In a breeze-block wall, a wire grille and a voice-box uttering
>   gobbledygook.
> (*IFN*, 34)

As efforts at spoken communication are replaced by mechanised gobbledy-gook, so in the poem 'Belfast Confetti', the mechanics of textuality – punctuation – obliterate rather than enable sense:

> Suddenly as the riot squad moved in, it was raining
>   exclamation marks,
> Nuts, bolts, nails, car-keys. A fount of broken type. And the
>   explosion
> Itself – an asterisk on the map. This hyphenated line, a burst of
>   rapid fire …
> I was trying to complete a sentence in my head, but it kept
>   stuttering,
> All the alleyways and side-streets blocked with stops and
>   colons.
>
> I know this labyrinth so well – Balaclava, Raglan, Inkerman,
>   Odessa Street –
> Why can't I escape? Every move is punctuated. Crimea Street.
>   Dead end again.
> A Saracen, Kremlin-2 mesh. Makrolon face-shields. Walkie-
>   talkies. What is
> My name? Where am I coming from? Where am I going? A
>   fusillade of question-marks. (*IFN*, 31)

The phrase 'Belfast confetti' appears several times in these two collections, referring to the miscellaneous ammunition thrown in street riots. Here punctuation becomes an equivalent violence on a linguistic level. If Carson's poems in *The Irish for No* tend to value constant movement, the ability to keep the flow of oral narrative going through the 'sprawling line', this poem explores the opposite sensation: the sense of being blocked, cut off, trapped, left empty of narrative. Here the associations of the street names are ominous and the poem is not allowed to veer off through linguistic inventiveness and the coils of etymology in order to transform the familiar into the new; everything is heavy and oppressive in its knownness but the labyrinth nevertheless yields no answers. Many of the characters in Carson's Belfast poems seem trapped and powerless, confronted with blocks and dead-ends at every turn.

But while Carson's poetry is on one level working *against* the city's violent 'full-stops' and its sense of enclosure, other poems reveal another side of Belfast: its mutability. This is an aspect of the city that Carson both celebrates and mourns. *Belfast Confetti* is overwhelmingly concerned with the city's metamorphoses, and this theme is set out most clearly in the opening poem, 'Turn Again':

> There is a map of the city which shows the bridge that was
>   never built.
> A map which shows the bridge that collapsed; the streets that
>   never existed.
> Ireland's Entry, Elbow Lane, Weigh-House Lane, Back Lane,
>   Stone-Cutter's Entry –
> Today's plan is already yesterday's – the streets that were there
>   are gone.
> And the shape of the jails cannot be shown for security reasons.[49]

Carson's Belfast is a city where nothing is stable and the mind's attempts to schematise or make sense of the city, whether through mental maps or physical maps, are always thwarted by the pace of change, the instinct towards secrecy and the degree to which maps incorporate ideological agendas. The textual materials that make up *Belfast Confetti* are as heterogeneous as the confetti of the title: prose pieces, translations of haiku, and quotations from historical sources are dispersed among the poems. The prose pieces allow a more discursive approach to the themes tackled by the poems. 'Question Time' asserts, 'No, don't trust maps, for they avoid the moment: ramps, barricades, diversions, Peace Lines'

(*BC*, 58). Since the moment is all in a context in which anything may at any time be 'sliding back into the rubble and erasure', maps are useless, and the only adequate representation is the thing itself: '*The city is a map of the city*' (*BC*, 69). Yet at the same time Carson's poetry recognises the necessity – and inescapability – of the human effort towards representation, and much of his poetry is concerned with the workings of memory: the continuous construction and reconstruction of mental maps of the past and the present. The mental map, as opposed to the physical one, has the potential to be fluid and provisional, continually responsive to the contingencies of event. Some mental maps can be adaptive, self-protective, such as the one which allows Mule in 'Dresden' to accomplish his 'careful drunken weaving' through the 'baroque pyramids of empty baked bean tins' which are 'as good as a watchdog' (*IFN*, 11–16). The self-protectiveness is born out of trauma here; the careful avoidance of collapse is opposed to the wholesale destruction which Mule's brother Horse witnessed in the bombing of Dresden.

In the prose piece 'Question Time', the narrator relates an incident in which he is interrogated by men who have seen him cycling an unusual route around the Falls and Shankill areas; here the mental street map of his childhood is the key to convincing them of his Catholic origins and harmlessness:

> I am this map which they examine, checking it for error, hesitation, accuracy; a map which no longer refers to the present world, but to a history, these vanished streets; a map which is this moment, this interrogation, my replies. (*BC*, 63)

Here the ideological content of mental maps and representations is revealed, as the mental maps have to correspond exactly to confirm membership of the same community. The same process is seen in 'The Exiles' Club' in *The Irish for No* and in 'Schoolboys and Idlers of Pompeii' in *Belfast Confetti*; in both pieces a group of Irish in Australia spend their evenings collectively reconstructing the area of their childhood in Belfast:

> After years they have reconstructed the whole of the Falls Road, and now
> Are working on the back streets: Lemon, Peel and Omar,
> Balaclava, Alma. (*IFN*, 45)

While there is a sense that such nostalgia might be debilitating, producing only comfortable escapism, there is also a fascination with the way in which mental maps and systems are more dogged in survival than the bricks and mortar of the city, even though they may have no particular claim to accuracy: 'who will sort out the chaos? Where does land begin, and water end? Or memory falter, and imagination take hold?' (*BC*, 54).

Carson's maps are not only of the past or the present, but also the future. 'Revised Version' details the many attempts to plan for the transformation of the city, most of them appearing ironically out of the touch with the realities of the present, including the most recent attempts to transform Belfast into a postmodern, business-friendly metropolis:

> The jargon sings of leisure purposes, velodromes and pleasure parks, the unfurling petals of the World Rose Convention. As the city consumes itself – scrap iron mouldering on the quays, black holes eating through the time-warp – the Parliamentary Under-Secretary of State for the Environment announces that *to people who have never been to Belfast their image of the place is often far-removed from the reality.* No more Belfast champagne, gas bubbled through milk; no more heads in ovens. Intoxication, death, will find their new connections. Cul-de-sacs and ring-roads. *The city is a map of the city.* (*BC*, 69)

While many of the plans mentioned here are satirised for being founded on a lack of engagement with reality, Carson is no enemy of imaginative transformation. Between *Belfast Confetti* and *Breaking News*, Carson published three major collections, each of which moves further in an exploration of the way in which language can effect a radical transformation in the way we see things: *First Language* (1993), *Opera Et Cetera* (1996), and *The Twelfth of Never* (1999). (*The Alexandrine Plan*, a collection of translations from Mallarmé, Rimbaud and Baudelaire, was also published in 1998.) These collections are all challenging for the reader, and this challenge is at times made explicit: 'I am a dash or a void. It's up to you to make me up. Wake up, / You, the reader! I have some tales to tell you, and the night is but a pup'.[50] These poems are indeed filled with gaps and jumps for the reader to negotiate, as they open themselves up to the connections suggested by rhyme and arbitrary systems like the alphabet, and revel in the freedom of language let loose. As Steven Matthews says, *First Language* is Carson's response to the state of closure and dissolution evoked so vividly in *The Irish for No* and *Belfast Confetti*; it emerges out of his 'determination to keep the casual speaking voice alive against such suddenly and violently punctuated conditions'.[51] All of these collections are playful in tone and method despite the seriousness of much of the subject-matter. 'Letters in the Alphabet', for example, the first section of *Opera Et Cetera*, performs formal gymnastics to achieve cheeky rhymes ('The French gunrunner Arthur Rimbaud is said to have par- / Taken of it, especially when he felt a little bit under par' (*OEC*, 27)), and while the reader searches each poem for its title letter, surrounding letters creep in, as if to demonstrate the irrepressibility of language in the face of efforts to establish borders and controls.

Out of these three collections, it is perhaps *The Twelfth of Never*, a sequence of seventy-seven sonnets written in alexandrines, which most reveals the real potential of his free-wheeling yet densely crafted style. In *The Twelfth of Never* Carson tackles all the icons of Irish nationalism, republicanism and loyalism, mixing them in a heady brew with drugs and magic. Coleridge reappears throughout the collection, imbuing it with the spirit of 'Kubla Khan', and Yeats's occultism and Celtic Revivalism are also a strong presence. Carson's relationship with the otherworldly beings of Irish myth and fairy tale is, however, pointedly different from Yeats's. While Yeats's poem 'The Stolen Child' allows just a hint of menace to colour the seductiveness of the fairy call, Carson's fairies are simply cruel:

> I know a woman was away for seven years.
> When she returned, it seemed she'd little left to lose:
> They'd drawn her teeth and danced the toes off her. They'd
>   docked her ears.[52]

All of the familiar figures and symbols of the various political mythologies are 'made strange' in this book. The focus is more firmly on the icons of nationalist discourses, but those of unionism and loyalism are also present; the title, of course, plays with the centrality of the Twelfth of July to Protestant culture in Northern Ireland. The *Shan Van Vocht* or Poor Old Woman of nationalist convention, who, representing Ireland, traditionally pleads with the young men to fight for her and thus revive her youth and strength, appears in 'The Rising of the Moon', urging the narrator 'to go out and revolutionize Hibernia, and not to fear the guillotine'. But the narrator opts instead for the 'People of No Property' and the 'fragrant weed' (*TN*, 19).

The scope of *The Twelfth of Never* is vast: Ireland past and present, contemporary Japan, the opium wars and the Napoleonic wars all contribute material. The juxtaposition of such different contexts and sources facilitates a defamiliarising effect, and the jumbling of history and fantasy allows Carson to explore what he calls 'the underworld, the otherworld, the in-between worlds [sic] that is not ostensibly the real world'.[53] *The Twelfth of Never* is, then, a continuation of Carson's determination to explore the inconclusive and the ambiguous, to probe fantasy, memory and imagination to discover the workings of thought and to uncover possibilities for new ways of seeing. In this collection, it seems that the responsibility of the artist – and reader – is to remain open to change, debate and reconsideration:

These words the ink is written in is not indelible
And every fairy story has its variorum;
For there are many shades of pigment in the spectrum,
And the printed news is always unreliable. (*TN*, 89)

Having become so used to Carson's long line – the sprawl of *First Language* and *Opera Et Etcetera* and the even, jogging alexandrines of *The Twelfth of Never* – readers were no doubt shocked to open Carson's latest collection, *Breaking News*, and see pages minimally marked by poems of only a few words per line. *Breaking News*, which won the Forward prize for poetry in 2003, shows Carson experimenting with a style influenced by William Carlos Williams, where line breaks and blank spaces are crucial, and single words shiver in white space on the page. The exceptions to this minimalist style are 'The Forgotten City', which is also indebted to Williams, and the poems which draw heavily on the war journalism of the Anglo-Irish war correspondent William Howard Russell (1820–1907). These are the sequence 'The War Correspondent' and the single poem 'The Indian Mutiny', which use longer lines and regular stanzaic patterns. Carson's notes to the collection point out that although Russell's presence is found in other poems as well, these poems are especially indebted to Russell's writing: 'in many instances I have taken his words *verbatim*, or have changed them only slightly to accommodate rhyme and rhythm.'[54]

Readers might have noted the associations of some of the street names listed in 'Belfast Confetti', quoted earlier: 'Balaclava, Raglan, Inkerman, Odessa Street'. These are all linked with the Crimean war (Baron Raglan was the first British commander-in-chief in that conflict), and in *Breaking News* Carson further pursues Belfast's deep involvement in British imperial history, in part through a sensitive recovery of Russell's reporting of the Crimean war and what was known as the Indian Mutiny. Obviously there are crucial connections being drawn between British imperialism in Ireland and in other parts of the world, but some of the poems based on Russell's journalism, with their evocation of the violent jumble of cultures and nations engaged in the Crimea, might also suggest other contemporary war zones upon which international contingents of soldiers, peacekeepers, bureaucrats, gold-diggers and opportunists have descended:

> then populate this slum with Cypriot and Turk,
> Armenians and Arabs, British riflemen
> and French Zouaves, camel-drivers, officers, and sailors,
> sappers, miners, Nubian slaves, Greek money-changers,
> plus interpreters who do not know the lingo;
> …
> O landscape riddled with the diamond mines of Kimberley,
> and all the oubliettes of Trebizond,
> where opium-smokers doze among the Persian rugs,
> and spies and whores in dim-lit snugs
> discuss the failing prowess of the superpowers,
>
> where prowling dogs sniff for offal beyond
> the stench of pulped plums and apricots,
> from which is distilled the brandy they call 'grape-shot',
> and soldiers lie dead or drunk among the crushed flowers –
> I have not even begun to describe Gallipoli. (*BN*, 57–8)

In other poems in this sequence ('The War Correspondent') Carson ventriloquises Russell's contained, precise but haunted description of the human atrocities of war:

> I will never forget one man
> whose head rested
> on a heap of apples,

his knees drawn up
to his chin, his eyes wide
open, seeming to inspect

the head of a Turco or Zouave
which, blown clean off,
lay like a cannonball in his lap.

What debris a ruined empire
leaves behind it! (71)

In this sequence and in 'The Indian Mutiny' Carson lets us view
Russell as both sensitive to the carnage inflicted upon cultures and
peoples by the British forces, but at the same time curiously –
perhaps defensively – involved in the minutiae of the military
system. In telling of the great fire in Varna, he mentions that 'The
howls of the inhabitants, / the clamour of women, horses, children,
dogs, the yells / of prisoners trapped in their cells, // were
appalling' but spends more time listing the material losses of the
British and French armies, including 'Lord Raglan's portable library
of books, / and 19,000 pairs of soldiers' boots' (59). Nevertheless, his
patient descriptions of everyday beauty and everyday brutality
convey the gravity of what has been done, aided at times by a
nineteenth-century idiom which is not afraid of solemnity:

And we spread terror and havoc
along the peaceful seaboard
of that tideless sea. (67)

This collection juxtaposes these poems imitating Russell's
nineteenth-century idiom with poems in Carson's new manner,
many of them holding on, however, to his consistent obsession,
Belfast:

Breaking

red alert
car parked
in a red
zone

about to

disintegrate
it's

oh

so quiet

you can
almost

hear it rust (16)

These poems achieve a variety of effects, not necessarily having much in common with the effects we find in a famous (and super-ficially similar) poem like Williams's 'So much depends', which relies on visual symmetry and the breaking up of compound words. 'Belfast' relies on a similar visual symmetry and balance, but some of the best of Carson's poems embody their content in their form in a more dramatic way, as in 'Breaking', where the sep-aration of the words suggests a voice breathing words out one by one, afraid to speak too loud or too fast for fear of triggering the explosion, with the isolated 'oh' particularly powerful in its sug-gestion of panic. 'News' (following 'Breaking') works to imitate the staccato of yet another explosion and of the news itself, with its never-ending volley of stories about violence:

alarms
shrill

lights
flash

as dust
clears

above
the paper

shop

The Belfast Telegraph
sign reads
      fast   **rap** (17)

Other poems such as 'Wire', 'Trap' and 'Spin Cycle' seek to enact the fracturing or slowing-down of thought in a context of danger or surveillance. Some of these poems do take risks in their spareness, and one wonders whether the form will have enough scope for Carson to continue writing in a similar style. Often, and in contrast to the elegant verbosity of Russell's journalistic style, they convey in their hesitations and silences a sense of the difficulty of saying anything at all about Belfast. If *First Language* reflects, as Steven Matthews says, a 'determination to keep the casual speaking voice alive', *Breaking News* also keeps the voice alive (most of the poems, despite using forms which rely heavily on layout on the page, can be imagined as being spoken) but rather than being 'casual' this voice is attenuated, fractured, watchful.

The collection as a whole comes across as an effort to explore new and different ways of speaking about war, and emphasises in its inclusion of Russell's words (and in its use of Russell's observations in some of the poems in the first section) that there is no right way of doing this. Carson's borrowing of other voices in this collection is a way of making possible a jump in perception, something which he achieves strikingly in 'The Forgotten City', which takes the title, narrative, and key phrases from William Carlos Williams's poem. Williams's characteristic tone of wonder is skillfully deployed by Carson in his narrative of discovery of a whole area of suburban Belfast which seems immune from and utterly cut off from the violence. Carson is pointing here to the class divisions in Belfast society, the way in which certain suburbs full of 'pleasant cul-de-sacs' manage to seal themselves off from trouble. Here is a place where death is only seen in the decorous environment of the crematorium and the parks are so quiet 'that at one gatekeeper's lodge / I could hear coffee perking' (37). The equilibrium is surreal in comparison to the chaos of the rest of the city, and the poem achieves an ironic indictment of Belfast's middle classes in its tone of naïve questioning:

> How did they get
> cut off in this way from the stream of
> bulletins, so under-represented
> in our parliaments and media when so near
> the troubled zone, so closely surrounded
> and almost touched by the famous and familiar? (37)

Conclusion

Each of these poets has, then, chosen a very different way of responding through poetry to the pressures and exigencies of the

Northern Irish context. Seamus Heaney's consistent emphasis has been on the relationship between the individual and the group, and on the freedoms and responsibilities of the individual. Michael Longley's writing has primarily focused on the expression of grief and loss, seeking ways in which poetry can mediate an understanding of suffering and a sharing of grief. Ciaran Carson's poetry urges us to confront the disturbing, dislocating aspects of everyday experience and to be conscious of the provisionality of all our beliefs, interpretations and conclusions. Yet while their emphases and strategies differ, the work of all three poets is strongly, indelibly marked by the influence of the griefs, stresses, hopes and anxieties which have shaped life in Northern Ireland over the last four decades. The difficult, abstract question of the political responsibility of the artist perhaps appears simpler when we have absorbed this poetry in all its variety and richness; it is clear that this poetry, above all, heightens our awareness, sharpens our perceptions, and increases our self-consciousness about our own responses to violence and conflict. It may not provide any 'answers' but in its attention to nuance and subtlety of feeling and experience it provides, nevertheless, a model for political thought and dialogue.

The English word 'no' has, of course, been all too frequently heard in the political scene in Northern Ireland since these three writers began their careers. But the last decade has seen dramatic changes: ceasefires, the Good Friday Agreement of 1998, the establishment of the Northern Ireland Assembly and other political institutions, moves on decommissioning by the IRA. At the time of writing, however, the Assembly has not been reinstated since its suspension in October 2002, and the dominance of Sinn Fein and the Democratic Unionist Party in the 2003 Assembly elections means that getting it up and running again will be a difficult process. Nevertheless, optimism has still been consistently higher since the Good Friday Agreement than at any time since the 1960s, and the fact that there is even talk of a deal being reached between Sinn Fein and the DUP is quite astonishing. The new optimism that has been sporadically and tentatively felt and expressed throughout the last decade is reflected in a milestone poem by Seamus Heaney, dated September 1994 (the month after the IRA ceasefire was announced) and published in *The Spirit Level*. In 'The Tollund Man' of *Wintering Out*, the speaker promises 'Some day I will go to Aarhus / To see his peat-brown head' (*WO*, 36). In 'Tollund' the speaker remembers a visit to the swamp in Denmark in which the Tollund Man's body was found. But whereas in 'The Tollund Man' the speaker had been compulsively drawn to the site of ritual violence, in 'Tollund' he finds a modern, commonplace landscape,

> With tourist signs in *futhark* runic script
> In Danish and in English. Things had moved on.
>
> It could have been Mulhollandstown or Scribe.
> The byroads had their names on them in black
> And white; it was user-friendly outback
> Where we stood footloose, at home beyond the tribe,
>
> More scouts than strangers, ghosts who'd walked abroad
> Unfazed by light, to make a new beginning,
> And make a go of it, alive and sinning,
> Ourselves again, free-willed again, not bad. (*TSL*, 69)

Although there may be a touch of ironic regret at the homogenisation caused by globalisation, the dominant feeling of the poem is relief at the release from the imperatives of tribe and place, along with the feelings of guilt and entrapment that they produced. The urge to purity is rejected – this speaker will have a flawed and free life instead of a pure sacrificial death. There is a sense of tentative excitement at the possibility of a new beginning and a readiness for change. Heaney is celebrating and urging an openness to those 'big soft buffetings' which 'catch the heart off guard and blow it open' (*TSL*, 70).

Notes

1 'Man and the Echo', in *The Collected Works of W.B. Yeats: Volume 1: The Poems*, revised edition, ed. Richard J. Finneran (New York: Macmillan, 1989), p. 345.

2 Conor Cruise O'Brien, 'A slow north-east wind', *Listener*, 25 September 1975, pp. 404–5 (p. 404).

3 Seamus Heaney, *Door into the Dark* (London: Faber, 1969), pp. 41–2.

4 'A raindrop on a thorn', interview by Robert Druce, *Dutch Quarterly Review*, vol. 9 (1978), pp. 24–37 (p. 30).

5 Seamus Heaney, *Preoccupations: Selected Prose 1968–1978* (London: Faber, 1980), p. 57.

6 Edna Longley, ' "Inner emigré" or "artful voyeur"?: Seamus Heaney's *North*', in *Poetry in the Wars* (Newcastle upon Tyne: Bloodaxe, 1986), pp. 140–69 (p. 159).

7 Ciaran Carson, 'Escaped from the massacre?', *Honest Ulsterman*, vol. 50 (1975), pp. 183–6 (pp. 184–5).

8 Longley, 'Inner emigré', p. 151.
9 Seamus Heaney, *Wintering Out* (London: Faber, 1972), p. 37. Henceforth referred to as *WO*.
10 Longley, ' "Inner emigré" ', p. 151.
11 Seamus Heaney, *North* (London: Faber, 1975), p. 38. Henceforth referred to as *N*.
12 One of the most succinct discussions of the Biblical contexts for 'Punishment' is Neil Corcoran's in *The Poetry of Seamus Heaney: A Critical Study* (London: Faber, 1998), pp. 72–4.
13 David Lloyd, *Anomalous States: Irish Writing and the Post-Colonial Moment* (Durham, NC: Duke University Press, 1993), p. 32.
14 See Patricia Coughlan, ' "Bog Queens": The representation of women in the poetry of John Montague and Seamus Heaney', in *Gender in Irish Writing*, ed. Toni O'Brien and David Cairns (Buckingham: Open University Press, 1991), pp. 88–111 (p. 103).
15 Seamus Heaney, *Field Work* (London: Faber, 1979), p. 22. Henceforth referred to as *FW*.
16 Seamus Heaney, *Station Island* (London: Faber, 1984), p. 85. Henceforth referred to as *SI*.
17 Seamus Heaney, *Seeing Things* (London: Faber, 1991), p. 50.
18 Seamus Heaney, *The Spirit Level* (London: Faber, 1996), p. 30. Henceforth referred to as *TSL*.
19 Harry Clifton, 'Peat smoke and Byzantium', *Poetry Review*, vol. 91, no. 1 (2001), pp. 43–5 (p. 44).
20 Ibid., p. 45.
21 Seamus Heaney, *Electric Light* (London: Faber, 2001), p. 22. Henceforth referred to as *EL*.
22 Seamus Heaney, *Beowulf: A New Translation* (London: Faber, 1999), p. xxx.
23 Michael Longley, *Tuppenny Stung: Autobiographical Chapters* (Belfast: Lagan Press, 1995, first published 1994), p. 24.
24 Heaney, *Preoccupations*, p. 56.
25 Michael Longley, *An Exploded View: Poems 1968–72* (London: Gollancz, 1973), pp. 40–1.
26 Peter McDonald, 'From Ulster with Love', *Poetry Review*, vol. 81, no. 2 (1991), pp. 14–16 (p. 14).
27 Ibid., p. 16.
28 Longley had drawn on the classics before, but not with the scale and ambition that we see in *Gorse Fires* and *The Ghost Orchid*.
29 Michael Longley, *Gorse Fires* (London: Secker and Warburg, 1991), p. 40. Henceforth referred to as *GF*.
30 Peter McDonald, *Mistaken Identities: Poetry and Northern Ireland* (Oxford: Clarendon Press, 1997), p. 136.
31 The title alludes to the notorious 'Shankill Butchers', who tortured and killed many people from 1975 to 1977. They belonged to the UVF, a loyalist paramilitary organisation. See Jonathan Bardon, *A History of Ulster* (Belfast: Blackstaff, 1992), p. 728.
32 Longley, *Tuppenny Stung*, p. 27.
33 These lines are based on a different *Odyssey* passage, from Book XXIV.
34 Michael Longley, *The Ghost Orchid* (London: Jonathan Cape, 1995), p. 37. Henceforth referred to as *TGO*.

35 Steven Matthews, *Irish Poetry: Politics, History, Negotiation: The Evolving Debate, 1969 to the Present* (Basingstoke: Macmillan (now Palgrave Macmillan), 1997), p. 2.

36 Robert Fagles's version, for instance, is 'I have endured what no one on earth has ever done before – / I put to my lips the hands of the man who killed my son'. Homer, *The Iliad*, translated by Robert Fagles (New York: Viking Penguin, 1990), p. 605 (Book XXIV, lines 590–1).

37 See my article 'Learning about dying: Mutability and the classics in the poetry of Michael Longley', *New Hibernia Review*, vol. 6, no. 1 (Spring 2002), pp. 94–112. Since writing this article I have revised my view of 'Ceasefire' slightly.

38 Ruth Ling remarks that '*The Weather in Japan* ... registers not greater acceptance, but, conversely, an increased fear of the dark' ('*The Weather in Japan*: Tact and tension in Michael Longley's new elegies', *Irish University Review*, vol. 32, no. 2 (2002), pp. 286–304 (p. 288)). *Snow Water* does not have this feeling of closeness to terror.

39 Michael Longley, *The Weather in Japan* (London: Jonathan Cape, 2000), p. 45. Henceforth referred to as *WJ*.

40 Michael Longley, *Snow Water* (London: Jonathan Cape, 2004), p. 41. Henceforth referred to as *SW*.

41 Michael Murphy, 'Review of *The Weather in Japan*', Critical Survey, vol. 13, no. 3 (2001), pp. 120–3 (p. 123).

42 Ling, '*The Weather in Japan*', p. 292.

43 Ibid., p. 286.

44 Robert Johnstone, 'The Longley Tapes', *Honest Ulsterman*, no. 78 (1985), pp. 13–31 (p. 14).

45 'Inventing Carson: An interview', interview by David Laskowski, *Chicago Review*, vol. 45, nos 3–4 (1999), pp. 92–100 (pp. 92–3).

46 Carson, 'Escaped from the massacre?', p. 186.

47 Ibid., p. 183.

48 Ciaran Carson, *The Irish for No* (Newcastle upon Tyne: Bloodaxe, 1988; first published 1987), p. 50. Henceforth referred to as *IFN*.

49 Ciaran Carson, *Belfast Confetti* (Newcastle upon Tyne: Bloodaxe, 1990, first published 1989), p. 11. Henceforth referred to as *BC*.

50 Ciaran Carson, *Opera Et Cetera* (Newcastle upon Tyne: Bloodaxe, 1996), p. 24. Henceforth referred to as *OEC*.

51 Matthews, *Irish Poetry*, p. 199.

52 Ciaran Carson, *The Twelfth of Never* (London: Picador, 1999), p. 45. Henceforth referred to as *TN*.

53 'Inventing Carson', p. 99.

54 Ciaran Carson, *Breaking News* (Oldcastle: Gallery, 2003), p. 74. Henceforth referred to as *BN*.

6

'A rustle of echoes': Self, Subjectivity and Agency

David Dabydeen, Paul Muldoon, Denise Riley

Romanticism's elevation of the lyric has meant that for the last few centuries our very idea of poetry has been intimately tied up with the idea of the authentic, personal, speaking voice. Although throughout this period (and indeed within Romanticism itself) there have been myriad challenges to the notion that poetry can be the direct expression of a unified and autonomous self, the most forceful questioning of this idea has emerged in modernist and postmodernist poetry. In the case of postmodernism this has been energised partly by poststructuralist theories of selfhood and subjectivity. Over the last few decades, the term 'subject' has been used more and more commonly as an alternative to 'self' and 'individual'. This is because the term 'subject' suggests the way language assigns us roles – the 'subject' position is the position of the actor in the sentence – and also suggests the way people are *subjected* to various operations of power within culture. As Paul Smith puts it,

> The 'individual' is that which is undivided and whole, and understood to be the source and agent of conscious action or meaning which is consistent with it. The 'subject', on the other hand, is not self-contained, as it were, but is immediately cast into a conflict with forces that dominate it in some way or another – social formations, language, political apparatuses, and so on.[1]

Smith goes on to note, however, that this apparent opposition has not dissuaded people from using the phrase 'the individual subject' in an effort to capture the sense that human beings are never entirely subjected.[2]

Poststructuralist formulations of subjectivity as a contingent effect produced by language, diffuse and discontinuous, have, then, undermined traditional notions of personal choice and agency which depend on the self having some degree of unity, autonomy and transparency. Yet these kinds of theoretical positions seem to conflict with an intuitive belief in our capacity to actively shape our lives and selves, and to take responsibility for our actions, at least to some extent and within constraints. Currently many theorists are seeking new ways of conceiving of agency that can recognise the instability and socially embedded nature of the self. Meanwhile, the exploration of self, subjectivity and agency proceeds in the parallel realm of poetry, where it is possible to see many fascinating interconnections with theory, particularly in the case of the three poets included in this chapter, all of whom are very aware of contemporary theoretical debates.

David Dabydeen

It is a reflection of the complexity and depth of David Dabydeen's poetry that it could have been included in so many of this book's chapters, most obviously those on gender, sex and embodiment, and race and ethnicity. My decision to include it in this chapter will, I hope, allow me to establish a slightly different critical context from that adopted by other critics, most of whom consider Dabydeen as a postcolonial poet. While the postcolonial paradigm is relevant to my discussion, I want to forge links between the postcolonial discussion of concepts such as hybridity and the broader debate on self and subjectivity in contemporary poetry.

Dabydeen was born in 1955 in Guyana and moved with his parents to Britain in 1969. He studied English at Cambridge and is now an academic at the University of Warwick. *Slave Song*, which Dabydeen began when he was only 22, is fascinating in its use of a critical apparatus and illustrations alongside the text of the poems. A full half of the book is taken up by such material, so that the poems themselves are decentred. Whereas the poems are written in creole, the rest of the material – extended critical notes and translations – is in a very decorous standard English. The notes do not convey the usual tone of a poet explaining his or her poems, but rather reproduce the discourse of academic literary criticism. The illustrations, which are mostly eighteenth- and nineteenth-century European images of the Caribbean, also contribute to a sense of disparity between the poems and the other material. Overall, the collection conveys a strong sense that the creole voice of the poems is being interpreted, controlled and filtered for a Western audience. Some have condemned Dabydeen for this, while others have argued that his shifting between the 'masks' of interpreter, translator, slave and so on is a complex strategy used to reveal the power politics inherent in the business of literary criticism. As Mark McWatt notes, the critic may

> feel uneasy, perhaps, when the poet deliberately puts on this [literary critical] mask and grins at us from behind it. It seems mockingly to invite us to criticize the criticism, along with the poem.[3]

McWatt encourages us to see the collection as presenting a series of masks, the juxtaposition of which actually has the effect of drawing our attention away from the creole-speaking personae in the poems, and towards the consciousness that is behind all the masks – David Dabydeen the poet.

Although some critics assume that the voice of the notes and translations can be unproblematically identified as the authorial voice, whereas the creole poems are distanced dramatic monologues,[4] there are moments in the notes that make us question this approach. Mario Relich points to the oddity of the notes to 'The Canecutters' Song'; the notes dwell on the white woman's feelings, while the poem itself is written entirely from the perspective of the canecutter. The notes state that 'She wants to be degraded secretly (the long lace frock is temptingly rich, and it hangs loose, suggestively; also the chaos of her hair), to be possessed and mutilated in the mud. The tragedy is as much hers for her desires too are prevented by social barriers.'[5] As Relich says, 'The observations about the white woman's desires read like an unwarranted interpolation, a highly ironic one because the fantasies are now those of the poet rather than those of the canecutters. The poet thereby draws attention to his own alienation and psychic divisions.'[6] These kinds of moments, combined with the rather pompous tone of some of the notes and their reiteration of colonial clichés about the rawness and savagery of creole, suggest to us that the voice of the introduction, notes and translation should not be simply identified as the authorial voice. Dabydeen himself has provided backing for this perspective in interviews:

> I thought of three things in writing an extensive introduction and a series of notes: it was a literary joke – hence I referred twice in *Slave Song* to T.S. Eliot, because Eliot had also joked and provided a kind of spoof gloss to *The Waste Land*. On another level, we had been arguing for a long time that Creole was a distinctive language. ... If we were going to take that seriously we should provide translations to our poems. But the third reason is the most serious. I wanted to write in a minimalist fashion, and I wanted to question the relationship between the work of art and the critical industry that arises because of that work of art. In other words, I was being the critic and the artist together in one book. ... It posed the question, which is so central now with Derrida and others, as to the relationship between the artist and the critic, the creative work and the critical work.[7]

In another interview he comments that he is 'concerned about the critical business that thrives upon the expression of poverty or of dispossession, which is what the Caribbean voice ultimately is'.[8] These comments raise many interesting questions about cultural imperialism and the power dynamics within literary criticism, but here I want to focus on the implications of Dabydeen's strategies for concepts of self and subjectivity.

In his use of the competing voices in *Slave Song*, Dabydeen begins his poetic career as he will continue: with a recognition of the way in which subjectivity emerges in and through a jostling of competing discourses, all of which have particular material effects and historical causes and consequences. For Dabydeen the central discourses are those of colonialism and postcolonial resistance. Without the additional materials of introduction, notes, translations and illustrations in *Slave Song*, the collection would have been read as an effort to represent lyrically and authentically the subjectivity of the peasant canecutters and slaves of Guyana, with the focus turned away from the author and towards the speakers. As it is, the collection focuses our attention on the subjectivity from which all of this material emerged; it becomes clear that the 'author' concedes the constitutive role of both the discourses of Western literary criticism and of peasant/slave oral literature in his subjectivity. We are reminded that the peasant and slave songs are written by Dabydeen, a British-based academic and critic, and the juxtaposition of the different voices reminds us that even the actual songs sung by canecutters and slaves emerged in a context of dialogue, exchange, competition between discourses. The slaves' songs take on – and respond to – colonial notions about blackness and whiteness. No subjectivity is autonomous; all necessarily feed off one another (in fact, Dabydeen's 1994 poem 'Turner' takes the image of cannibalism and uses it to explore power relations). It becomes difficult to assess whose subjectivity we are accessing when we read, for example, the controversial and disturbing suggestion that both white colonial women and slave women have a secret desire to be raped by the 'other' – is this Dabydeen's view of the actual erotics of the relationship of oppression which constituted slavery (after all, one of the poems suggesting this is voiced for the slave women)? Is it to be read as the masculine fantasy of the colonisers, perpetuated through the voice of the 'colonising' anthropologist/ poet, translator and critic? The difficulty of assessing this reflects Dabydeen's wider suggestion that patterns of thought and relationship inhabit us and shape us whether we want them to or not, so that the task of assessing the 'ownership' of ideas becomes extremely difficult if not impossible.

Dabydeen's second collection *Coolie Odyssey* (1988) continues this meditation on the way in which an individual subjectivity can be shaped – and perhaps even trapped – by the metanarratives that have driven the historical phenomenon of colonialism. The collection contains a wide mixture of poems, some in creole and some in standard English, and right from the beginning it signals its desire to interrogate the paradoxes of a colonial inheritance. The first and title poem, 'Coolie Odyssey', begins with a wry glance at the success of poets like Harrison and Heaney:

> Now that peasantry is in vogue,
> Poetry bubbles from peat bogs,
> People strain for the old folk's fatal gobs
> Coughed up in grates North or North East
> 'Tween bouts o' living dialect,
> It should be time to hymn your own wreck,
> Your house the source of ancient song[9]

Like *Slave Song*, then, *Coolie Odyssey* is still painfully conscious of the question of audience and the dangers of peddling the 'post-colonial experience' as literary capital for 'congregations of the educated sipping wine' (13).

The poems I am most interested in here are set in contemporary times and focus on a West Indian who has settled in Britain. They explore the way in which intimate relationships are shaped and shadowed by the historical narratives that they inhabit imaginatively. Thus in 'The Seduction', a poem whose monorhymed stanzas convey a sense of circularity and entrapment, the initiation of a sexual relationship between a black man and a white woman is thwarted by the historical roles they are struggling with and trying to avoid. The man fears that he cannot live up to the image of the black man's potency, and is 'lost in shame' (*CO*, 31). The woman asserts her independence from colonial history, saying that she is 'Unblighted by colonial reign' and accusing him of wallowing in historical oppression: 'all he wanted was some pain / To wrap himself in mythic chain / And labour in his self-disdain' (*CO*, 30). But her ominous choice of simile for herself ('sweet as sugarcane'), the uncertainty about whether she is giving her real name, her grandiose accusations, and the fact that when she leaves he 'whimpered, bled in deference' suggests that she might not have avoided playing the colonial role she so robustly denies.

In contrast, 'The Sexual Word' affirms the woman's right to reject the man's efforts to haul himself out of the historical mire; interestingly, his only available strategy for emergence is a replication of the gendered paradigm of colonisation – rebirth through the domination of a feminine other. He is 'desperate to colonize her / In images of gold and fertility' but she 'refused the embrace of fantasy, / Unable to be torn up, transplanted, / Stripped, raped, broken and made to bear / Beautiful bastard fruit' (*CO*, 32). The end of the poem, however, qualifies her refusal a little by the suggestion that she was nevertheless 'ravished by the poetry'. This poem, and others in *Coolie Odyssey* including 'Miranda' and 'Caliban', explore the way in which the individual is shaped by the roles which have been established by generations of historical relationships. Subjectivity is experienced as divided and conflicted, internal and external become blurred, as these roles are recognised as belonging to narratives which have a prior existence to the individual, are experienced as deeply oppressive, but are deeply embedded in selfhood. Thus in 'Rebel Love' the black man has only to put his hand to a white woman's breast to be overcome by a powerful vision of the violence of white men against slaves, as he awaits 'The whiplash, white man bellowing pain' (*CO*, 34).

'Turner', the long poem sequence giving the title to Dabydeen's 1994 collection (the other poems in the collection are republished from *Slave Song* and *Coolie Odyssey*) exposes the issue of the relationship of the self to history even more clearly. The title sequence takes its point of origin from J.M.W. Turner's painting 'Slavers Throwing Overboard the Dead and Dying', a Romantic painting in the sublime mode. In 1840 when Turner painted it, the slave trade was outlawed in Britain but was still being practised elsewhere. In the preface to *Turner* Dabydeen explains how Ruskin's essay on the painting relegated the actual subject of the painting, the shackling and drowning of Africans, to a footnote: 'The footnote reads like an afterthought, something tossed overboard.'[10] It is necessary to quote extensively from Dabydeen's description of his project:

> My poem focuses on the submerged head of the African in the foreground of Turner's painting. It has been drowned in Turner's (and other artists') sea for centuries. When it awakens it can only partially recall the sources of its life, so it invents a body, a biography, and peoples an imagined landscape. Most of the names of birds, animals and fruit are made up. Ultimately, however, the African rejects the fabrication of an idyllic past. His real desire is to begin anew in the sea but he is too trapped by grievous memory to escape history. Although the sea has transformed him – bleached him of colour and complicated his sense of gender – he still recognises himself as 'nigger'. The desire for transfiguration or newness or creative amnesia is frustrated. The agent of self-recognition is a stillborn child tossed overboard from a future ship. The child floats towards him. He wants to give it life, to mother it, but the child – his unconscious and his origin – cannot bear the future and its inventions, drowned as it is in memory of ancient cruelty. Neither can escape Turner's representation of them as exotic and sublime victims. Neither can describe themselves anew but are indelibly stained by Turner's language and imagery. (*T*, ix–x)

Because the poem itself is also written in standard, literary English, and because this preface overtly presents the voice of the

author ('My poem focuses ...'; 'I believe ...') we can read it more
straightforwardly than the introduction to *Slave Song*, as an
authorial (but not authoritative) interpretation or description.

Dabydeen's comments on memory and the desire for transformation provide a useful starting point. They direct us to the
question of whether an individual has any autonomy or agency in
self-creation, or whether the 'self' is merely a passive construction
of historical and cultural forces. It is this tension that Dabydeen
explores in 'Turner', in the particular context of the postcolonial
experience. The head of the black African slave is a symbol of the
postcolonial self: detached from his origins and family, freed, at
least physically, from the direct oppression of the coloniser, floating in a sea of cultural detritus and signs of violence, and seeking
to establish a new and autonomous identity. For years and years
the speaker has been in a state of emotional limbo, watching and
learning from all the subsequent shipwrecks and the bodies (and
texts) that are tossed into the sea, but not seeking to create anything
new for himself. The stillborn or 'partborn' child who is tossed into
the sea forces him to 'wake' because it is a symbol of origins, family, newness, birth, his own truncated history, and of hybridity,
because the child is born of a union between a slaver and a slave.

The African longs to recapture his own childhood ('I dream to be
small again' (*T*, 4)), and the first few sections of the poem are
devoted to accounts of his childhood in Africa. The odd thing,
though, is that his remembered childhood is not entirely African –
Indian words like 'savannah' are included, and most of the names
of fruit and so on are made up, as Dabydeen explains. In fact, the
slave himself has become hybrid, in-between, as he absorbs the
texts of the world ('scrolls in different letterings / Which, before
they dissolve, I decipher / As best I can' (17)) and the histories of all
the displaced people whose bodies find their way to the ocean.
Even sexually he has become a hybrid, androgynous, as he takes on
the role of mothering the child: 'My breasts a woman's which
I surrender / To my child-mouth' (16). Interestingly, the name of
the prophet-figure Manu, whom the speaker invokes in memory, is
actually the name of a figure in Hindu mythology.

In interview Dabydeen has commented on this in the context of
the necessity for Caribbean writers to look at all strands of
Caribbean culture. He comments that it is 'outrageous' and a kind
of 'self-apartheid' to leave it up to the different ethnic groups to
write their own history and culture.[11] He remarks that his own use

of the name Manu was a 'total accident'; it was 'just a name I'd plucked out from memory', and he didn't know of its Indian origin until an English scholar pointed it out. But he sees it as a sign of how 'it's only in revising [writing] that you get clues to a much deeper meaning or a deeper structure. Now the deeper sense of Indianness did not reside with Manu but in descriptions of planting and reaping. Manu was just a kind of trigger, which in some peculiar way forced me to express an Indianness.'[12] Effectively the memories of the speaker's childhood become a blended image of a traditional society that is both African and Indian.

The subjectivity of the speaker in the poem, then, provides an image for the creolisation that has occurred in the Caribbean and to a greater or lesser extent in all colonial and postcolonial contexts. The question the speaker faces is whether it is possible to 'start again', to create a new identity. In this effort he is almost viciously undermined by the voice of the child (who represents, of course, his memory, origins and unconscious, as well as the potential for change and rebirth), who throws the word 'nigger' at him:

'Nigger,' it cries, loosening from the hook
Of my desire, drifting away from
My body of lies. I wanted to teach it
A redemptive song, fashion new descriptions
Of things, new colours fountaining out of form.
I wanted to begin anew in the sea
But the child would not bear the future
Nor its inventions, and my face was rooted
In the ground of memory, a ground stampeded
By herds of foreign men who swallow all its fruit
And leave a trail of dung for flies
To colonise; a tongueless earth, bereft
Of song except for the idiot witter
Of wind through a dead wood. 'Nigger'
It cries, naming itself, naming the gods,
The earth and its globe of stars. (39)

The child is called 'Turner', after the paedophilic captain of the slave ship in the poem, in turn named after the painter; yet at the same time the child is part of the African slave. This is a neat way of indicating that we are produced by representation – we are all products of the texts, paintings, and other symbolic systems of the past that make up our cultural heritage and thus the lens through which we see the world. The reiteration of the name 'Turner' (with its suggestions of circularity and hypocrisy) underlines the sense of entrapment within existing symbolic systems. This is most powerfully evoked by the child's cry of the word 'nigger', which signals that the vicious system of degradation and violence which slavery represented has an inevitable continued existence within the minds of those whom it oppressed. Thus the poem ends with a sense of being entrapped, enclosed, smothered by the symbol of colonialism in the poem, 'Turner' in the guise of Zeus raping Leda: 'the white enfolding / Wings of Turner brooding over my body, / Stopping my mouth, drowning me in the yolk / Of myself' (39). All the stories the African has told as part of the process of self-creation are finally negated:

> No savannah, moon, gods, magicians
> To heal or curse, harvests, ceremonies,
> No men to plough, corn to fatten their herds,
> No stars, no land, no words, no community,
> No mother. (40)

While one cannot underestimate the power of this final vision of emptiness and aloneness, one does not leave the poem without some sense of hope, and most of this resides in the words spoken by Manu about the future of his scattered tribe:

>   in the future time each must learn to live
> beadless in a foreign land; or perish.
> Or each must learn to make new jouti,
> Arrange them by instinct, imagination, study
> And arbitrary choice into a pattern
> Pleasing to the self and to others
> Of the scattered tribe; or perish. Each
> Will be barren of ancestral memory
> But each endowed richly with such emptiness
> From which to dream, surmise, invent, immortalise.
> Though each will wear different coloured beads
> Each will be Manu, the source and future
> Chronicles of our tribe. (33–4)

The suggestion is there, then, that the sense of emptiness the African slave descends into at the end of the poem might possibly be the necessary starting point for a new self-creation. At the same time, the whole poem has in itself demonstrated the speaker's capacity to create something new and hybrid. It is as if the emptiness, the sense of the absence of the stable point of origin and nurture which is imaged finally by the mother, must be continuously faced, felt, understood, in order to turn again to the process of attempting to create future 'chronicles of our tribe'. Ultimately the poem does leave us uncertain as to whether such creation is possible or whether the sense of smothering and of absence will dominate.

'Turner' reflects the anxiety, pervasive in modern culture and particularly in the discourses of critical theory, over whether an acceptance of instability and the absence of any fixed point of origin, and an awareness of the way in which the self is constructed by historical narratives, will lead to despair or to a creative hybridity. Dabydeen does not celebrate hybridity (or the post-colonial/diasporic condition) in an unthinking way. It is in his poetry, rather than in his interview comments (which tend to be rather more upbeat[13]) that we see a full encounter with the devastation associated by the loss of a sense of self that is a result of a forceful amputation of links with the past, and the subjection to the words of the other:

> He fished us patiently,
> Obsessively, until our stubbornness gave way
> To an exhaustion more complete than Manu's
> Sleep after the sword bore into him
> And we repeated in a trance the words
> that shuddered from him: *blessed, angelic*
> *Sublime*; words that seemed to flow endlessly
> From him, filling our mouths and bellies
> Endlessly. (38)

The sublimation of paedophilic desires into religiosity is analogous to J.M.W. Turner's incorporation of the scene of the drowning slaves into the Romantic discourse of the sublime. The trance engendered by these manoeuvres is difficult to wake from.

Paul Muldoon

Paul Muldoon's sense of the elusiveness of human agency is, like Dabydeen's, informed by a postcolonial context. Muldoon, a poet from Northern Ireland who moved to the United States in 1987, has cultivated crossovers and comparisons between the Irish experience and the experience of other colonised peoples, particularly native Americans. In the nineties Muldoon was indisputably the single most influential figure in contemporary British and Irish poetry, and he perhaps still is today; his distinctively casual-clever voice, his dense use of allusion and self-reference, and his obsession with puns and intricate formal experimentation have influenced writers like Simon Armitage, Glyn Maxwell, Don Paterson, and many others. Muldoon himself is fascinated with the notion of poetic influence – many of his lectures trace convoluted trails of relationships between poets and texts – and counts Frost, MacNeice and Heaney among the major influences on his own writing. Muldoon, born in 1951, shares a rural Northern Irish Catholic background with Heaney, and the older poet was a mentor and advocate for Muldoon in his early years as a writer. The ongoing relationship has been almost mythologised by critics, aided and abetted by Muldoon himself who has playfully displayed his debts to and differences from Heaney in his insistently allusive poetry.

Muldoon's poetry plays out a complex ambivalence about the relationship between the self and language. His extravagantly complex rhyme systems, and his capacity to stretch the concept and function of rhyme to its limits and beyond, seem to dramatise a kind of struggle with the issue of control and agency. As an example, we might consider the ninety endrhymes of the 'twelve, intercut, exploded sestinas' of 'Yarrow', in itself a formal tour de force,[14] which are then transferred to 'Incantata', written later and also included in *The Annals of Chile*. Muldoon, however, doesn't stop there; as Clair Wills notes, the same ninety endrhymes are used in the three long poems in *Hay* – 'The Mud Room', 'The Bangle (Slight Return)' and 'Third Epistle to Timothy' – revealing, in Wills's words, 'an increasing obsession on Muldoon's part with arbitrary formal constraint as such'.[15] *Within* a poem like 'Incantata', with its *ababcddc* rhyme scheme (what Muldoon called the 'stadium stanza'[16]), Muldoon's use of an idiosyncratic and expansive consonantal-based rhyming principle (which Andrew Osborn has labelled 'fuzzy rhyme'[17]) enables him to accentuate the excessiveness and exuberant mobility of language, so that the fluent skip between part-rhymes, from 'cloth' to 'cliff', from '*Krik!*' to 'Karaoke', comes to seem at once surprising and inherent in the nature of language itself. But the connections *between* poems, and the use of 'rhyme' in a poem like 'Yarrow', where the rhyming words are placed far apart, draws our attention instead to issues of control and authority.

The choice of such extravagantly complex patterns seems to be a bravura attempt to proclaim control as an artist over the medium of language. By comparing two separate interview comments we can see that Muldoon is pulled between this idea of authorial power and a contrasting stance of submission to language. In the first of these comments rhyme is the focus:

> I believe that these devices like repetition and rhyme are not artificial, that they're not imposed, somehow, on the language. They are inherent in the language. Words want to find chimes with each other, things want to connect. I believe ... I was almost going to say 'I accept the universe!' I believe in the serendipity of all that, of giving oneself over to that.[18]

On the other hand, in an interview with Clair Wills Muldoon asserts the ultimate control of the writer over his or her work:

> I think that the writer should be alert to all these possible readings. And alert to the curtailing of possible readings that are not productive. And I don't care what people say, it's the writer who does that. And the points at which he doesn't do it are the points at which there is confusion ... . Because that's what the process of writing is about. It's about opening himself, or herself to the floodgates, what it's about is discovering the extent of limits, the confinement, the controlling of readings, of possible readings.[19]

'People' in this context refers to theorists and critics who assert the 'death of the author'; Muldoon is much vaunted as a postmodernist but his comments on authorial control and about the 'confusion' which can ensue if the author does not exercise adequate control, must at least complicate this classification. Muldoon *is* postmodernist, however, in the sense that he is hyperaware of these issues, and his poetry as a whole reflects a troubled fascination with the issue of agency, both in the context of poetry and of life more generally.

Muldoon's third collection, *Why Brownlee Left* (1980) (after *New Weather*, 1973, and *Mules*, 1977) is the first to explore this issue in any extended way, though the earlier books also touch upon it. The long concluding poem in *Why Brownlee Left*, 'Immram', takes its model from the traditional medieval Irish voyage narratives or *immramma*, and in particular the voyage of Muldoon's namesake Máel Dúin. 'Immram' uses the quest narrative as a parodic template that highlights the lack of agency experienced by the narrator and ostensible protagonist, who undergoes a series of bizarre and disconnected experiences. The poem is full of violence, both directed at the narrator and at others (particularly women) and it seems to seek to highlight the way in which power operates in society at the expense of the individual: colonialism, the drug trade, sexual abuse, and cult religion are all instances of manipulative and oppressive power relations.

The particularly interesting feature of this poem is the way in which we seek to locate desire in the protagonist in order to make sense of events; his ostensible motivation is to 'know more about my father',[20] but this is strangely unconvincing. The blank and unemotional tone of the narration, the passive verbs, the unexplained sequences of events which happen *to* the narrator, the use of dream and drug imagery to suggest the lack of conscious control, the emphasis on repetition, circularity, and intergenerational cycles of violence: all this works together to ensure that the strong impression is of passivity and lack of agency. The narrator seems dogged by an 'original sin' which appears to have been laid upon him by his birth, but the nature of his inheritance, his origins, is no clearer at the end of the poem – except for the fact that they are enmeshed in relations of domination. At the end of the poem the narrator is left 'going along with, happily', the 'steady stream of people / That flowed in one direction, / Faster and deeper' (*WBL*, 47); despite the use of the adverb 'happily', this suggests homogeneity, circularity and passivity.[21] The narrator begins and ends in Foster's pool-room, with no additional knowledge, insight or strategies in place to prevent the whole bizarre, inexplicable sequence of events from happening again. 'Immram', then, dramatises the subjective experience of being pushed and pulled, controlled and swayed by history and by external forces; the experience of being unable to access the emotion that is needed to drive action.

'Immram' set the pattern for Muldoon's next collection, *Quoof*, which also closes with a major long poem, 'The More a Man Has the More a Man Wants'. This poem adopts a slightly different strategy to 'Immram' but evinces the same concern with the issues of agency and desire. 'The More a Man Has' blurs the boundaries of personhood through deliberately ambiguous use of personal pronouns. The first three stanzas already create in us a sense of uncertainty about our ability to correctly identify – and separate – the agents involved in the narrative. The 'He' of the first word of the third stanza seems at first to refer to Mangas Jones, the subject of the second stanza, but by the end of the stanza we have changed our minds, judging retrospectively that the 'He' must refer to Gallogly.[22] This process continues throughout the poem, with the reader continually struggling to work out who is responsible for the narrated events. Even names do not function to maintain stable identities; the arrested man is described as 'Gallogly, or Gollogly, / otherwise known as Golightly, / otherwise known as Ingoldsby, / otherwise known as English' (*Q*, 58).

The 'shape-shifting' character of the apparent protagonist, Gallogly, and his alter ego Mangas Jones, is reinforced by allusions to the Trickster figure in Native American mythology, and particularly in the Winnebago cycle of tales. This connection is noted in the blurb on the back of the first edition of *Quoof* and indicated in the poem by the recurrent use of animal imagery in describing Gallogly ('hared / among the top-heavy apple orchards'; 'a baggy-kneed animated / bear'; 'His eye like the eye of a travel-ling rat' (44, 45, 47), and so on), as well as the typically Muldoonian insertion of a Winnebago camper (51). Trickster in native American mythology is a complex amalgamation of qualities; straddling animal and human, natural and supernatural, he is sent to earth to help humans, but only manages to get himself into a series of scrapes. He is portrayed as instinctive, undifferentiated, unethi-cal, irresponsible, clumsy and ignorant – but at the same time he is humorous, likeable and well-meaning.[23] He is notorious for running away from responsibility, and the question of agency and responsibility becomes particularly significant in this poem because it is set in Northern Ireland and is full of violent event. Gallogly is on the run and *may* be a terrorist, but we are never sure. The question of who is responsible for the violence which occurs on a daily basis in Northern Ireland (and which was at a peak when Muldoon was writing this poem, at the time of the 'dirty protests' in the Maze prison) is highlighted by this poem in which motivation and purpose are elusive, and individuals blur into one another so that responsibility cannot easily be assigned.

As in 'Immram', we find ourselves looking for emotion and
desire, in order to ascertain that what is happening is not simply
random or instinctive. Unlike in 'Immram', where the narrator
remains emotionally blank, there *are* suggestions of emotional
intensity in the portrayal of Gallogly. The following passage, for
example, is suggestive:

> His six foot of pump water
> bent double
> in agony or laughter.
> Keeping down-wind of everything. (47)

'Bent double in agony or laughter' recalls the mischievous
Trickster, who in Paul Radin's account is described as 'laughing at
them till he ached'.[24] It is the kind of affection one can feel
for Trickster that seems to emerge here in the narrator's portrayal
of the person we think of here as Gallogly. This is particularly
clear when we visit him in private, intimate moments, like when
he lies down in the sheugh 'to munch / through a Beauty of /
Bath' and enters the Heaneyesque moment of finding 'that first
"sh" / increasingly difficult to manage. / *Sh*-leeps' (49).[25] Likewise,
the allusions to Sweeney, the legendary cursed king turned bird-
man from Irish myth, suggest the lonely, passionate intensity and
self-pity of the outcast.[26]
    Clair Wills suggests that the description of Gallogly's escape
from jail, in which he seems to turn himself into a beaver, 'perhaps
signifies the bestial, nihilistic origins of violence. Gallogly is forever
hungry, greedy for food and sex, without responsibilities or
allegiances, driven by desire.'[27] Yet Wills also notes that Gallogly
may be seen as 'Everyman' and may also be seen as a figure for
the poet himself, who is also notorious for his slipperiness and
all/el-usiveness. The lines quoted above, which picture Gallogly
'bent double / in agony or laughter / Keeping down-wind of
everything' (47) do not evoke 'bestiality': paired with laughter
'agony' takes on connotations of a pain which is more than simply
physical, and, because of this, 'keeping down-wind of everything'
seems to imply more than simply the animal's instinct for self-
protection. Muldoon hints at a subjectivity that is (like Trickster)
simple, clumsy, violent, but also hurt and vulnerable. The rather
intimate portrayals of Gallogly – such as the 'one low cry of
anguish' (58) he gives when he is arrested – conflict starkly with

the matter-of-fact accounts of the violence which we uncertainly attribute to him in the absence of any other convincing actors. We look for political motivation in order to develop a sense of individual desire and agency. A political agenda seems attributable to Mangas Jones, who is at one point described as 'busily tracing the family tree / of an Ulsterman who had some hand / in the massacre at Wounded Knee' (48). The existence of possible motivations – revenge or reconciliation – may make us feel comfortable attributing agency to him. With regard to Gallogly it is the difficulty of fixing any motivation (besides the physical stimulus of hunger) that causes doubt about his capacity to act as a human agent. The allusions to political motivations are presented in such a fragmented, free-floating manner that we are uncertain about linking them to Gallogly in any definitive way; 'The Croppy Boy', for example, is sung by 'Beatrice' and it is *she* who wants to shave 'his' (Gallogly's?) head in memory of '98 and the French Revolution (52). We can attribute motivations to Gallogly, such as the desire for a united Ireland, in order to fit him neatly into a particular category – that of Republican terrorist – yet all such agendas seem somewhat imposed. The narrative tracks Gallogly on a journey, but the goal of the journey remains obscure. Gallogly remains enigmatic, and our thought processes with regard to him mirror our struggle to interpret the violence that breaks up our communities. We can dismiss him as 'mindless' or 'bestial' or we can attribute complex ideological motivations to him, but neither response seems entirely satisfactory. Our powerlessness to penetrate to the causes of violence is symbolised as well in the image of the sixteen-year-old 'whose face is masked by the seamless / black stocking filched / from his mum' (52).

The most disturbing and emotive account of violence is linked not to Gallogly but to a husband who suspects his wife has been unfaithful. Muldoon leaves us uncertain as to whether Gallogly has raped the wife, simply slept with her, or merely stolen the husband's clothes, but the husband's response is brutal:

Someone on their way to early Mass
will find her hog-tied
to the chapel gates –
O Child of Prague –
big-eyed, anorexic.
The lesson for today

is pinned to her bomber jacket.
It seems to read *Keep off the Grass.*
Her lovely head has been chopped
and changed.
For Beatrice, whose fathers
knew Louis Quinze,
to have come to this, her perruque
of tar and feathers. (43)

In the central role the church plays in this stanza, and in the
stanza's engagement with Heaney's 'Punishment', the motivation
behind this very public violence seems clear: society's need to
control and regulate female sexuality and to stake out aggressively the boundaries of acceptable and non-acceptable behaviour. The implication is that a society whose established and
respected institutions, such as the church, are seen as condoning
or even advocating such brutal means of 'control', should not be
surprised by the violent behaviour of a Gallogly.

The poem has the effect of stimulating self-consciousness about
the processes involved in assessing cause and responsibility. It
makes us aware of the urgency and intensity of our desire, as
readers, to identify a pattern of causation, to attribute moral
responsibility and to locate agency within the individual rather
than to explain events and behaviour as the 'effects' of a network
of discourses or the play of language. While Muldoon is certainly
drawing our attention to the role of cultural institutions in producing individual behaviour, as reflected in his use of the chapel
as a backdrop for intolerance and brutality, I do not read him as
turning away from the concept of individual agency; instead, 'The
More a Man Has', through its silences and gaps, directs us *towards*
the issue of what makes individuals choose violence. The question is not simply abstract. As Clair Wills comments, the use of
'you' in the seventh stanza effects an interpellation of the poem's
male readers, 'only to suggest that Gallogly has assumed their
identity – he is wearing "your" jacket'.[28] At the same time the
overtones of affection or intimacy in the narrative voice when
describing Gallogly – along with the hints of emotional trauma –
ensure that we as readers cannot entirely distance ourselves from
the central character. The use of a broken-up, disjointed picaresque
narrative, full of event and action, draws us towards those two
fundamental questions, *who* and *why*. While these two questions
remain unanswered, their urgency is undiminished.

I have concentrated on these 'dramatic' narratives from Muldoon's middle period because, in their destabilising use of 'character', they lead us to question the nature of human agency. Since *Quoof*, Muldoon has published five major new poetry collections. *Meeting the British* (1987) and *Madoc: A Mystery* (1990) both develop Muldoon's interest in America, and in the colonial parallels between America and Ireland. In the case of *Madoc* this is achieved through a grand and typically convoluted vision of what would have happened if Coleridge and Southey *had* in fact carried out their plan of emigrating to America to establish a 'Pantisocratic' community. Both collections are characterised by the same teasing, ironic voice which dominated the earlier books, but in *The Annals of Chile* (1994) we see a decisive shift in tone, which, if not replicated in the later collections, leaves its mark on Muldoon's style. *The Annals of Chile* contains two major elegies, 'Incantata' and 'Yarrow', and as Tim Kendall notes, 'it is no coincidence that *The Annals of Chile*, Muldoon's most elegiac collection to date, is his most candidly autobiographical,' as 'such personal loss does not so easily allow for mischief'.[29]

'Incantata' is at once accessible and allusive, direct and convoluted, giving the impression at once of spontaneity and of intricate craft. It is a lament for the artist Mary Farl Powers, but it also presents a fascinating image of subjectivity and of relationship. It evokes the way in which subjectivity may be *shared*, while at the same time persistently reminding us of the separateness, on another level, of individual existence. Muldoon uses the device of the 'potato-mouth' to produce a voice which is neither his own nor Mary's, but evokes their shared existence, the brimming catalogue of events which made up their common experience. The potato-mouth is 'all that's left':

That's all that's left of the voice of Enrico Caruso
from all that's left of an opera-house somewhere in Matto
  Grosso,
all that's left of the hogweed and horehound and cuckoo-pint,
of the eighteen soldiers dead at Warrenpoint,
of the Black Church clique and the Graphic Studio claque,
of the many moons of glasses on a tray,
of the brewery-carts drawn by moon-booted drays,
of those jump-suits worn under your bottle-green worsted
  cloak.[30]

As Kendall points out, the fact that the tag 'all that's left' is dropped, leaving only 'of' to remind us 'that these various items are being reduced rather than eulogized', means that the list becomes as much a celebration as a record of loss.[31] In one sense the poem seems to affirm the poststructuralist description of the 'self' as contingent, diffuse, unstable and non-autonomous, since it overwhelmingly presents subjectivity as *made up of* the multiplicity of experience, and of shared experience, so much so that when Mary dies, a whole world of shared subjective meaning is, on one level, lost. But at the same time, the poem asserts first the separateness of individual subjectivity, in, for example, the continual implied disagreements between the two about fate and determinism, and in its continuity – in the fact that the poet-persona has the capacity to remember and thus reconstitute, in a different form, the experience of the past. The 'I' and the 'you' in this poem still retain a degree of separateness so that the death of Mary does *not* imply the death of the poet; subjectivity has an overlapping element but an ultimately individual basis.

'Yarrow', which is an oblique elegy for Muldoon's mother as well as a complex meditation on childhood and origins, also suggests interesting ways of conceiving subjectivity. The temporality of the poem has a stable basis in that the present tense always relates to an American, contemporary scene, but the 'I' voice moves back and forth at great speed and without any linking material between this contemporary scene and childhood and teenage scenes in Northern Ireland. Within these different periods, the poem's subject shows himself capable of moving himself rapidly, in imagination, between settings and historical periods, mostly inspired by the narratives of the many adventure stories which he devours as a child. As Kendall notes, this 'scattered' narrative has its complement in the poem's form: 'The scattered sestinas of 'Yarrow' … correspond to the poem's "intercut, exploded" time-schemes and locations.'[32]

The poem certainly affirms the importance of discourse, and particularly of *narrative*, in the construction and experience of subjectivity, in the sense that the speaker persistently lives out the narratives, and lives *in* the characters, of the adventure stories and historical narratives he reads and hears. However, the emphasis is less on the way in which the self is *subjected* to these pre-existing discourses, and more firmly on the way in which the speaker creatively adapts, enacts, mixes and transforms these narratives so that they provide an enabling – if sometimes also evasive – resource, a distinctive and creative strategy for coping with a world which is often experienced as threatening and oppressive in its restrictions and prejudices. The capacity to move between contexts imaginatively and in memory is presented as liberating, even if, as Kendall notes, the references to the actual time on the VCR clock in the contemporary scene do remind us 'that in one inescapable sense time is constant and linear, relentlessly devouring the short span of life'.[33]

Hay (1998) and *Moy Sand and Gravel* (2002) continue the more personal and autobiographical tone of *The Annals of Chile*. Taking these three collections together, we see an intense interest in the strange conjunctions of childhood and adulthood, of Ireland and America, and of the disparate cultural histories of Muldoon's own Irish family and his wife Jean's Jewish-American family. Muldoon's poetry in these collections is just as technically ingenious, semantically provocative, and demanding of the reader as any of his previous work, and perhaps increasingly prone to self-reference, but there are fewer dramatic characters and the reader feels that the 'I' of the poems is gradually revealing more and more of the poet Paul Muldoon himself, in his everyday life in America and in his memories of Northern Ireland.

I would like to comment in particular on the long concluding poem to *Moy Sand and Gravel*, entitled 'At the Sign of the Black Horse, September 1999'. This poem is a rewriting of Yeats's poem 'A Prayer for My Daughter', the rhyme scheme of which Muldoon has used before in 'Incantata'. 'At the Sign of the Black Horse' may be interestingly compared with Dabydeen's 'Turner', as both poems use the imagery of water – the ocean, in 'Turner', and a flooded canal in Muldoon's poem – to represent the flow and flood of history. Both poems also place a baby at the centre of the poem, and raise the question of the baby's relationship to the history that precedes and surrounds it. Muldoon's poem responds to Yeats's sense, asserted in the midst of a physical storm and the political turmoil of the Civil War, of the importance of tradition, custom, permanence and inheritance. In 'A Prayer for My Daughter' Yeats prays that his daughter might 'live like some green laurel / Rooted in one dear perpetual place', and that her bridegroom might

> bring her to a house
> Where all's accustomed, ceremonious;

For arrogance and hatred are the wares
Peddled in the thoroughfares.
How but in custom and in ceremony
Are innocence and beauty born?
Ceremony's a name for the rich horn,
And custom for the spreading laurel tree.[34]

Reflecting the older Yeats's enchantment with the Anglo-Irish
aristocracy as well as his disdain for and impatience with the middle classes, 'A Prayer for My Daughter' advocates (especially for
women) a retreat from the bluster of politics and of opinion into a
charmed circle of peaceful gentility and traditional values, in
which the soul 'recovers radical innocence / And learns at last
that it is self-delighting'.

Muldoon's poem stringently questions this notion of 'radical
innocence', a phrase that he uses several times in the poem, and it
suggests that such a retreat is impossible and self-deceiving.
Asher, the baby whose pram is 'wheeled to the brim' of the
flooded canal while his parents watch the floodwaters pass with
all their cargo of chaos, 'sleeps on' like Yeats's daughter for most
of the poem, but he wakes at a crucial point and, throughout the
poem, the poet-persona is preoccupied by the way in which
Asher's face is ghosted by his forebears, 'a slew of interlopers',
and in particular

> the likes of that kale-eating child on whom the peaked
>   cap, *Verboten*,
> would shortly pin a star of yellow felt,
>
> having accosted him on the Mosaic
> proscription, Please Secure Your Own Oxygen Mask
> Before Attending To Children, on the eating of white-lipped
>   peccary.[35]

The poem is scattered with interjecting commands and public
notices as in the above quotation; these range from the trivial and
everyday ('Please Leave A Message After The Beep' (*MSG*, 83)) to
those which in the context of this poem carry the weight of the
Holocaust (*Verboten, Halt* (75, 89)). Edna Longley has questioned
the wisdom of these conjunctions, suggesting that

> it seems glib to juxtapose everyday hectoring with the pre-
> scriptions of the concentration camp: this tonal blip being an

indication that Muldoon's comedy and his seriousness are for once, slightly at odds.[36]

There is certainly humour in the poem (as in the suggestion that Asher might be 'dreaming of a Pina Colostrum' (81)), but I doubt that there is any intent of comedy in Muldoon's use of these very various commands and announcements. The implication is surely not any kind of equivalence, but rather extreme disparity: the banality of the contemporary American experience of public control and communication in comparison to the viciousness of the life suffered by Asher's 'child-kin' in the ghetto. Yeats's love-affair with 'custom', 'ceremony' and ancestral values is implicitly critiqued through the references to Jewish relatives and ancestors who criticise the parents' decisions for their children – 'By which authority did we deny Asher a mohel?' (80) – and generate an ongoing obsession with the status of the trapped and killed peccary (a hoofed pig-like mammal) as forbidden food. The killing of the young peccary becomes a focus for guilt partly because of these strictures but also because of the way in which it gradually comes to stand for, or remind the speaker of, the deaths of other young things, in particular children in the Holocaust.[37] Yeats's politics are also critiqued as we are reminded of how his love of custom and tradition blurred into a dubious attraction to forms of political authoritarianism.

If we compare this poem with Dabydeen's 'Turner' I think we note a similar sense of the inevitable embeddedness of the self within history. Muldoon's poet-speaker and his son do not face the kind of complete and violent dissolution of self that Dabydeen's drowned slave does. The poet-speaker, his wife, son and daughter, are not actually carried off by the waters; because of this he is able to be

> happy that the house I may yet bring myself to call mine
> is set on a two-hundred-and-fifty-year-old slab,
> happy that, if need be, we might bundle a few belongings
> into a pillow slip
> and climb the hill and escape, Please Examine
>
> Your Change, to a place where the soul might indeed recover
> radical innocence. (73)

But as the poem progresses, and the stream of ancestral visitors, memories and images brought by the flood waters increases, it becomes obvious that this kind of solidity (the kind that Yeats also set great store on in his Anglo-Saxon tower) is illusory and that no 'radical innocence' is possible. Whereas the drowned slave is confronted with the severing of all roots, forced upheaval, the speaker in 'At the Sign of the Black Horse' has not only retained his own possessions in the flood but is confronted (as in the clutter of 'The Mud Room' in *Hay*) with an abundance of inheritance; but this, in the end, brings the poem to a place which is not all that distant from that which *Turner* reaches. 'At the Sign of the Black Horse' questions whether Asher is the holder of a 'radical innocence', whether it is possible to 'begin again' entirely; the answer seems to be an emphatic 'no'. The 'baggage' of history – the Irish navvies who built the canal, the 'child-kin' who died in the Holocaust, as well as innumerable relatives and ancestors, both famous and unknown – already surrounds and inhabits Asher. Whether this history is somehow present in the child himself already or is projected onto him by his parents is unimportant, since the effect will be the same. The obtrusiveness of the public world, whether violent or trivial, also seems to work against any concept of a truly individual space.

This does not necessarily imply the absence of agency, but Muldoon in this poem does not confront in quite the same way as Dabydeen the question of whether something 'new' can be actively forged from the hybrid inheritance of history. In a sense, like all Muldoon's poems, it suggests that the new is inevitable – just as the conjunction of Irish and Jewish-American histories produces something new in Asher without any apparent 'agency' on his part, so language provides a model for the seeming inevitability of new and surprising conjunctions in the world. Muldoon's speakers tend to experience this newness with a mixture of bewilderment and fascination. In this poem there is much less of a sense of the creative agency of the experiencing subject than there is in 'Yarrow'; the dominating violence of the Holocaust context perhaps enforces this. Instead, we have a sense of the speaker gradually becoming more aware of and overwhelmed by the flow of historical events, until the end of the poem enacts this sense of pace and flow in the repetition of the subordinate clause introduced by 'when', a technique familiar from 'Incantata', whose rhythms are echoed in the ending of this poem, right down to the 'deh-dah' instead of 'arrah' in the final stanza.

Muldoon *is* postmodernist in his interest in the constitution of the self and the elusiveness of a sense of subjective agency, but in his approach to these issues he differs from the poets associated with postmodernist and 'experimental' poetry in both Britain and America. He does not radically disrupt syntax. If he uses a first-person speaker, the speaker tends to retain some degree of continuity and at least superficial consistency, while in a dramatic narrative like 'The More a Man Has', despite the actual destabilisation of such fundamentals as character and plot, the poem proceeds *as if* it were a perfectly easy-to-understand narrative. Rather than confronting the reader with explicit disruption and fragmentation, Muldoon soothes us into a sense of smoothness and readability, only to proceed to discomfort, provoke, confuse, and fascinate. As he put it in an interview:

> Of course I sometimes make little jokes and I do, quite often, engage in leading people on, gently, into little situations by assuring them that all's well and then – this sounds awfully manipulative, but part of writing is about manipulation – leaving them high and dry, in some corner of a terrible party, where I've nipped out through the bathroom window.[38]

Denise Riley

Denise Riley (b. 1948) differs from Muldoon in exactly this respect; her poetry for the most part does not even *pretend* to be 'easy'. Sometimes, as in 'Laibach Lyrik', Riley does use the strategy of attempting to lull the reader into a lyrical mode of reading, only to break into this with a very different, edgy voice ('Cut the slavonics now. Cut the slavonics'[39]) but this is unusual.[40] More often, a Riley poem confronts the reader early on with syntactical complexities and ambiguities that signal her association with the more 'experimental' side of poetry in Britain today. The nature of such labels ('experimental', 'avant-garde', 'mainstream') will be discussed more generally in the next chapter, but I want to note at this point the extent to which questions of subjectivity and self-hood are crucial and pressing concerns for many poets associated with the experimental scene internationally. Much of this poetry is marked by a radical scepticism about the conventional use of the 'I' voice in poetry. As Marjorie Perloff puts it, in the work of Language poets like Charles Bernstein, 'it is often impossible to decide whether the speaker is a "he" or an "I" or a "you", much less what the "I" or the "you" might be like'. Perloff suggests that these poets may be feeling that

> at a time when the spoken and written word are more pervasive than ever, when our visual fields are bombarded by billboards and manuals, and our aural fields by overheard snatches of conversation and catchy television jingles, the individual voice can no longer be In Charge. Rather, the text gives the impression that the story is telling itself, that it is available for communal use – a kind of score that we can endow with meaning by 'speaking it' ourselves.[41]

Riley's poetry is less formally disjunctive than many of the poets associated with Bernstein and Language poetry, and in many of her poems we *do* find the first-person voice, but it is not the first-person voice of the traditional lyric. For Riley the nature of the self and of the speaking 'I' is a knotty, endlessly compelling problem that her poetry stubbornly and inventively investigates. Riley is a particularly intriguing figure in this regard because she has recently published *The Words of Selves: Identification, Solidarity, Irony*, a theoretical text which is closely concerned with issues of selfhood and identity – in particular the question of self-description – and her recent poetry closely intersects with this theoretical work. Riley teaches literature and philosophy at the University of East Anglia, and her academic writing is notable for its capacity to range across the boundaries of academic disciplines.

One of the much-vaunted features of postmodernist writing is that it foregrounds self-reflexively the actual process of writing. While some traditional modes of lyric and narrative poetry allow the reader to immerse her or himself in the created world of the poem and forget the fact that this world was crafted out of language by a particular person at a particular time, postmodernist poetry constantly breaks into this kind of experience with a reminder of the actual process of writing. As Lyn Hejinian puts it, 'By emphasizing its writtenness, its literariness, the poem calls attention to the complexity of its constructedness.'[42] Naturally this kind of self-reflexivity is not *new* – earlier traditions of poetry have incorporated it as well, in various ways – but it has been a dominant feature of what has been described as postmodern writing, in both poetry and prose. We find this self-reflexivity in Muldoon's work, of course, with his ubiquitous self-referencing and the formal tricks that seem to draw attention back playfully to the ingenuity of the author. When there is a first-person and seemingly autobiographical voice in the poems, these features seem to remind us that this first-person voice cannot be *simply* identified with 'the poet', although it may be closely related to that elusive entity. However, Muldoon's work tends to incorporate such self-conscious reference to the process of writing alongside or within a strong narrative or descriptive element. In Denise Riley's work, a meditation on the process of writing or on the construction of the self in poetry is often the only or explicit focus. Where Muldoon tends to draw the reader in by creating an apparently uncomplicated first-person or third-person identity, only *then* to disrupt or subvert this, in Riley's poetry the reader is often confronted immediately with a sense of difficulty concerning identity or subjectivity. The 'authorial I' voice is actually more prominent in Riley's poetry than in Muldoon's, but it is nearly always drawing attention to its own instability.

Although in many of Riley's poems the 'I' does, however awkwardly, find a place, on some occasions it is prominent through its pointed absence, as in the poem 'Summer' from *Mop Mop Georgette*. The poem begins with a present participle, avoiding the use of a pronoun: 'Looking in pools to see things flick' (*SP*, 46). We expect a pronoun to emerge at some point to clarify *who* is doing the looking, but the poem moves through various verbal forms – 'Lean in a head wind', 'should not pin down' – without ever specifying a subject. The third stanza is simply descriptive, while the fourth stanza unsettles us the most by finally emerging with two pronouns, both of which are objects rather than subjects within the poem's strange grammar:

> Moon, its industrial light. What though
> the dark thee cumber:
> Glow, worm. Say to her.[43]

The poem refuses unification through viewpoint, because of the lack of a subject (an 'I'/eye), or through scene, and its strangeness underlines the dependence of our conventional reading strategies on the clear attribution of all language to *someone*. As Perloff notes, such elision of subject pronouns gives us the sense that the poem is 'available for communal use'. When this elision is placed in combination with disjunctive images, the reader is in fact forced to actively create meaning, to forge, discard and re-forge connections and interpretations, since none is plainly offered (or imposed) by the poem itself, and also hesitantly to inhabit various rather shaky positions as subject or object within the poem's world. Such strategies only work if the detail of the poem repays the considerable attention it demands. In 'Summer' the linguistic surface of the poem does reward readerly creativity. In the second stanza, the words 'should soar' are opposed to the 'biscuit rock stare over water' but 'should soar' sits immediately above 'over water', creating the alternative 'should soar over water'. The same occurs with the words 'stare' and 'down', which connect vertically across the lines to suggest hostility. 'Pin' and 'head' connect vertically to create a sense of shrinkage and smallness, while 'wind' and 'down' suggest entropy. Such connections only appear once the reader accepts the absence of a controlling, expressive subjectivity and accepts the challenge of 'making' the poem her or himself.

In 'Summer' Riley seems to perform the absence of the subject almost neutrally; in 'When it's time to go', also from *Mop Mop Georgette*, the subject is almost as elusive, but there is more of a sense that this is being tackled as a problem. As Clair Wills comments, the poem 'explores the ways in which public forms of knowledge both shape and are shaped by the domestic and personal environment'.[44] The first section portrays a kind of worldview which reads the political and ideological into every experience, so that even the 'kitchen colander shells out a neat / wehrmacht helmet of brown rice' (59), and every action or gesture is self-consciously identified according to a particular ideological position – someone's 'professional unhappiness / taps on its wristwatch "as a realist I ... " '. Note that this 'I' is in fact not linked straightforwardly to a person but to someone's unhappiness. If translated literally, 'Das schmeckt nach mehr' suggests (as Wills notes) that the rice tastes of more than just rice, but in colloquial German usage it means actually 'That tastes good,' or 'I would like some more of that.' Hence the relentless politicisation is at once attractive and negatively narcissistic and self-serving, reading 'a personal threat in everywhere'. Into this scene intervenes an apparently romantic voice – 'set this boy

free' – followed by a disclaimer, 'No this isn't me, it's just my
motor running'. As Wills notes, 'Even the poet's disclaimer is
ironic since we already know "this boy" is not "me", the author
Denise Riley, in any simple fashion, if only because he has the
wrong gender.'[45]

The last three lines enact a strange apostrophe:

> O great classic cadences of English poetry
> We blush to hear thee lie
> Above thy deep and dreamless.

This ending uses one of the favoured techniques of Language
poets – manipulating line breaks or removing words in order to
reveal hidden meanings in familiar phrases, thus 'renovating'
the language. Wills notes that 'Here Riley foregrounds the
strange upside-down image latent in the lines from "O Little
Town of Bethlehem": "How still we see thee lie / Above thy
deep and dreamless sleep" '.[46] With 'sleep' also removed, and
the great classic cadences of English poetry substituted for
Bethlehem, we get an odd mixture of impressions. English
poetry may be duplicitous ('We blush to hear thee lie') but at the
same time the removal of the word 'sleep' works to put more
emphasis on the beautiful adjectival phrase 'deep and dreamless', which is now floating without a noun, meaning that,
despite the awkward 'thy', we seek to attach it to poetry itself, or
even to the prior mentioned 'We', so that as readers we might
feel ourselves to be floating 'deep and dreamless'. The 'I' voice
has never been found, and the 'We' is borrowed from the sentimental communality of Christmas – a sentimentality that perhaps causes the blush of embarrassment. The poem acknowledges
the attractiveness of both the heady rhetoric of politicised discourse and the idea that one could break out of this and achieve
a kind of youthful, non-ideological innocence. Both, though,
have the quality of a 'motor running' rather than any sense of
personal agency – what hint of personal agency we do find in
the poem is surely present in that final thought-provoking
disruption of the Christmas carol.

On this question of the personal agency of the human subject it
is worth referring to Riley's theoretical work. In the introduction
to *The Words of Selves* she dismisses in her characteristically lively
way the idea that either language or the speaker has a hold on

power:

> If words are rendered their own head, it's often hastily assumed that speakers must be rendered abject, as if any consideration of language's own affect must lead straight to human dejection. This false choice of loyalties – either to the word or else to the speaker – is encapsulated for easy swallowing. Fast thought has, like fast food, its uses – but, by a languorous fatalism, prêt-à-penser may slide prematurely into prêt-à-mourir.

Of course, Riley's own view on the matter, presumably not being fast thought, is less easy to summarise, but, like other poststructuralist-influenced thinkers, she places great emphasis on irony as a means for the subject to achieve a degree of agency.

Riley argues that, while we look towards possible categories of self-description with great hope, self-description is always dogged by a sense of inadequacy and unease, as we can never effect a complete identification between linguistic description and self:

> I labour under what must be a common compulsion; that once I'm forced to speak about myself at all, I must through my own efforts make it sharply true – yet cannot. As if even the most subdued self-reference steered close to a demand for precision it must dangerously fail. In the same breath I fear and feel its fundamental lie.[47]

Language in its social circulation – 'what's expectantly in place, already chatting about me before I appear on stage'[48] – offers potential self-descriptions and sometimes enforces them. Nevertheless, Riley doesn't consider language as constraint:

> what releases language from the suspicion that its overarching emotional architecture should be considered as a constraint is another of its inherent elements: its blessed capacity for self-reflection. Irony is one manifestation of speech which notices itself out loud. … This is not irony as a deliberating parody or as the irritating knowingness which so easily tips into being arch – but irony as language presenting itself to itself.[49]

In Riley's comments on poetry (even if these are found in the context of an ironic exegesis of a poem she wrote for the occasion) it is clear that the writer must accept the 'linguistic unease' (or guilt, or shame) which comes with the attempt to define and describe oneself, and must also accept that poetry is 'an affair of high speed autodictation and half-conscious gluing':[50]

> Every time I open my mouth, I'm insinuating myself into some conversation which preexists me and to which my contribution is only a rustle of echoes – on paper, which is where we must all live. Nevertheless, writing moves through its own simulacrum of originality; for even if its 'creativity' is conceived as really a matter of endless refashioning and involuntary plagiarising, it still retains, in the lonely fact of the signature, its final flourish of individuation.[51]

Through irony – the self-consciousness that gives the repetition of some linguistic structure a mocking edge and opens up the possibility of change – the speaking subject can exercise some agency. Riley seeks to demolish the polarity between the interiority of self and the exteriority of language, and to argue that we are always both speaking and being spoken.

In the final section of the *Selected Poems* Riley includes the whole of 'The Castalian Spring' and excerpts from 'Affections of the Ear', the poems which she uses as playful material for her argument in Chapter 3 of *The Words of Selves*, indicating that she sees this work and the corresponding theoretical discourse as integral to her poetic project. So in 'Affections of the Ear' the figure of Echo, from the Narcissus story, is used to convey the negative feeling of being a mere sounding chamber for others' words: 'Echo's a trope for lyric poetry's endemic barely hidden bother: / As I am made to parrot others' words so I am forced to form ideas by rhymes, the most humdrum' (*SP*, 96).

Riley's philosophical narrative verse is entertaining, but a poem in *Mop Mop Georgette*, 'Wherever you are, be somewhere else', enacts the crisis of subjectivity more effectively. The opening of the poem introduces a body, and we are not told whether the body is that of self or other: 'A body shot through, perforated, a tin sheet / beaten out then peppered with thin holes' (*SP*, 47). Light and voices leap and fly through these holes, and then it becomes clear that the first-person voice does identify problematically with this body-image of the self: 'whichever / piece is glimpsed, that bit is what I am, held // in a look until dropped like an egg on the floor / let slop, crashed to slide and run, yolk yellow / for the live, the dead who worked through me'. These lines capture the feeling that the self only exists in interaction with others and in other's perceptions; it has no solidity in and of itself, and risks collapse every time another's attention is turned away. The next stanzas seem to offer more images for the frayed, stretched, permeable self: 'just scrappy / filaments lifting and lifting over in the wind'. In conversation with Romana Huk, Riley herself noted that 'The body, by the end of the first five stanzas, has been reduced to a blur of interruption, a film.'[52]

The poem then moves toward a wish for a dissolution or gentle death of the 'I' – 'Draw the night right up over my eyes so that I / don't see and then I'm gone; push the soft hem / of the night into my mouth so that I stay quiet' and then towards the dual fears of being abandoned and being trapped in relationships. The poetic voice becomes more and more rhetorical and self-dramatising, in contemplating death, until it slides into self-mockery – 'I can try on these gothic riffs' (48) – and a recognition of the failure of self-expression. There is a longing to 'be only transmission', to speak the world without the constraints of individuality:

> in sleep alone I get articulate, to mouth the part of
> anyone and reel off others' characters until the focus
>
> of a day through one-eyed self sets in again: go into it.
> I must. (48–9)

Here the longing for expression does not orientate itself towards an authentic individuality, but towards the casting-off of individuality, towards the ability to absorb the words of the other into oneself and effectively to *be* other.

The entering into the individual self which seems to occur on waking, on the move into consciousness, leads only to a fraught sense that the self is characterised by lack, in opposition to the luxuriant words which 'belong' to others. The quotation of a Chuvashi poem serves to generate only envy. The 'speaker' lurches towards the idea that perhaps modernity, even if it can't achieve that kind of lyricism, has a particular capacity for dialogue, but even this 'plea for mutuality' is rejected as 'not true' (49).

Instead the poem returns to the image of dissolution:

> It's more ordinary that
> flying light should flap me away into a stream of specks
> a million surfaces without a tongue and I never have wanted
>
> 'a voice' anyway, nor got it. Alright. (49)

Riley's own description of what the poem does next is useful:

> And then what it does is flip back to exaggeratedly lush quota-
> tions from old Chuvash and Gaelic poems blurred into a long
> glistening stream of traditional possibilities of lyrical writing,
> which is then checked by some contemporary censor who
> urges the delirious, glossolalic persona to achieve a balance.
> The poor speaker fails to do this, and says in the last line that
> none of this is, for her, manageable – 'You hear me not do it'.
> Now of course 'you hear me not do it' is, in the cadence of that
> short line, almost self-negating because it's a very poised, very
> balanced sentence which has got the direct appeal to the audi-
> ence that is positively showy – it's a piece of self-cancellation
> and of showmanship at one moment. [Laughs.] And it's some-
> what difficult to re-read, you know, realising that paradox.[53]

It seems that the 'self-negating' quality of that last phrase was
not apparent to Riley when she wrote the poem, but of course this
last phrase is not the only one (besides the explicitly borrowed
phrases) which displays poetic virtuosity and flair; 'push the soft
hem / of the night into my mouth so that I stay quiet', for example, is sensual, melodic, and indeed lyrical, reminding us perhaps
of Keats's 'To cease upon the midnight with no pain'.[54] The
poem's form is also relatively traditional, being composed of regular tercets with some use of half-rhyme, and all of this serves to
underline Riley's own comment about the inescapability of the
lyric mode:

> I don't have the choice to 'abandon' it. You get formed in a cer-
> tain way. You get formed with attachments to, for instance,
> Blake – the prime example of somebody who uses the lyric
> form to carry a savagely distressed content.[55]

'Wherever you are, be somewhere else' is clearly an engagement
with lyric poetry from a place that is neither inside nor outside, in
keeping with the poem's title. It plays with the convention that the
'I' voice of a poem should be called the 'speaker'. Riley herself,
when commenting on the poem, uses the term 'speaker', but
despite the conversational character of the poem ('what // I really
mean to say instead is, come back / won't you' (48)), the ambiguous final lines draw attention to the fact that the reading experience is in fact a textual one in which an imaginary speaker is
constructed: 'I can't talk like any of this. / You hear me not do it' (49).
This textual subject seems to feel torn between an oppressive
notion of originality as necessarily located in the individual, which
leaves her feeling empty and void of meaning (I am following
Riley's gendering, for convenience), and an alternative dissolution
of self and embracing of others' voices, which veers between
nihilism and delirium. A little like Dabydeen's speaker in 'Turner',
the 'I' ends up rejecting all her efforts to talk, experiencing 'linguistic unease' about the lack of 'fit' between self and words, but in
a sense the poem itself, in its very portrayal of this unease, stands
as a proof that speech/writing nevertheless can and should go on.

Riley's poetry exhibits a clear suspicion of the kind of writing
which places a 'poetic' self in a controlling position, centre stage.
In an interview she commented that she tries to avoid a 'violent or
seductive appeal back towards the writer',[56] and in 'Dark Looks',
from *Mop Mop Georgette*, Riley satirises the way in which contemporary poets draw attention to the self despite asserting that 'Who
anyone is or I am is nothing to the work':

> What forces the lyric person to put itself on trial though it
>   must stay rigorously uninteresting?
> Does it count on its dullness to seem human and strongly
>   lovable; a veil for the monomania
> which likes to feel itself helpless and touching at times? Or
>   else it backs off to get sassy
> since arch isn't far from desperate: So take me or leave me.
>   No wait, I didn't mean leave
> me, wait, just don't – or don't flick and skim to the foot of a
>   page and then get up to go – (74)

Poetry as attention-seeking is what Riley wants to avoid,
though some element of this is perhaps inevitable. Even attempts
to get rid of the self can be 'self-magnifying', as 'Disintegrate me'

suggests:

> No single word of this
> is any more than decoration of an old self-magnifying wish
> to throw the self away so violently and widely that
>   interrogation
> has to pause since its chief suspect's sloped off to be cloud,
>   to be
> wavery colour bands (83)

'Disintegrate me' is the sixth of seven poems in the sequence 'Seven Strangely Exciting Lies', the lie in question in this poem being presumably the seductiveness of disintegration, dispersal, 'drained / abandon, in mild drift out over some creamy acre studded with / brick reds' (82). This poem encapsulates precisely Riley's most characteristic poetic stance, her readiness to self-critique and her continual attention to possible cognitive and emotional laziness. Simply to 'throw away the self' would be to abdicate the responsibility of investigating the paradoxical experience of being at once self and other, of speaking words that are at once one's own and the world's. Instead, Riley has determined to interrogate relentlessly the self's desires and self-consciousness.

Some poet-critics from the experimental scene have suggested that in doing so she fails to encounter otherness often enough – she is too obsessed with the self, even if this obsession is entirely focused on the self's construction, instability and elusiveness. John Wilkinson, in a *Parataxis* article, expresses this feeling:

> trapped within the narcissistic orbit; one yearns for release, for a writing which does not so repeatedly reassemble the writer's looking-glass, no matter how lovely the fleeting figure of self-invention there revealed, no matter how suggestive the finely-tuned points of surpassing, no matter how deft the founding of each name. What this reader chiefly remembers are those more modest, epiphanic chinks where a real exchange – with landscape, with another – briefly occurs … .[57]

Asked by Romana Huk about this accusation of 'narcissism', Denise Riley replies,

> I'd say: perhaps there's been an oversimplification of Freud's theory of narcissism. Narcissism is a condition of being fragmented, but it's through that fragmentation and that lack of a

boundary that you become aware of and respond to other people's differences: you're constantly struggling with those differences, and you don't suffer from illusions about your own finished quality. That gives you, at least at the level of its own theory, the grounds for some notion of exchange among or between people, which is the grounds for any political understanding.[58]

In fact Wilkinson does see the potential and value of Riley's project, but longs as well for more moments (like those of 'Laibach Lyrik', which he finds 'a fine poem') in which the poetry reaches 'beyond the travails of the narcissistic ego'.[59] Many complex philosophical questions are embedded in these exchanges, but it is clear that for Riley it is neither possible nor responsible to 'forget herself', as Wilkinson seems to urge at one point;[60] any experience of the other is necessarily refracted through the labyrinth of the self's rigorous examination of selfhood. The last poem in the sequence 'Seven Strangely Exciting Lies' enjoins the reader to the same degree of rigour, underlining also the necessity of relationship: 'do keep me company' (84).

Conclusion

In Peter Middleton's essay 'Who am I to speak? The politics of subjectivity in recent British poetry', he argues that expressivist or mainstream poetry (he identifies the two, and defines them as poetry which 'assumes that a poem is the record of an "I" speaking its loves and losses'[61]) is dominated by nostalgia and seeks to hold on to the self as the one fixed point in an unstable world. He argues that

The difference between dominant poetries and those where subjectivity is put into question, is not between a happy and a decentred self, but between a paralysed self-division and an engagement with contemporary event by a participant subjectivity. A reading of recent British poetry excluded from the public sphere shows that far from rejecting the expressive self it actually gives it much play, negotiating complex tensions between the pronouns of self, community and state. The exclusions are political, and they are made possible by the identification of refusals of the right kind of poetic authority.[62]

Middleton's division between 'dominant poetries' and 'excluded poetries' is far too crudely drawn (a point I will return to in the next chapter) – even a cursory glance at the poetry of Muldoon, for instance, who has been given all the 'mainstream' rewards of publication, professorships, and prizes, reveals a rejection of nostalgia and a questioning of subjectivity. But Middleton's broader point is still useful; he emphasises that a poetry which values the idea of a coherent self does not necessarily reflect a confident, active and engaged relationship with the world and political reality; instead, such a poetry can be (Middleton would say *is*) mired in nostalgia and self-obsession in the face of a seeming failure to achieve such coherence. Similarly, a poetry which embraces the idea of the fragmentation or decentering of the self need not reflect failure and disengagement, but can instead convey a sense of willingness to enter into all forms of engagement with the world and with others, even those which provoke instability.

As a counterbalance to simplistic attacks on postmodernism Middleton's point is valid, even if it in turn simplifies poetry that prefers a more conventional use of the first-person voice. It is also valuable in reminding us that an interest in 'expression' is in fact strong in 'experimental' poetries, although it is manifested in different ways. Denise Riley's poetry certainly provides support for this assertion; her interest in the question of the relationship between the self and language, and the way in which desire and agency operate along this interface, is the driving force for much of her 'experimental' poetry. Dabydeen and Muldoon are not normally considered 'experimental' (although Muldoon is sometimes cited as a possible bridging figure between 'mainstream' and 'experimental'), but their use of both first-person voices and third-person characters is complex and challenging, and they cannot be dismissed as mired in nostalgia. All three poets are ready to ask the hard questions about the nature and extent of human agency, and to throw open the whole notion of self-expression. But the work of all three poets does, I think, suggest that we should not ignore or repress the extent to which 'putting subjectivity into question' is a difficult and fraught process; if the self that values coherence has no monopoly on happiness, nor does the self that is willing to embrace fragmentation.

Notes

1   Paul Smith, *Discerning the Subject*, Theory and History of Literature vol. 55 (Minneapolis, MN: University of Minnesota Press, 1988), pp. xxxiii–xxxiv.

2   Ibid., p. xxxiv.

3   Mark McWatt, 'His true-true face: masking and revelation in David Dabydeen's *Slave Song*', in *The Art of David Dabydeen*, ed. Kevin Grant (Leeds: Peepal Tree Press, 1997), pp. 15–25 (p. 17).

4   So Benita Parry argues that Dabydeen is trying to 'articulate in the local idiom the perceptions and dreams of the historically muted … . But "speaking for" others is a fiction, and although it is Dabydeen's stated intention to "describe" ways of being and seeing based on a "jumble of fact and myth, past and present", ("Introduction", p. 10) what he does is reinvent the speech and reconceive the fantasies of slaves and peasant canecutters – and often in verse form that can owe as much to manipulating or parodying English modes as to oral traditions.' Benita Parry, 'Between Creole and Cambridge English: The poetry of David Dabydeen', in *The Art of David Dabydeen*, pp. 47–66 (pp. 49–50).

5   David Dabydeen, *Slave Song* (Oxford: Dangaroo Press, 1984), p. 53.

6   Mario Relich, 'A labyrinthine Odyssey: Psychic division in the writings of David Dabydeen', in *The Art of David Dabydeen*, pp. 123–40 (p. 125).

7   Frank Birbalsingh, 'Interview with David Dabydeen', in *The Art of David Dabydeen*, pp. 177–98 (pp. 182–3).

8   Wolfgang Binder, 'Interview with David Dabydeen', in *The Art of David Dabydeen*, pp. 159–76 (p. 169).

9   David Dabydeen, *Coolie Odyssey* (London: Hansib Publishing and Dangaroo Press, 1988), p. 9. Henceforth referred to as *CO*.

10 David Dabydeen, *Turner: New and Selected Poems* (London: Random House, 1994), p. ix. Henceforth referred to as *T*.

11 Kwame Dawes, 'Interview with David Dabydeen', in *The Art of David Dabydeen*, pp. 199–221 (p. 203).

12 Ibid., p. 204.

13 For example, in interview with Frank Birbalsingh Dabydeen comments, 'One of the old themes in West Indian literature is the crisis of identity. I have a multiple identity. There is no crisis. There is a kind of delight as well as a kind of an anguish in jumping from one identity to the next.' Later he asserts that even if one is open to multiplicity, 'The amoeba never breaks it [sic] boundaries, it always has a skin, a shell. You always have the nucleus of your soul.' Birbalsingh, 'Interview with David Dabydeen', pp. 195, 198.

14 Tim Kendall notes the intricacy of 'Yarrow', explaining that the order in which Muldoon uses his twelve sets of endrhymes is not arbitrary: 'Each page of "Yarrow" fits one of the twelve units, but Muldoon's patterning is not random: ignoring the envoi, it is apparent that the same end-words are employed by the opening and the concluding page, the second and the penultimate, and so on, with the result that the second half of the poem is a mirror image of the first half. Effectively, "Yarrow" consists of a series of concentric circles.' Tim Kendall, *Paul Muldoon* (Bridgend: Seren, 1996), p. 228.

15 Clair Wills, *Reading Paul Muldoon* (Newcastle upon Tyne: Bloodaxe, 1998), pp. 207–8.

16 Quoted in Kendall, *Paul Muldoon*, p. 209.

17 Andrew Osborn, 'Skirmishes on the border: The evolution and function of Muldoon's fuzzy rhyme', *Contemporary Literature*, vol. 41, no. 2 (2000), pp. 323–58.

18 John Redmond, 'Interview with Paul Muldoon', *Thumbscrew*, 4 (Spring 1996), pp. 2–18 (p. 4).

19 Personal interview with Clair Wills, 2 June 1987, quoted in Clair Wills, *Improprieties: Politics and Sexuality in Northern Irish Poetry* (Oxford: Oxford University Press, 1993), p. 202.

20 Paul Muldoon, *Why Brownlee Left* (London: Faber, 1980), p. 38. Henceforth referred to as *WBL*.

21 It is possible to read these last lines as affirming a positive postmodern consciousness. For example, Richard Kirkland argues that the hero manages to escape from atavistic and brutal historical forces and 'can return to a sense of living within the community and resume his existence in the pool-room which continues to bear the label of a celebratory mixed inheritance' ('Paul Muldoon's "Immram" and "Immrama": Writing for a sense of displacement', *Essays in Poetics*, vol. 17, no. 1 (1992), pp. 35–43 (pp. 41–2)). However, I would suggest that kind of potentially positive reading needs to admit a tension produced by the sense of pointlessness, anonymity and entrapment which remains. See my article 'Leaving Main Street?: Agency and responsibility in Paul Muldoon's "Immram" ', *The Australian Journal of Irish Studies*, vol. 3 (2003), pp. 91–101.

22 Paul Muldoon, *Quoof* (London: Faber, 1983), p. 41. Henceforth referred to as *Q*.

23 Paul Radin, *The Trickster: A Study in American Indian Mythology*, new introduction by Stanley Diamond, commentaries by Karl Kerényi and C. J. Jung (New York: Schocken Books, 1972).

24 Ibid., p. 26.

25 See Kendall's *Paul Muldoon* for an explanation of the link between Heaney's 'Broagh' and this moment in 'The More a Man Has' (p. 111).

26 The most obvious allusion is found in the second half of the 'sheugh' stanza, in which the milk-drinking episode is directly taken from the story of Sweeney. Gallogly also eats watercress like Sweeney, and names the forgotten names of apples in a rather pallid, slightly parodic version of Sweeney's poetic celebration of nature.

27 Wills, *Reading Paul Muldoon*, p. 108.

28 Ibid., p. 108.

29 Kendall, *Paul Muldoon*, p. 209.

30 Paul Muldoon, *The Annals of Chile* (London: Faber, 1994), p. 21.

31 Kendall, *Paul Muldoon*, p. 217.

32 Ibid., p. 229.

33 Ibid., p. 231.

34 *The Collected Works of W.B. Yeats, vol. 1: The Poems*, revised edition, ed. Richard J. Finneran, (New York: Macmillan, 1989), pp. 188–90.

35 Paul Muldoon, *Moy Sand and Gravel* (London: Faber, 2002), p. 75. Henceforth referred to as *MSG*.

36 Edna Longley, 'Twists and turns', review of *Moy Sand and Gravel*, *Poetry Review*, vol. 92, no. 4 (2002–03), pp. 62–6 (p. 66).

37 As Robert MacFarlane notes in his review of *Moy Sand and Gravel*, the dead peccary becomes a counterpoint to Asher, 'who is himself shadowed by a nameless Jewish baby which we are led to suppose perished in Auschwitz. Astrakhan – the wool taken fatally from lambs between 3 and 10 days old – also crops up, and the poem becomes overtly preoccupied with infanticide. Its veiled subject appears to be the nature of proxy grief. More precisely, it attempts an examination of the emotional mechanisms by which we come to understand tragedies in which we had no part.' Robert MacFarlane, 'Review of *Moy Sand and Gravel*', *Times Literary Supplement*, no. 5193, 11 October 2002, p. 24.

38 Clair Wills, Nick Jenkins and John Lanchester, 'An Interview with Paul Muldoon', *Oxford Poetry*, 3.1 (Winter 1986–87), pp. 14–20 (pp. 19–20).

39 Denise Riley, *Selected Poems* (London: Reality Street Editions, 2000), p. 30. All references to Riley's poetry will refer to the *Selected Poems*, as many of the other collections are not easily available. Henceforth referred to as *SP*.

40 Of the opening of 'Laibach Lyrik', John Wilkinson admits that 'this reader felt foolish to have taken on trust a passage which began "*The milky sheen of birch trees*" (the sort of thing only Tarkovsky is allowed by sophisticated Westerners). But then, a poem of shifting frames is unprecedented in Riley's writing, where always the voice has been trustworthy through its constant admission of untrustworthiness ("love me").' John Wilkinson, 'Illyrian places', review of *Mop Mop Georgette*, *Parataxis*, vol. 6 (1994), pp. 58–69 (p. 64).

41 Marjorie Perloff, *Poetry On and Off the Page: Essays for Emergent Occasions* (Evanston, IL: Northwestern University Press, 1998), pp. 138–9.

42 Lyn Hejinian, *The Language of Inquiry* (Berkeley, CA: University of California Press, 2000), p. 329.

43 The phrase 'What though the dark thee cumber' is an allusion to Robert Herrick's poem 'The Night Piece, to Julia' ('Let not the dark thee cumber / What though the moon does slumber') in which a glow-worm also features. The allusiveness (signaled by the use of 'thee', even if one doesn't recognise the allusion) suggests a mind in the process of free association, the self as echo chamber, as elsewhere in Riley's work, but the absence of any subject pronouns, especially in the odd verbal constructions of the first two stanzas, makes us uncertain about this paradigm as well.

44 Clair Wills, 'Contemporary women's poetry: Experimentalism and the expressive voice', *Critical Quarterly*, vol. 36, no. 3 (1994), pp. 34–52 (p. 44).

45 Ibid., p. 45.

46 Ibid., p. 45.

47 Denise Riley, *The Words of Selves: Identification, Solidarity, Irony* (Stanford, CA: Stanford University Press, 2000), p. 17.

48 Ibid., p. 7.

49 Ibid., p. 14.

50 Ibid., p. 96.

51 Ibid., pp. 100–1.

52 'Denise Riley in Conversation with Romana Huk', *PN Review*, vol. 21, no. 5 (1995), pp. 17–22 (p. 19).

53 Ibid., p. 19.
54 John Keats, 'Ode to a Nightingale', in *Keats: Poetical Works*, ed. H. W. Garrod (Oxford: Oxford University Press, 1970), p. 208.
55 'Denise Riley in Conversation with Romana Huk', p. 19.
56 Ibid., p. 17.
57 Wilkinson, 'Illyrian places', pp. 68–9.
58 'Denise Riley in Conversation with Romana Huk', p. 20.
59 Wilkinson, 'Illyrian places', p. 67.
60 Ibid., p. 64.
61 Peter Middleton, 'Who am I to speak?: The politics of subjectivity in recent British poetry', in *New British Poetries: The Scope of the Possible*, ed. Robert Hampson and Peter Barry (Manchester: Manchester University Press, 1993), pp. 107–33 (p. 119).
62 Ibid., pp. 119–20.

7

The Tribes of Poetry

Tom Raworth, Geraldine Monk,
Catherine Walsh, Peter Reading,
Patience Agbabi

To most people, the idea that any poet might be described as 'mainstream' seems slightly odd; the whole of the poetry world appears to the majority to be an esoteric and marginal enterprise. However, marginality is always relative, and within the current poetry scene in Britain – and to a lesser extent in Ireland – the debate over whether certain sections of the poetry-writing population have been unfairly excluded and marginalised by the dominant publishers and institutions has reached a new level of intensity. A combination of events has catalysed this; firstly, and most importantly, the publication of several new books which have a clear revisionist agenda and seek to redress a perceived repression of the experimental poetry scene;[1] secondly, the success of new Cambridge-based publisher Salt, which is publishing large amounts of new and existing experimental poetry and criticism of such work; and thirdly, the impact made between 2002 and 2005 by the editors of the London-based *Poetry Review*, a magazine which has been decidedly mainstream for the last few decades[2] but has recently taken a strikingly different approach in seeking to expose work from all sections of the poetry continuum. Robert Potts, one of the editors since 2002,[3] comments that

> In *Poetry Review*, we try to see poetry not as an archipelago of mutually hostile factions, but as an art which people do very different things with. So we try to represent quite a few of those different approaches (but without calling attention to them as

aspects of tribes; just as things in their own rights). We want the magazine to be an open space for these approaches (all of which have audiences and fans, all of which also have their detractors); to avoid lapsing back into old boring dichotomised debates. And we think maybe if people could see more of the 'terrain' they might make new discoveries, which is what culture is all about (for me, anyway).[4]

The signs of rapprochement are all to the good, in my opinion; the experimental poetry community, which can sometimes appear self-absorbed and insular (whether this is partly chosen or entirely forced upon them is a fraught point) can only benefit from a broader readership and vigorous debate about their work, while mainstream poetry will also gain if it allows its assumptions to be more strenuously examined and challenged. This view is not, however, shared by all, as the fighting introduction to Don Paterson and Charles Simic's anthology *New British Poetry* (2004) indicates. This book was published in America and acknowledges its role as an 'alternative' (but not a 'corrective')[5] to Keith Tuma's revisionist *Anthology of Twentieth-Century British and Irish Poetry* (published by Oxford University Press's New York offices in 2001). The introduction, written by Paterson (and discussed also in Chapter 1), declares its intention 'to discuss the threat currently presented by the Postmoderns and their general ubiquity, and give some defence of Mainstream practise'.[6]

To Paterson, then, 'the Postmoderns' (who are, along with 'Mainstream' poets, given a capital letter throughout the introduction, as if to accentuate the binary opposition and the sense of antagonism) are a real 'threat'. What poets and what kind of poetry does he feel so threatened by? Here we should step back a little to examine the terms of the debate. 'Experimental' or 'avant-garde' are terms which are frequently used to describe poetry which is deliberately disjunctive in its procedures and draws attention to the materiality of language in a manner more radical and overt than other poetries.[7] Poets associated with the experimental scene also tend to be interested in the relationship between text on the page and other media; so-called visual poetry, sound poetry and mixed-media performances enact this interest. Poets in the experimental scene trace their influences through the permutations of international modernism (including neglected British modernist poets like Hugh MacDiarmid, David Jones and

Basil Bunting) and many would acknowledge links with the American $L=A=N=G=U=A=G=E$ poets and earlier Americans including Charles Olson's Black Mountain group and the New York school.

Many of the poets associated with the experimental scene are interested in and cognisant of developments in literary theory, and much of the poetry lends itself to readings informed by post-structuralism. On the other hand, there are modes of experimentalism that are determinedly anti-theoretical. Poetry which is identified as experimental tends to make use of what Charles Bernstein, one of the pivotal Language poets, described as 'anti-absorptive' techniques:[8] methods which make it difficult for the reader to become entirely absorbed in the 'world' of the poem and which act to remind the reader of the process of writing. This poetry works to combat the notion that language is a transparent medium for communicating meaning from poet to reader. If the idea of communication is retained at all, it becomes problematic.[9] Experimental poetry is frequently impossible to paraphrase, and therefore poses great problems for conventional criticism. Although the idea that the poem 'should not mean but be' has long been a touchstone for mainstream criticism, most criticism nevertheless relies on suggesting possible 'meanings' for poems in a manner that often verges on paraphrase. Much experimental poetry resists this process strenuously.

There have been arguments over whether some forms of experimental poetry reject 'meaning' altogether. However, it is difficult to think of any poem which eludes 'meaning' entirely; even a sound poem which is based on phonemes and avoids all words derives 'meaning' from the associations we attach to various sounds – 'soft' sounds, 'hard' sounds, and so on. Most experimental poetry does not even go this far; it utilises words, phrases and sentences that cannot be described as meaningless no matter how resistant they are to paraphrase. I think most Irish and British experimental poets would agree with Bernstein and Andrews's dismissal of this idea in their introduction to *The L=A= N=G=U=A=G=E Book*:

> ... the idea that writing should (or could) be stripped of reference is as bothersome and confusing as the assumption that the primary function of words is to refer, one-on-one, to an already constructed world of 'things.' Rather, reference, like the body

itself, is one of the horizons of language, whose value is to be found in the writing (the world) before which we find ourselves at any moment. It is the multiple powers and scope of reference (denotative, connotative, associational), not writers' refusal or fear of it, that threads these essays together.[10]

Perhaps the most commonly remarked upon feature of experimental poetry is a characteristic suspicion of the lyric 'I', something which I have already discussed in relation to Denise Riley's poetry in Chapter 6. This reflects a postmodernist or poststructuralist conception of the self as fragmented, conflicted, dispersed; it generates a poetry which does not place the lyric voice in a central and authoritative position, as an origin beyond language, but views the 'I' as a position generated and solidified by its operation within a linguistic system. There are of course many different 'takes' on this both vexed and fascinating question of the nature of the self and its role in language, and many different ways of exploring it, but a high degree of self-consciousness regarding this issue is characteristic of many poets in the experimental scene.

Of course these characteristics are not limited to poets who are identified as experimental. Many of them are associated generally with postmodernism and can be identified in the work of mainstream poets who are viewed as postmodernist, such as Paul Muldoon. Whether poets are associated with experimentalism tends to come down to the distance they go in the direction of disjunction and the disruption of conventional reading strategies. At the same time, there is a degree of self-identification; poets who publish with small presses and participate in the conferences, joint publications, performance circuits and internet discussion groups associated with the experimental scene will inevitably be labeled experimental even if in other contexts their work could be viewed as on the edge of mainstream. Denise Riley's poetry is a case in point.[11] For many poets, self-identification as 'experimental' or avant-garde is politically important, as many see mainstream poetry as shoring up conservative and/or oppressive tendencies in society.

In experimental forums, the political significance of poetic form is often viewed in the context of capitalism and consumerism; many experimental poets argue that mainstream poetry invites the reader to 'consume' a poem without questioning its nature, construction, and situation in history, just as modern capitalism seeks to seduce the consumer to buy goods without questioning the system in which they operate. Influential experimental poets argue that poetry which, through its disjunctive and disorienting procedures, forces – or invites – the reader to participate in the production of meaning (the Marxist imperative of reclaiming the 'means of production' is one influence here) has the capacity to alert the reader to the insidious way in which language is used by powerful individuals and institutions in order to make certain oppressive systems and ideologies seem 'natural'. In other words, what is said in language no longer feels smooth and self-evident, inviting easy assent; the reader is instead invited to experience the fissures in perception and expression, the moments when the process of creating meaning and pattern is experienced as tenuous, volatile and unstable. There is a kind of cognitive Puritanism to this kind of description of experimental poetry, with its emphasis on the reader's *work* and its suspicion of easy enjoyment. Other descriptions might emphasise more heavily the idea of release into a kind of free associative experience, a letting go of the intellectual need for logical connection and linear narrative in favour of a more emotional or sensual experience of sound, pattern and free-wheeling association.

All of these ideas are of course found, at times, in mainstream criticism and accounts that mainstream poets give of their intentions and writing processes. Clearly the binary opposition between 'mainstream' and 'experimental', although it does reflect important differences along a continuum of poetic practice, is frequently too emphatically and rigidly drawn. As Andrew Michael Roberts says in a very useful article, the avant-garde tends to demonise and homogenise the mainstream as a way of coping with their own marginalised position; this in fact seems to go against its own principles, which generally emphasise diversity over homogeneity and oppose hierarchies of value.[12] Certainly such homogenisation is rife in the anthologies representing the avant-garde or experimental scene. Richard Caddel and Peter Quartermain, for example, in *Other: British and Irish Poetry since 1970*, describe the 'mainstream' in the following way:

> It is not the function of this introduction to describe in detail the development of this 'mainstream,' nor is it our intention to dismiss it as devoid of worth. However, it is necessary to

suggest why it has appeared such an alienating experience for so many of the writers here, and why, finally, most of them reject it: 'mainstream' in this context may be said to include the narrow lineage of contemporary poets from Philip Larkin to Craig Raine and Simon Armitage, and encompassing their attendant 'collectives' (Movement, Martians, New Generation). Generalisation about such (often nebulous) groups is fraught with difficulties, but it nevertheless holds that in each case the typical poem is a closed, monolineal utterance, demanding little of the reader but passive consumption. Such a cultural vision has obviously been privileged not simply by the major publishing houses but also by their attendant infrastructures of reviewing journals, 'literaries' and other elements of the media.[13]

This is somewhat disingenuous. Caddel and Quartermain are careful to say that the mainstream *includes* rather than *is* the groups they have named, but do not mention figures who are indubitably 'mainstream' but clearly stand outside the indicated 'narrow lineage'; we might think of Paul Muldoon, Medbh McGuckian, Geoffrey Hill and Ciaran Carson. The New Generation itself was hardly homogeneous, and figures like Peter Reading and David Dabydeen, who were named in that list, have little in common with a 'Movement' aesthetic. Even if we accept that a poem by Larkin, Raine or Armitage is relatively (though not absolutely) closed and monolineal, it is clear that other poets whose work is much more open and multilineal are rewarded and lauded in the mainstream; obviously Muldoon is a case in point. Homogenisation of either 'mainstream' or 'experimental' work from either side is clearly unhelpful. On the mainstream side the problem is ignorance and (confirmed nicely by Paterson's introduction) defensive anxiety, and from the experimental side the problem is a sense of neglect or even systematic persecution.[14]

The current climate suggests a possible movement towards a greater knowledge of experimental poetry by poets and critics working in the mainstream, which can only be a positive thing. This has been propelled in part by the work of Keith Tuma, an American critic who has launched himself into the role of an evangelist for British poetry (and especially experimental poetry) in America. There is a need for this, Tuma says, because in America 'British poetry is dead', having been 'crossed off our maps, or relegated to the zones of the quaint and antiquarian'.[15]

Tuma argues that this is partly to do with the relative invisibility of formally innovative poetry in Britain, and the lack of critical and poetical trans-Atlantic dialogue. In America, experimental poetry has had a much higher profile, and a much easier ride in terms of relationships with institutions; Tuma urges Americans to read British experimental poetry 'to see what happens to a poetry which more often has had to go it alone, as it were, without being able to depend quite so heavily on the artificial economies created by the academy and other institutions such as grants-awarding agencies'.[16] Tuma's effort has received a predictably mixed response in Britain; one of the first things Robert Potts and David Herd did when they took over the editorship of *Poetry Review* in 2002 was to print a new and more sympathetic review[17] of Tuma's *Anthology of Twentieth-Century British and Irish Poetry*, which had been savaged by Sean O'Brien under the previous editorship of Peter Forbes. O'Brien's review was disappointing in its failure to engage seriously with the issues at stake, straining readers' credulity by aligning Tuma with George W. Bush's American imperialism, and labelling the entire avant-garde community 'post-imaginative'.[18]

While American influence on British experimentalism is strong, there is also a consciousness among British experimental poets of the need 'to speak to the British contexts British exploratory poetics emerge from'[19] rather than to become overly immersed in the American context. Tuma notes that this desire to look to British models has been more characteristic of the poets associated with the Cambridge scene than of those associated with London.[20] All such groupings are problematic, but certainly one can see the influence of J.H. Prynne in the work of a group of poets who live or have lived in Cambridge, while the London poets, influenced perhaps more by Eric Mottram, have shown a shared interest in performance and mixed-media productions. Naturally there are many poets who are associated with neither of these groups. Although most of the poets who identify themselves as experimental or avant-garde are published by small presses, the exclusion of experimental poets from major publishers' lists has perhaps shown signs of easing in recent years; J.H. Prynne's *Collected Poems* have been published by Bloodaxe and Tom Raworth's by Carcanet. *New* experimental poetry, however, is rarely published by major publishing houses.

The situation in Ireland is rather different from that in Britain. Several of the key modernist figures behind current experimental writing were, of course, Irish (Joyce and Beckett, particularly) and there has been what Alex Davis calls a 'broken line' of modernist writing in Ireland since then:

> the poetry of the 'Thirties generation', which would include that of Thomas MacGreevy, Coffey, Beckett and Sheila Wingfield, as well as [Denis] Devlin, can be read as a reactive, second-generation modernism. Subsequent to the 1930s poets, there is a rich vein of modernist and postmodernist poetry in Ireland, a lode which includes Eugene Watters's *The Week-End of Dermot and Grace*; Thomas Kinsella's poetry from *Nightwalker* and *Notes from the Land of the Dead* through his Peppercanister series; Hugh Maxton's *The Puzzle-Tree Ascendant* and other works; the preponderance of the poetry published by Michael Smith's New Writers' Press, that of Trevor Joyce, Geoffrey Squires, and Augustus Young; and the writing of a number of younger poets, including Randolph Healy, David Lloyd, Billy Mills, Maurice Scully and Catherine Walsh, whose formally innovative work bears points of comparison with that of North American Language poets.[21]

I have quoted Davis's list in its entirety because it is important for readers to be aware of this tradition of modernist writing in Ireland. Strangely enough, after Joyce and Beckett, and with the limited exception of Kinsella, modernist writing in Ireland has struggled to gain a profile internationally and in Ireland itself. Many critics and poets have laid the blame for this squarely at the foot of Ireland's fraught sense of national identity, arguing that poetry which does not easily allow itself to be read as part of a tradition of specifically *Irish* poetry, which does not possess an 'Irish content', tends to be excluded from the cultural conversation. Catherine Walsh says that '[y]ou are only supported if you are part of that tradition, that same tradition which must celebrate above all else your sense of Irishness and your sense of being part of an ongoing linear tradition of Irish writers, writing out of a sense of bondage almost.'[22] Experimental writers in Ireland tend to feel too that the idea of the 'Irish poem' is also highly restricted in terms of form, linked historically to the Revivalist lyric and more recently to the Movement-influenced aesthetic of the popular Northern Irish poetry of the 1970s and 1980s, and in general hostile to modernism.

While, as in Britain, there is a degree of exaggeration in experimental writers' portrayal of the mainstream,[23] it is true that even mainstream and well-supported poets in both the Republic and the North of Ireland do at times become exasperated with the tendency for critics and readers to view them *only* in terms of 'the matter of Ireland' or the conflict in Northern Ireland. This is partly driven by overseas academic and popular audiences, who read Irish poetry as part of a general interest in or study of Irish culture and politics. Poetry that engages with questions of Irish identity is easily exportable. Experimental writers tend to prefer to view themselves as part of an international community of avant-garde writers, and adopt formal methods which make their poems resistant to assimilation into any narrative of identity – in fact, any narrative whatsoever.

Ireland's rapid entry into global capitalism in the 1990s (the birth of the 'Celtic Tiger') has provided a context which makes dialogue between Irish experimental poets and American Language poets even more potentially fruitful, and makes arguments about the relationship between avant-garde art and modernism, postmodernism and capitalism particularly and suddenly relevant. Alex Davis argues that the poetry of the Irish neo-avant-garde poets 'pays witness to the divergent, and often contradictory, discourses of contemporary Ireland: the anachronistic rural idyll markets by Bord Fáilte; the forward-looking nation at the heart of Europe promoted by governmental and corporate interests'.[24] In this context it is regrettable that, as John Goodby says, the 'separation between the "realms" [of mainstream and experimental poetry] is noticeably greater, at an institutional level, in Ireland than in either Britain or the USA, with their relationship characterised not so much by polemic as by ignorance and dismissal'.[25] The publication of Goodby and Davis's critical books, however, perhaps signals the beginning of a broader debate on the issue of this separation.

After all this talk about the experimental scene it is obviously high time to look at some poems. In this chapter I want to look, firstly, at poems by three experimental poets, Tom Raworth, Geraldine Monk and Catherine Walsh. Rather than giving an overview of their work, as I have done with poets in previous chapters, I would like to focus on one or two poems or excerpts from sequences by each poet. This enables me to introduce several

experimental writers and also allows close and detailed demon-
stration of the particular formal qualities of individual poems.
This chapter will also seek to contribute towards the bridging of
the gap between 'experimental' and 'mainstream' poetry by discussing the poetry of Peter Reading alongside these three, and
noting some important similarities and differences. Another
major divide in poetry in Britain and Ireland is between poetry
which is written primarily for the page and poetry which is
oriented towards performance, and in an effort to address this
issue I will finish the chapter by considering the poetry of
Patience Agbabi. Although performance poets like Agbabi (and
Zephaniah, included in Chapter 2) are celebrated and enjoyed,
there is a tendency to see such poetry as in some way lesser – less
serious, less deserving of academic recognition or critical discussion, less *complex* – than poetry which is page-based. Although the
vitriol which emerges in the exchanges over experimental poetry
is not as marked in this divide, a patronising attitude towards
performance poetry among critics and some poets reflects a serious undervaluing of the skills and specific accomplishments of
this poetry. A willingness to explore seriously the particular
demands and opportunities of performance is much more common
in the experimental scene than in the mainstream.

Tom Raworth

Tom Raworth has been an influential figure in the British experimental scene since the publication of *The Relation Ship* in 1966, and
is famous for his high-speed, high-impact performances. He was
born in London in 1938 and since 1977 he has been based in
Cambridge. His early poetry was influenced by the 'projective
verse' and open form aesthetic of Charles Olson, Robert Creeley
and Ed Dorn of the Black Mountain school. For the most part it
includes more recognisable narrative elements and speech-like
progressions than his later poetry, which has become more
disjunctive and paratactic in the manner of the Language poets.
Throughout his *Collected Poems* Raworth's sense of humour is
evident, as in a poem like 'Read Me', whose full text is 'Thanks'.[26]
As William Wootten says, 'Slight as it is, the poem, which one has
already read before realising that one has been told to do so, manages to say something useful about the demands and processes of

reading, to tell a home truth about authors' egos, and to be endearingly polite.'[27] At the same time, Raworth can be both grim and mordant in his political critiques, as in his oft-quoted take on the Thatcher period in 'West Wind' in the section beginning 'colourless nation / sucking on grief' (*CP*, 360–1).

I would like to discuss a poem called 'That More Simple Natural Time Tone Distortion'. This was originally published as a stand-alone pamphlet in 1975, but can now be found in *Tottering State: Selected and New Poems 1963–83*, in the *Collected Poems* and in the anthology *Other: British and Irish Poetry Since 1970*. The *Publishers Weekly* reviewer of *Other* describes the poem as 'a sonic joy-ride of one- to three-word lines that bristle with pixilated narrative'.[28] This is a good description of a poem that invites us to experience momentary, volatile, fleeting flashes of what might be called narrative or at least continuity, and then to let them go and open our minds to revisions and rearrangements, or move on to seek more possibilities. In fact, moving on is inevitable, as the poem consists of two thin parallel columns that draw the eye ever downwards even as our habit of reading left-right keeps us searching for horizontal connections. At least, this is the way we encounter it in the texts which are most readily available. When the poem was originally published as a pamphlet, however, it was printed as one long column,[29] and Raworth says that that is how he wrote it and usually thinks of it. Later publishers printed the poem with two columns on each page in order to save space, so the horizontal alignment of words is determined only by the number of words which fit on a page in a given edition. This is surprising information, perhaps, to the reader who has first encountered the piece in the layout of two columns on each page, as the horizontal connections can seem just as important as the linear downward direction.

Raworth's comments on this phenomenon are interesting. He comments that he usually reads the poem (and others like it) as he wrote it,

> but I don't see that as a definitive reading – simply how I, myself, read them. The poem that arises from a horizontal scanning of two randomly-placed (because of page-length) columns seems no less interesting, and at the very least a glance at another facet of the piece. I can see it as a variant of the reader who sees something in a poem (and it's happened to me) that had never been seen, nor intended, by the author.

For many years one of the things that has interested me in writing is the way that certain words, being in their positions syntactically ambiguous, can direct a multitude of readings of a work: how it seems to flicker, unfixed, in levels.[30]

The poem is too long to reproduce in full here, but I have included the final page of the *Collected Poems* version (excerpting inevitably does violence to the poem):

TREMOR
stillness
of
my present
moves
within
me
chill sheets
chime
stained
ice
shatter
shadows out
without
falls
in
to memory
edmund
dante
caught
by a thought
nature
inclines
towards
risk
no
further
than you
can go
tempo
moon
(*CP*, 240)

my tube
moon
slow behind
silence
peace
or play the
game
I love
your music
muse
nor will
silence
slide
those fibres
of my love
for vanity
disfigures me
why cold
if ay
reflection
flames
to memory
games memory
of games
then silence
wakes me
with a break
in waves

It is indeed the syntactical ambiguity of the vertical arrangement of words that allows the poem to acquire a horizontal dimension when printed in double columns, and Raworth's openness to
the possibilities engendered by layout which he does not control
is reflective of his broader openness to multiple and shifting
meanings. In one sense this poem is 'easier' or less threatening for
the reader new to experimental poetry than many of the poems
which present themselves visually as traditional forms, because,
by signaling difference so explicitly, Raworth helps the reader to
let go of conventional reading strategies and expectations. It is
immediately clear that this poem demands a more fluid and
non-linear approach to meaning.

The ways in which meaning emerges in this poem may be seen
in the excerpt above. If we read the poem as Raworth originally
intended it to be read, in a single vertical column, then we read
down the left-hand column and then jump up to the top of the
right-hand column to continue. Even reading in this manner there
is considerable fluidity in the reading experience, as we perceive
multiple ways to arrange the words; thus we can read either 'stillness of my present moves within me' or 'within me chill sheets
chime'. Both these phrases are simultaneously present. Once we
allow ourselves to move between the two columns horizontally as
well, the possibilities proliferate. Some possible word strands are:
'my present silence moves within me'; 'stillness of my present
silence'; 'chime your music stained muse'; 'nor will ice shatter
silence'; 'silence shadows out'; 'shadows slide without those
fibres of my love'; 'nature inclines to memory'; 'risk then silence',
and so on. One could go on, and this is only using a small section
of the poem. One of the poem's achievements is to show us how
to enjoy the flitting of meanings and images, reading as an experience that is wholly given up to the movement of time. Standing
entirely alone, any of the above phrases might seem like flimsy
nonsense (although some have considerable resonance in their
own right), but in context they achieve the subtlety of the play of
light and shadow on a wall.

As Kit Robinson says of the single-column version of
Raworth's 'Ace',

[it is] an exploration of discontinuous language in continuous
time. The language of the poem is composed of bits (short
lines) which, by virtue of a polyvalent syntax, can point
forward or back. There is no punctuation. Meaning is dependent

on where the mind locates its attention within the continuum and how it groups the particles. Each language event (line) qualifies what has come immediately before and violates any totalization prior to it. Time destroys fixed ideas.[31]

So, earlier in 'That More Simple Natural Time Tone Distortion', there is an apparent affirmation of art's endurance – 'but this is clear this area this never ending song to last' – which is undermined immediately by the next word, 'gasp' (237). Later we grasp at an apparent narrative strand of a Gothic or horror scenario – 'direction of icy moon howl scratch soft knuckles at the door' – before hoarding it as the poem moves relentlessly on: 'above the tempo flesh tuner shriek right we slide out into …' (238). In the long extract quoted above, we will probably read 'edmund dante caught by a thought' before considering the possibility of 'caught by a thought nature inclines towards risk', and then 'risk no further than you can go'.

Even reading the title necessitates this kind of revision process. 'That More Simple Natural Time' is the object of much conservative nostalgia; this poem, the title seems to suggest, will have no part in such disenchantment with the present and idealisation of the past. We are not allowed to settle, to dwell, in or on that idea of the past, but are swept on into the rest of the phrase which, through its own obliquity, seems to create 'tonal distortion'. Distortion could be viewed positively here, as every word is altered according to the combination in which it is viewed, and memory never seems to evoke anything 'simple' or 'natural'. The poem as a whole seems to suggest a kind of struggle with the capacities of memory, imagination and self-reflection; with desire and loss and their evocation in the mind:

> reflection
> flames
> to memory
> games memory
> of games
> then silence
> wakes me
> with a break
> in waves

Reading the poem, we experience a process of creating and then letting go of or losing fragments of meaning which mimics the process of grasping for coherence and strands of narrative in memory and in dreams. This poem should not be read with any feeling that the poet has provided some kind of puzzle for us to decipher; the focus of the poem is not on any endpoint of interpretation, but on the *process* of reading and making meaning.

New readers of Raworth's poetry should begin with poems like this or with his early work from the beginning of the *Collected Poems*, where his casual, impressionistic and humorous style is at times reminiscent of Frank O'Hara. The much later sonnet sequences like 'Eternal Sections' demand patience, but they do reveal most clearly the breadth and scope of Raworth's concerns, from capitalism and mysticism to the media, domestic life and the nature of the self and the body. The sonnets of 'Eternal Sections' differ radically from each other in diction and tone, recalling both John Ashbery and Charles Bernstein in their exploration of the range and instrumentality of different linguistic discourses. This kind of work demands careful and attentive reading, and its *difference* from the kind of 'mainstream' poetry most often given exposure in the public sphere is marked. In contrast to 'That More Simple Natural Time Tone Distortion', the coherent syntax of the sonnets creates an expectation in the reader of narrative or description. This expectation is challenged and unsettled but never entirely relinquished as the reader juggles, drops, retrieves and constantly reassembles fragments of narrative, pattern or argument.

Catherine Walsh

Born in 1964, Catherine Walsh is one of the younger Irish experimental poets. Both Alex Davis and John Goodby, in their recent books on the Irish modernist tradition, cite her as one of the most interesting experimental poets writing in Ireland today. Her four major publications – *Making Tents* (1987), *Short Stories* (1989), *Pitch* (1994) and *idir eatortha and Making Tents* (1996) – are exceedingly difficult to excerpt from. They are not really 'collections', as one cannot see them as a group of separate poems herded together; even 'sequence' is not quite right, as there are, with few exceptions, no clear boundaries between poems. At the same time, the writing within any book ranges so widely, with abrupt style changes, that it is difficult to think of each book as consisting of 'one' long poem. This is of course all part of Walsh's attempt to draw attention to the limitations of conventional ways of thinking about poetry and to explore the possibilities of alternative approaches.

Walsh's poetry has much in common with American Language poetry, although, as Alex Davis remarks, a 'crucial point of divergence can be glimpsed in the persistence of "the I" in Walsh's poetry'.[32] Although 'the I' is present, however, it provides no unifying perspective, no centre, for the work, which disperses itself across different overheard discourses and fragmented experiences, and distributes itself spatially across the page in unpredictable, uneven ways which encourage multiple readings. Much of Walsh's work seems to mimic the processes of the mind in perception and cognition; in this sense, and like Joyce and other modernists, it strives for a kind of realism – of the mind rather than of the world. A section from *idir eatortha* (the Irish means 'between two worlds') demonstrates this:

> "it's coming down any minute now where? well?
> where is it then? (SHOUTS) *where's the jacket?*"

> [scrabbling]

> "they do but they don't"

> "the council, The Council. The Local Borough Council.
> no corpo and county here. no craic
> the greetings ..."

> "here's a likely looking pair"
>
> [politely, respectfully]

> [shovelling sounds]

> [accelerating footsteps
> female voice]

> "*I* don't know George, drunk"
> "this time of the morning dear? don't know"
> "well, Irish, Scottish perhaps"

> [sniffing]
> "ah well, and up yours to with a, stop there. stop right there.
> here. here, there, anyplace. space. stop right there, that's
> here, was there, was here there any where – what a load of.

doesn't mean. or we only want to feel – are –
incapable – world happening –
Johnson adrift. it's all animate
poetry struggling to contend with
a lack our socializing instincts gone apeshit
thinking we *know*

credo inanimatus

green leaf, sound, wheels on pavement –
no – footpath – contending with space we box it, label it, extend
language fencing effect to move, ourselves, we extend
bridges of words – to pass over – instead of ourselves

that's it,   misnomer, space.
space a misnomer.
space is.[33]

This is actually one of the most accessible sections of *idir eatortha*, because there are extended fragments of conversational language and there is the possibility of constructing a context; the text seems to capture the processes of the mind as it overhears street sounds but at the same time continues to work on the words of a poetic text. The section immediately before this seems to make the poetic process more prominent, as we witness an internal dialogue (though we can't rule out the possibility that this is a 'real' conversation between two people) that ruminates over variations on the phrase 'a green leaf on a grainy grey pavement' (*ie*, 37). This is also interrupted by overheard street sounds, but in the section quoted above, the street sounds have begun to take over, and the text only returns to the poetic image at the end of the quoted passage, as the thinker reminds her or himself that she/he had already emphatically rejected 'pavement' for 'footpath'. The fragments of overheard speech which interrupt and blur into the thinker's thoughts do impinge on questions of nationality; at least one of the people involved in the exchanges is Irish, but the scene is set in England, where he(?) has to be reminded not to speak of the 'corpo' (Dublin Corporation) but of the 'Local Borough Council'. Meanwhile, an English couple, perhaps elderly, walk past with 'accelerating footsteps', drawing on prejudices against the Irish and Scots in their distaste for the man's behaviour. As far as we can tell, all he has said about them is 'here's a likely looking pair', and that '[politely, respectfully]'. The Irish man and his (possibly Irish) companion could be the builders who have been making all the sounds which have dotted the last few pages, but this is only a guess based on the prevalence of itinerant Irish construction workers in Britain before the 1990s boom in Ireland; they could equally be simply standing and having a conversation while others make the building sounds in the background.

The last part of the quoted section begins with quotation marks but these are never closed, suggesting that this text begins in overheard – or imagined? – speech but is interrupted and taken over by the thoughts of the poet/thinker with the words 'stop there'. It is perhaps the effort to construct an all-too-familiar narrative around national identity which the speaker/thinker wants to break off; the imagined or overheard speaker begins with an aggressive rejoinder to the English couple 'ah well, and up yours to with a', and it is perhaps this circularity of predictable prejudice and predictable aggressive response which the speaker confusedly and confusingly interrupts. The only clear part of this following section is the phrase, 'thinking we *know*'; Walsh seems to be critiquing poetry that creates a narrative it presents as known, as understood.

The next section, which returns to the 'green leaf, sound, wheels on pavement' image cluster the poet was working on earlier, suggests that we 'extend bridges of words' instead of extending ourselves. In other words, we pass over the gaps, the indeterminacies and contradictions within language in order to create narratives that make smooth sense. This poetry makes it well-nigh impossible for us to do this; it is not clear, for example, how the final three lines connect with this idea, while the section before 'thinking we *know*' is typically indeterminate, with a lack of punctuation, for example, making us unsure whether we should read 'animate' as an adjective linked to 'poetry' or make a break between these two words. Even when the text seems to reach some kind of certainty at the end of the quoted passage, indicated by the phrase 'that's it', this is undermined by the ambiguity of the final line – does this indicate that 'space is a misnomer' or simply that 'space is'? – and also by the casually disparaging continuation on the next page: 'that. this. thisthat. what, where.' (40).

All in all, the poem presents thought or poetry 'struggling to contend with / a lack'; it presents the gaps in understanding as in themselves interesting and meaningful. In an interview Walsh commented that 'The kind of misunderstandings that crop up are as much a part of our lives and are as important as the understand-ings.'[34] Nevertheless, this text does not limit itself simply to making a point about indeterminacy; there is also a resistance to the 'fenc-ing effect' which language inflicts upon space, and this seems to connect to the narratives of nationalism which Walsh wants to avoid. She seems to want to resist the clarity of being either 'here' or 'there', instead searching for a position 'between two worlds'. At the same time, this section of *idir eatortha* breaks down the bound-aries between internal and external; it is frequently unclear whether words are generated by the poet or overheard. This participates in the wider project associated with experimental poetry (and post-modernism more generally) of undermining the traditional notion of the poet as originating, authoritative voice.

Much of the text of *idir eatortha* looks different on the page from the section quoted above; frequently it is spaced out in a manner influenced by Charles Olson's projective verse. A more typical passage is the following:

> another   in the long lore of
>
> > > traffic
>
> triteness
> > tripping lep
> > too old for this   unwillingness
>
> and too young and too young
> for
>
> > > > before
>
> they even began
>
> > > in every
> > > one   (19)

At times in Walsh's work (as here) one does feel that she errs on the side of too much indeterminacy and achieves only emptiness; the reader, after all, must be given enough *potential* significances to be able to begin to play with multiple and perhaps conflicting meanings. Walsh is known as a wonderful performer of her work, and it may be that the intonation of the voice helps with this problem. But this also creates limits, of course, and the advantage of encountering such work on the page is the reader's freedom to reread and alter her or his interpretations. The difficulty of producing such writing, however, lies in judging just where suggestive indeterminacy slides into a paucity of potential meanings. In the best parts of Walsh's texts, she gets this balance right.

Geraldine Monk

Geraldine Monk was born in 1952 and lives in Sheffield. Along with Caroline Bergvall, Denise Riley, Maggie O'Sullivan and Wendy Mulford, she is one of an increasingly influential group of British experimental women poets. Monk's texts use formal methods associated with experimental or avant-garde poetics, but they often also have a clear theme or context which they develop at length, such as the sequence 'Interregnum', which explores the 'imprisonment and execution of the Pendle Witches [in East Lancashire] in 1612'.[35] Monk's poetry is intense, sensual and startling. She is creative in her use of typography to achieve defamiliarising effects, as in the following short poem 'Return of Dream One***Pendulum', which is part of the sequence 'Long Wake':

> The fish are / dead / lying open / mouthed / I / walk
> village / streetdown / towards / deathwake / cure I /
> have / biscuits soaked in lemon / juicesky sea / at
> mostphere lem / onjuice / the fish / willwake / willmake /
> lively as Scaling / Dam in Spring /
> Above .... lemon .... skyjuice .... swings .... silently ....
> suspended .... a pendulum .... the time .... struggles ....
> it is .... I think .... (*SP*, 6)

The slash – conventionally used to indicate line breaks when quoting poetry – is here used to different effect, with the slashes enacting the fragmentation associated with dream content and, especially, with the attempt upon waking to retrieve a dream. At the same time the slashes are used to create breaks which produce multiplicity of meaning; the slash between 'open' and 'mouthed' means that we can link 'mouthed' either with 'open' or, alternatively, with 'I', achieving the strange phrases, 'The fish are dead lying open' and 'mouthed I walk'. Similar effects are achieved by cleverly worked line breaks, as in the break between 'at' and 'mostphere', with the extra 't' in 'atmosphere' creating a disruptive effect which makes us return again and again to the oddness of this juncture. These effects draw our attention to the materiality of language, making us see words as strangely wrought artifacts of sound and form, but at the same time there are strong, surreal images emerging in the piece: the dead, gaping fish, the lemon sky, the huge suspended pendulum. There is a sense as well of the tension between sleep and waking, an uncertainty over which is associated with death. The switch from slashes to dots in the final three lines suggests the more even, swinging effect of the pendulum and an effort not simply to describe but to work towards interpretation.

I would like to look now at a poem from the sequence 'Latitudes', entitled 'A Eulogy Written in an Unmarked Northern City Pub'. This sequence is tightly structured; the titles of the poems are as follows: 'An Elegy Written in an Unmarked Northern City Graveyard', 'A Eulogy Written in an Unmarked Northern City Pub', 'North Bound: Facing South', 'North', 'South Bound: Facing North', 'South', 'Eulogy in an Unmarked Southern County Graveyard by the Sea', 'An Elegy in an Unmarked Southern County Pub'. This sequence is a good place to start for readers unfamiliar with experimental poetry, as it provides a clear sense of context, obviously setting out to explore the experiential differences between the North and the South of England. The differences in the titles are, of course, crucial; the Southern pub does not elicit a eulogy from the poet, but rather an elegy, and an atmosphere is evoked which is both violent and insular:

> The snug. The warm sickly draught. Of insularity.
> Stagnation. Exclusion. Pick yer winda.
>   Pick any
>   thing
>   to throw and smash the
>   winged and
>   wounded.
>   Dragon.
>   Fly. (*SP*, 96)

In contrast, the Northern pub elicits a celebration:

> It is night. Or. It is day. It is timeless.
> Sporadic fighting breaks. Is quickly quelled.
> All things considered. Proximity excites. Generating passion.

Desirability. To have contact. To consume. To drink deep.
Long. Soft. Hard. Break and.
Soak.
Bread.

Green light from shaded pool. Tables of time without tide.
The lilt of tower blocks with awakenings in the sky or
hibernations entrenched in basement undergrowths.
Rarely at street level. Few wise. Most nibble and peck.
Nuts.
Seeds.

It is see-saw-jig-saw.
　　　　　Endless pieces. Parties of choice. And much.
　　　　　Wet squelch littered. Concrete. Jolly kiss o' life.
　　　　　Painted paddock. Balls. Bells. Tail backs. Feathers.
　　　　　Dashes. Exhausts. Upside. Turnaround. Roundabout.
Let's take away.
Buttercross.
Hot fried fishes.

It is still night. It is still day. It is moving. Timeless.
The traffic.
The cues.
The ebb and flow and chink of glasses.
The spills.
The queues.

All jam. All runny.
Cherry cake. (*SP*, 89)

The simple use of 'fishes' instead of 'fish', and the use of 'Break'
with 'Bread' in the first section, suggest together both the Biblical
parable of the loaves and the fishes *and* the communion ritual of
breaking bread together. The allusion to the parable of the loaves
and the fishes helps to produce the sense of abundance; in this
Northern pub life is overflowing. Even the towerblocks 'lilt',
while the pool-table is spoken of in terms suggesting shady tropical
warmth. Where the Southern pub is characterised by exclusive-
ness, this Northern pub is all about inclusiveness and the excitement of being together, an excitement that has an erotic element to
it. The scene is jumbled and unruly, 'see-saw-jig-saw', a proliferation of sense-impressions in which everything is incorporated.

Even 'Wet squelch littered' and 'Concrete' are incorporated into this celebration of the actual. This poem does not incorporate many defamiliarising techniques; in fact, formally, it is relatively conservative. However, the very first line marks the poem out as experimental; not many mainstream writers would construct the 'or' in this way. It is this kind of disruption of ordinary conventions of syntax (also seen in the phrase 'Break and.') that Monk uses to jolt the reader into seeing things differently. In the case of the first line, the phrase 'It is night. Or. It is day.' makes the reader stop and feel the symmetry and the undecidability of these two possibilities in a way which 'It is night or it is day' would not.

Nostalgia for the North is seen as dangerous in 'North Bound: Facing South'; the way in which 'Alchemical minds' can turn 'cold boreal winters to molten / gold'[36] and give them 'The lick of Eden' is 'Dangerous magic' (90). But although the North is presented as rough and at times harsh – 'Even love is flung / gathering in the throat's pit / a stomach's empty growl' ('North', 91) – it is never described with the antipathy which the South elicits: 'All narrowness. All fear' ('South', 93). The only positive evocation of a Southern scene is found in 'Eulogy in an Unmarked Southern County Graveyard by the Sea', but even this celebration of the Southern coast ('Feet deep on a warm summers day. / Skipping tussocks' (94)) is shadowed by a sense of deathly oppression within life: 'opposition to life is / massive and sustained' (95).

However, any attempt to draw out phrases from these poems radically diminishes their complexity, since Monk's poems gain much of their effect from the subtle interactions of phrases juxtaposed and jostling against each other. In the following section from 'Eulogy in an Unmarked Southern County Graveyard by the Sea', the verb 'sucks' gets its ominous quality in this context from the closeness of 'rictus' and 'skeletal':

Skeletal craft. Skimming. Sea lap.
Harbour lips. Rictus. Kiss.
Sucks slowly.
Sucks.
Gulls. (94)

There are also moments that seem overwhelmingly resistant to interpretation, as in the phrase immediately subsequent to this: 'Growth gang. Ging and. Blue chipped. Marble.' (94). Moments like this, where individual words seem to resist meaning, are unusual in this sequence; more often we are challenged by our desire to find connections between different words, phrases, or sections. But these poems challenge without frustrating the reader, because they are full of strange images and striking phrases; these lines, for instance, are more arresting than most in contemporary poetry:

the thick hiss and prodding fingers
of sun and subways
                    long
and burn for damp bronchial skies (92)

If one continuum of difference between 'mainstream' and 'experimental' poetries is the extent to which experimental poetry works to prevent the reader from slipping into the role of passive, admiring consumer, do lines like this actually allow this to happen? Alone, they might, but in context they do not; from the quoted lines we move on immediately to the following phrases, which we perhaps struggle to link with the established subway imagery before letting this image go and working on new possibilities:

Listen: on the downwind
            wheezing amphibians
        full   fuff   fuff
wet-glass-hoppers
crawl and cluck (92)

Monk's language is always *interesting*, meaning that even when we are perplexed and troubled by her poetry, we are simultaneously intrigued, compelled and drawn along in the poetry's audacious linguistic adventures.

Peter Reading

In America in the 1990s, the 'New Formalism' was championed by a group of poets who believed that free verse had become so dominant in the United States that there was a need to champion a return to traditional metrics and rhyme. In Britain and Ireland free verse has never been so dominant as in the States, and there has been a greater variety of approaches to form reflected in mainstream poetry. Nevertheless, the problem the New Formalists are seeking to respond to in American poetry is sometimes also seen in British and Irish poetry; at times poets writing in free verse (i.e. poetry which does not adhere to traditional formal patterns such as metre and rhyme) seem to ignore not only metre and rhyme, but form altogether. As Marjorie Perloff says,

> No doubt, the New Formalists do have a genuine grievance against the dominant lyric mode of the seventies and eighties, with its repetitive dwelling on delicate insight and 'sensitive' response, its nostalgia for the 'natural', and its excessive reliance on simulated speech and breath pause as determinants of line breaks and verse structure.[37]

Here I am primarily interested in the last phrase – the 'excessive reliance on simulated speech and breath pause as determinants of line breaks and verse structure'. As indicated by the fact that this quotation comes from Marjorie Perloff, one of the foremost critics and promoters of avant-garde poetry in the United States, the New Formalists and the avant-garde or experimental poets, while they may seem opposed in many ways, have in common their interest in form, and together they stand against the kind of free verse poetry which tends simply to imitate speech rhythms and gains little from being laid out on the page like a poem. While the New Formalists counter this with a return to traditional forms (and a tendency towards narrative rather than lyric), experimental or avant-garde poets respond with more varied procedures, often (but not always) connected with how the poem looks as text on the page (Raworth's columns, Monk's use of slashes, Walsh's scattered lines).

Peter Reading is a surprising figure because he uses both of these strategies. Born in 1946 in Liverpool, and now living in Ludlow, Shropshire, he is not part of the experimental poetry scene in Britain, and while he is often seen as something of an outsider in general, he has always been published by major publishers, has frequently reviewed poetry for major publications like the *TLS*, has a devoted if not vast readership, and has won major prizes. Reading trained as a visual artist, and his work reflects an interest in the visual aspects of the text, incorporating various different typefaces and layouts, handwritten sections, cut and pasted documents, diagrams, and crossed-out type. He is also extremely unusual among contemporary poets in his wide-ranging approach to prosody. In his twenty-five separate collections (beginning with *Water and Waste*, 1970), Reading ranges between syllabic, classical and stress metres; he writes alliterative verse in the Old English style, haiku and tankas. He has had particular success in approximating (in English stress-based metre) classical quantitative metres like the dactylic (heroic) hexameter, the Alcaic stanza, the Alcmanic stanza and the elegiac distich. Sometimes he sticks very closely to these metrical forms, and at other times he bends and blends them to create his own forms, what Isabel Martin calls his 'metra episyntheta'.[38]

Reading's 1989 collection *Perduta Gente* is one of his most interesting in formal terms, and one of his most successful overall. It presents a collage-like collection of texts: poems, handwritten diary excerpts, fragments of newspaper clippings and official documents, and prose sections. The world Reading evokes is grim; the central scenes are of the homeless, the 'perduta gente' or lost people, the derelict who are constantly shoved off from every place of shelter. In his descriptions of this lifestyle there is no shrinking back from its despair and squalor; one of the handwritten diary entries reads as follows:

> terribly sick with her meths, but who kept on and on vomiting through the night, but with nothing left to sick up (the front of her scraggy overcoat covered in the methsy, vegetable-soupy slime – the stench abominable) so that between honks she screamed horribly. The only sleep we got was after one of the old hands dragged her off, still screaming, and dumped her in the alley round the corner where the dustbins are. Today is <u>Monday</u>: in St. Botolph's crypt they give out free clothes to us[39] (for layout see original)

These scenes are juxtaposed with advertisements for top-range properties ('London's most exciting apartments all have river views, £330,000 to £865,000' (*CP2*, 161)) which emphasise the social and economic chasms in Thatcher's Britain, as does the fact that many of the homeless people live *under* the Royal Festival Hall while above them the more fortunate attend cultural events in warmth and comfort.

Parallel to this, Reading gives us another story, the story of a cover-up by the government of the dangers posed to workers and to the public by a damaged nuclear plant and by the transporting of nuclear materials through London. These two narratives are linked by a Russian scene which presents homeless people who have been afflicted by radiation from Chernobyl, and they are also linked through the figure of 'the poet'. The poet himself is homeless as he writes the poems included in *Perduta Gente*, and he is given secret documents about the effects of radiation illness from a physicist who, himself having 'ad a radio dose' (184) and got into trouble for leaking information about nuclear dangers to the media, also becomes jobless and homeless. The various strands are also linked (and clarified) by the writings of a biographer or literary critic who is apparently writing about the poet after his death, having gained access to all his papers. This writer declares that the fact that the poet himself was homeless

> seems to have concentrated his notion of the 'slurry-wallowing degraded dispossessed' as a metaphor for all of *H. sapiens* involuntarily subjected to that other 'excreta' and thereby, irrespective of position in society, dispossessed of (191)

Here the prose section is cut off. The fact that we only get fragments of the critic/biographer's text indicates that, within the fiction of the piece, *Perduta Gente* cannot be read as having been put together in this form by the critic/biographer, but must have been compiled by a third person. Peter Reading is at once this compiler and the (deceased) poet-figure who writes the diary fragments and the poems. This poet figure is deliberately blurred with the real-life Reading when the critic/biographer refers to the 'author's last review', and goes on to quote from a review which Peter Reading had in fact recently published of Maggie Gee's novel *Grace* (1988).[40] Even before *Perduta Gente*, Reading's poetry had shown a tendency to announce the poet's own imminent death or silence, and this would become a stronger and stronger motif as the collections, nevertheless, continued to pile up.

Both Dante's *Inferno* and Old Testament prophecies are echoed in the poet's words as he circles his own particular hell,[41] adding complexity to the debate over whether the poet actually embraces a pure fatalism and despair or whether his writing emerges out of some belief in the possibility of change. I do not have space to enter these debates here,[42] as I want to focus instead on the significance of Reading's formal strategies in the context of the debate over experimentalism. *Perduta Gente* is radical in its juxtaposition of classical metres with materials like advertisements and prose diary entries. As Isabel Martin notes, the collection uses the elegiac distich as the 'point of reference of the increasingly independent metres in this volume', but the 'weighty single hemiepes' (a fragment of the elegiac distich) is 'all pervasive'.[43] The following triplet, for example, consists of three hemiepes:

> After a gobble of meths,
> crunch up a Trebor Mint fast –
> takes off the heat and the taste. (203)

If any poet truly deserves the epithet 'experimental', with its implications of newness and originality, Reading is surely a candidate, because of his strikingly original combination of strategies derived from visual art, traditional verse, and postmodern poetics.

In terms of the treatment of narrative and of the self, however, we do note a clear difference between Reading's work and that of poets conventionally identified as 'experimental', like Raworth, Walsh and Monk. In *Perduta Gente* we are at first confronted with a confusing juxtaposition of fragmented texts, but as we read on (and certainly on a second reading) the connections become clear, and it is possible to construct a narrative to frame events, and to ascribe authorship of the various texts to certain personae. The 'I' present in the poems in *Perduta Gente* is complex. In the cases where there is no obvious dramatic monologue and when we might be tempted to feel we are hearing the voice of the 'author', the voice often seems to expand to a generalised voice of lament ('Gone are the youthfully beautiful whom I / loved in my nonage' (171)), or to avoid the 'I' by moving into the second person ('though their / glee was authentic / when you disburdened yourself / of that frayed ten-dinar note' (179)). At other times the voice shifts between the 'we' of the homeless and the 'we' of humanity:

> sometimes it seems like a terrible dream, in
>   which we are crouching
>   gagged, disregarded, unsought
>   in dosshouses, derries and spikes,
>   and from which we shall awake,
>
>   mostly, it seems, though, we won't. (180)

The only poem which has a straightforward 'I' is an apparent rec-
ollection from childhood; the speaker tells of experience as a child
in tormenting a gipsy woman who lived in a caravan near his
home. But this poem is so unusual in the collection that we are
unsure to whom it should be ascribed; within the fictional
narrative it must be authored by the homeless poet-figure and
may be his memory, but it seems to float free as if urging readers
to remember their own experiences of childhood distrust of and
even cruelty to the vulnerable. Many of the poems achieve a paradoxical sense of being both distanced and profoundly involved;
this is helped by the use of the language of Old Testament
prophecy with its tone of detached intensity.

The authorial self, then, is remarkably elusive and wily in
Reading's work. As if to assert this again, his most recent collection, which has as its title the marginal mark for delete, ends with
the single word 'I', crossed out in red ink with a red handwritten
delete mark next to it.[44] We are certainly never presented with the
kind of relatively direct autobiographical presentation that we see
in, for example, Seamus Heaney, Michael Longley, Jackie Kay or
Moniza Alvi. When intensely personal material *is* incorporated
into the poems, as in the section in *Stet* that deals with the death
of Reading's childhood friend Michael Donahue, the asides are
vicious:

> wants⎤
> [Who do you think you are whining to? No reader shares⎦ your
>   bereavement
>   and it's pathetic and mad to address yourself to the dead.]
>   (CP2, 104)

While Reading may at times seem to be similar to Muldoon in his
game-playing over the idea of the authorial self, the above quotation reveals the difference between them; despite the parodies and
slipperiness, Reading's poetry has, finally, a fierce earnestness
about it which Muldoon's does not. Reading does believe, as
Martin puts it, that 'the personal ego [is] best eliminated from the
writing process,'[45] and rather more than in Muldoon's case,
Reading's rejection of poetry as self-expression emerges from an
ethical and political position about the importance of looking out-
wards towards others. In this sense he has some motivation in
common with the experimental community. However, Reading

does not foreground the question of the construction of the self. Despite his use of radically diverse discourses his emphasis is not on the idea of the self's construction through language but, in a humanist sense, on the diversity of people and the range of linguistic and conceptual resources on which they draw in order to combat – and express – the sense of life's cruelty and hopelessness. Reading's middle-period collections (including *Perduta Gente*) tend to have a dramatic quality which emphasises character and voice; his later work has moved away from this a little and towards collections which are linked more by tone, theme and intertextuality than by plot or character. But Reading's poetry does not problematise the nature of the self as such; it takes the potential of the self to experience both individuality and community as a premise, and moves on to explore the scope and limits of the human capacity for both despair and hope. The fact that Reading continues to write, despite endless declarations of futility, imminent silence, and death, is his crucial, self-dramatising enactment of the compulsion to continue living and creating. As it is put by Viv from *Ukelele Music* (one of the many Reading characters who, on the verge of being parodied, also represent a commitment to survival and hope which he takes utterly seriously), *'well you has to LIVE don't you? / that's what I think, any road'*(CP2, 45).

Patience Agbabi

'Performance poetry' today reaches audiences which page-based poetry hardly even hopes to appeal to. Poetry slams draw huge young audiences, attracted in part by the overlaps between performance poetry and contemporary musical genres like rap and hip-hop. Of course, the easy classification of poets into two groups, 'performance' and 'page-based', has its problems, as it may limit our capacity to view a particular poet's work in various different ways. Nevertheless, the distinction does emerge out of important differences, and these differences are rarely given the critical attention they deserve. Too often, the judgment that a poem 'doesn't work on the page' is used as sufficient reason to dismiss a poem critically. But as Kwame Dawes points out, this reveals a double standard, as critics rarely dismiss a 'book poem' as a bad poem just because it doesn't work in performance.[46] In fact, the tolerance which audiences at conventional poetry readings extend towards poetry which either is manifestly impossible to perform effectively, or is simply appallingly read, is barely credible. To any reader of poetry who has attended far too many such events, the advent of poets who take performance really seriously, and whose work is in fact primarily, or at least equally, directed towards the performance context, is restorative and refreshing. There is a clear need for criticism which recognises the different aims, influences, demands and skills of poetry which is oriented around performance. While we should not think of the two kinds of poetry as mutually exclusive – clearly some poetry which is written primarily for performance does 'work' on the page, and vice versa, and some poets (Tom Leonard and Grace Nichols, for example) are equally respected in both contexts – the tendency for performance poetry to be denigrated is connected to the lack of a real appreciation of the artistry involved in writing and performing a really impressive performance poem.

As Kwame Dawes says, it also cannot be divorced from 'the politics of race and ethnicity which undergirds much of the relationship between "street poetry" and "book poetry" '.[47] Many of the most well-known practitioners of performance poetry are black, or non-white, and they often derive influence and inspiration from musical and oral literary traditions which are perhaps non-Western, or 'popular' and oppositional (reggae, rap). In this context the dismissal of the poetry as (for example) *not complex enough* takes its place in a long tradition of colonialist discourse. However, we do have to be careful not to make our description of performance poetry too narrow. Ruth Harrison comments that Apples & Snakes, which was founded to support and promote performance poetry, is commonly identified with black poetry, when it was actually trying to be much broader:

> people disregarded anything else that the organisation did, and what it was trying to put forward: the idea of performance poetry as being a very broad church, going from the very abstract poets like Bob Cobbing, all the way through to John Hegley, going right across the spectrum.[48]

The mention of the sound poet Bob Cobbing reminds us that the interest in the potential of sound, in the role of the body, in technology, and in breaking down the borders between different media and art forms are in fact points of connection between the most popular performance poets (Linton Kwesi Johnson, for example) and those associated with experimental modernist poetics.[49] Performance poetry is as diverse and varied as page poetry and it is important for a criticism to develop which reflects this; in the round-table discussion between Patience Agbabi, Jean Binta Breeze, Jillian Tipene, Vicki Bertram and Ruth Harrison, all the poets expressed a desire for more and better criticism of their work.

Patience Agbabi was born in London in 1965 to Nigerian parents, and was fostered to a white family in Sussex and Wales. She established a reputation as a performer before publishing in book form, but soon felt the pressure to publish:

> … it came to a stage where there were certain poems which were so popular that people were coming up to me with money … I didn't have a book and that was painful. And so, since then, the book's sold well, so it does work on the page.[50]

The book in question is *R.A.W.*, Agbabi's first, rap-influenced collection, published in 1995. *Transformatrix* was published in 2000, and in 2004 Agbabi was named as one of the Next Generation poets in the Poetry Society's promotion. Agbabi has commented that she does not like the rigid divide between performance and page-based poetry, and the 'Prologue' to *Transformatrix* makes it clear that she will do her best to break this down:

> Give me a stage and I'll cut form on it
> give me a page and I'll perform on it[51]

There is no reason why we should expect poetry that is oriented towards performance to work as well on the page; many people use a book simply as a trigger to help them remember and relive the experience of the poetry in performance. Many of Agbabi's poems are like this; if one encountered them on the page without having seen her perform them they would be interesting but certainly not nearly as effective as they are either in performance, or with Agbabi's voice and movements replaying in the imagination as they are read.

There are exceptions, however; Agbabi has consistently shown an interest in the visual aspects of form in her books, so that some poems are dependent on their physical appearance on the page for much of their effectiveness; for instance, 'Accidentally Falling' (written in the shape of a bottle), 'My Mother' (written in two columns separate and then merging to imply the separation and then unification of mother and daughter), and 'E (Manic Dance Mix A)' (set out in rectangles of text), 'Miss First World' (using columns and different typefaces), and '1996' from 'Weights and Measures and Finding a Rhyme for Orange' (set out in five vertical columns of text). Furthermore, there are poems whose conceptual complexity generously rewards the more extended attention of the reading process; 'Ufo Woman' and 'Ajax' from *Transformatrix* are examples of this. *Transformatrix* also contains a set of seven sestinas that work equally well, but differently, on the page and in performance. These sestinas are an impressive feat because all seven use the same six end-words but each has a radically different tone and setting. Because there is considerable enjambement, one would expect the sestina form to be less obvious in performance than on the page, but Agbabi's subtle emphasis on the end-words allows her to convey the hypnotic, circling quality of the sestina powerfully.

It is, however, important to convey a sense of the power of the poems that *do* very clearly make their greatest impact in performance. These include many of the early poems from *R.A.W.*, which Agbabi has been performing to appreciative audiences for years. A poem like 'Sex Is' is one of the most popular of these. A rapping meditation, sometimes lyrical and sometimes satirical, on the different things that sex means to different people, 'Sex Is' gains its power from Agbabi's distinctive style of performance. Using hand movements to emphasise the rhythm, Agbabi performs without reference to a text, keeping eye contact with the audience.[52] Here is the chorus:

> *Some like it with a he*
> *Some like it with a she*
> *some like to use the four-letter words*
> *and LOVE is a many splendoured thing*
> *but some like to stick to three and*
> *some like it O.T.T.*
> *some like to kiss*
> *sex is   sex is*[53]

Rhythmical musical notation would seem more useful than traditional poetic notation, as it indicates temporal values. Much of the effect in the performance of this poem is achieved not by stress but by lengthening certain syllables. In the first two lines, for instance, the word 'like' takes about twice as long as any of the other syllables, and this is a pattern that is repeated throughout the poem, giving it a syncopated feeling. The dominant rhythm, then, in musical notation, is:

The crucial central phrase 'sex is   sex is' achieves its syncopation through lengthening of the second 'is' and a pause after the first. Another prominent phrase is 'love is a many splendoured thing', which stands out in the poem not simply because of its surprising diction but because of its different rhythm and the more lilting tone of voice which Agbabi uses for this line. The poem moves on quickly; the rhythm and rhyme carry us along, and no line is intended to be a site for intense scrutiny and analysis. The listener is captivated by the poem's sounds and its quickness of thought, as it moves from celebration ('Sex is a thing you think of / when you're feeling warm and free') to satirical comedy ('some like it in / some like it out / some like in out in out / and think that that's what it's all about') to serious anger ('sex is an excuse to be a sexist / sex is an excuse to be a rapist') (*R*, 56–7). Agbabi's precisely modulated voice and expressive face and hands are a crucial part of her performance.

The page-poem looks pallid in comparison to its twin in performance, but it would be madness to assert that this lessens its value as poetry. Poets like Agbabi are revitalising something that has, to a large extent, been lost or marginalised in Western culture: the power of the poem as a specifically oral phenomenon. With this comes another dimension; the interface between poetry and drama. Poets who emphasise performance over the page are more likely to incorporate gestures and movement into their performances and to work hard at perfecting accents, something Agbabi does for certain of her impressive dramatic monologues, such as 'The Wife of Bafa', which demands a Nigerian accent. Music and visual effects can also be incorporated into the performance, as Agbabi has done in the past. Performance poetry allows us to let go of the idea that poetry is contained on the page and sealed off from other art forms, and to consider instead the ways in which poetry can work dynamically with different media and modes of expression.

Performance poetry also questions, of course, the poststructuralist-generated emphasis on the text and suspicion of the implied immediacy and authenticity of the spoken word. The feeling of authentic and direct speech is certainly one of the effects which performance poets powerfully exploit; many of the political poems in *R.A.W.* have the feeling of a passionate outburst of self-assertion. But this is only one of Agbabi's styles; more commonly she uses dramatic monologues and other such devices to create ironic distance between 'speaker' and performer. In many cases the audience is left feeling unsettled and unsure about the relationship between poet and character. But after Agbabi's performances the audience *is* left with a sense of personal connection with the poet, a sense that some kind of positive and enlivening bond between audience and poet has been achieved on an interpersonal level. This is a feeling that some forms of poststructuralism would perhaps distrust but which audiences everywhere seem to find energising, stimulating and profoundly satisfying.

Conclusion

Despite the range and diversity of the poetry presented in this chapter, every poet included pays a particular and intense attention to the effects of form, whether these effects are visual or aural in their dimensions. The variety of poetry that we see in this chapter, in formal and conceptual terms, is a powerful reminder of the dangers of the kinds of good–bad dichotomies that are all too often aggressively maintained by criticism. In particular, the effort to defend the mainstream against experimental and marginal poetic practices is dangerous in that it may lead to certain poets being accepted or even lauded purely because they are non-threatening, while poets who challenge our idea of what contemporary poetry is are not even read. Of course it is natural to have preferences as a poetry reader, and it would be rather too teacherly to insist that people should *always* allow these preferences to be challenged; after all, poetry *is* about pleasure as well as all those other more fashionable things such as self-questioning. However, new and unfamiliar forms of poetry often do require time and attention before their ways of working become comprehensible and pleasurable to the reader, and a literary discourse which dismisses a whole body of poetry out of hand discourages people from even taking the time to explore. In the case of performance poetry the issue is rather different, as audiences are in many cases easily captivated by the pleasure of the poetry; the issue is instead the relegation of this poetry to the margins in the public discourse of literary criticism and in the teaching of poetry at a tertiary level. As poetry slams and other 'spoken word' events become more popular there is a tendency among literary critics to rush to defend 'real poetry' against the populist version, but poets like Agbabi who speak to both worlds, writing sestinas and performing in rap groups, show that the gulf is not as wide as it might appear. Given the pace of globalisation and the strength of oral forms among non-Western cultures as well as in popular culture in the West, it seems likely that in the next few decades we will witness a rediscovery or reinvigoration of the art of performance by poets in the West.

Notes

1 These books include, most recently: Keith Tuma, *Fishing by Obstinate Isles: Modern and Postmodern British Poetry and American Readers* (Evanston, IL: Northwestern University Press, 1998); Keith Tuma (ed.), *Anthology of Twentieth-Century British and Irish Poetry* (New York: Oxford University Press, 2001); Andrew Duncan, *The Failure of Conservatism in British Poetry* (Cambridge: Salt, 2003); Alex Davis, *A Broken Line: Denis Devlin and Irish Poetic Modernism* (Dublin: University College Dublin Press, 2000); John Goodby, *Irish Poetry Since 1950: From Stillness into History* (Manchester: Manchester University Press, 2000). The fight-back by experimental poets and sympathetic critics began, however, in the late eighties and the nineties with books such as: Andrew Crozier and Tim Longville (eds), *A Various Art* (Manchester: Carcanet, 1987); Gillian Allnutt, Fred D'Aguiar, Ken Edwards and Eric Mottram (eds), *The New British Poetry 1968–1988* (London: Paladin, 1988); Robert Hampson and Peter Barry (eds), *New British Poetries: The Scope of the Possible* (Manchester: Manchester University Press, 1993); Iain Sinclair, *Conductors of Chaos* (London: Picador, 1996); Richard Caddel and Peter Quartermain (eds), *Other: British and Irish Poetry Since 1970* (Hanover, NE: Wesleyan University Press, 1999).

2 *Poetry Review* and the Poetry Society figure strongly in the mythologised history of experimental poetry in Britain, as recounted for example by Eric Mottram in his essay 'The British poetry revival' in Hampson and Barry's *New British Poetries*. Mottram was editor of *Poetry Review* from 1971 to 1976 and during those years the experimental poetry scene experienced a period

of growth, activity and positive exposure. This ended when the Arts Council, objecting to the direction taken by *Poetry Review*, managed to force changes in the membership of the Poetry Society council. One of the current editors of *Poetry Review*, Robert Potts, comments that 'The split does go back to the 60s/70s. But I imagine many young poets today barely know the ins and outs of that history; they have inherited a situation where the division is so long established, they merely see it as orthodox.' Email to author, 21 October 2004.

3 Robert Potts and David Herd hand the editorship of *Poetry Review* over to Fiona Sampson in summer 2005.

4 Email to author, 21 October 2004.

5 Don Paterson and Charles Simic (eds), *New British Poetry* (Saint Paul, MN: Graywolf Press, 2004), p. xxv.

6 Ibid., p. xxiii.

7 Debates over the relative merits of the two terms 'avant-garde' and 'experimental' are common, with discussions of 'avant-garde' often centering around the relationship of current poetry to the early modernist avant-garde, represented by Dada, surrealism and artists like Duchamp. Peter Bürger's theory of the necessary demise of avant-gardism is frequently cited. Because I do not have time to go into arguments about the continuity or discontinuity of contemporary experimental poetry with the historical twentieth-century avant-garde, I have opted mostly to use the term 'experimental' instead of 'avant-garde'. Even this term is problematic, since it implies that *all* poets practising so-called linguistically oriented poetry are in fact *experimenting* constantly (i.e. trying out new things) and that no other poets are. This is clearly unsatisfactory since the 'experimental' scene is itself now part of a tradition – an 'avant-garde tradition', however paradoxical that phrase may sound. *As a group*, these poets are distinguishable from the mainstream by difference, but not absolute newness. Nevertheless, I have used 'experimental' throughout this chapter as a shorthand way of indicating the group of poets who are frequently identified as experimental, avant-garde, linguistically oriented, formally innovative, and so on.

8 Charles Bernstein, 'Artifice of absorption' (1987), in *A Poetics* (Cambridge, MA: Harvard University Press, 1992), pp. 9–89.

9 Peter Riley, one of the Cambridge-associated British experimentalists, says that the poem exists 'as an object between poet and reader which is both a means of communication and a barrier to communication'. From Riley's *Distant Points (Excavations Part One Books One and Two)* (London: Reality Street Editions, 1995). Quoted by Keith Tuma in *Fishing*, p. 220.

10 Charles Bernstein and Bruce Andrews (eds), *The Language Book* (Carbondale and Edwardsville, IL: Southern Illinois Press, 1984), pp. ix–x.

11 John Matthias notes that Riley is the only poet to be included in all three of the following anthologies: Sinclair's *Conductors of Chaos*, Caddel and Quartermain's *Other*, and Simon Armitage and Robert Crawford's *Penguin Book of Poetry from Britain and Ireland* (London: Viking, 1998). The first two are anthologies focusing on marginalised experimental work, and the third is much more mainstream. See Section 1 of 'British Poetry at Y2K', in the online journal *ebr*, no. 10 (2000), www.altx.com/ebr/ebr10/10mat/matbody1.htm, accessed 15 September 2004.

12 Andrew Michael Roberts, 'The rhetoric of value in recent British poetry anthologies', in *Poetry and Contemporary Culture: The Question of Value*, ed. Andrew Michael Roberts and Jonathan Allison (Edinburgh: Edinburgh University Press, 2002), pp. 101–22 (pp. 114–15).

13 Caddel and Quartermain, *Other*, p. xv.

14 Paranoia is apparent on both sides, and John Matthias captures one half of it neatly when he says that 'The problem among the *Others* and the *Conductors* is in part their unwillingness to understand that Simon Armitage and Robert Crawford are not Rupert Murdoch and Bill Gates.' See Section 1 of 'British Poetry at Y2K'.

15 Tuma, *Fishing by Obstinate Isles*, pp. 1, 3.

16 Ibid., pp. 19–20.

17 Andrew Duncan, 'The invisible museum', *Poetry Review*, vol. 92, no. 2 (2002), pp. 83–7. Duncan also takes Tuma to task for various exclusions, but his critique comes from the opposite side of the fence from O'Brien's.

18 Sean O'Brien, 'Bizarro's Bounty', *Poetry Review*, vol. 91, no. 2 (2001), pp. 109–10.

19 Tuma, *Fishing*, p. 208.

20 Ibid., p. 205.

21 Davis, *A Broken Line*, p. x.

22 Catherine Walsh, interview in *Prospect into Breath: Interviews with North and South Writers*, ed. Peterjon Skelt (Twickenham: North and South, 1991), pp. 171–89 (p. 188).

23 Alex Davis, who is very sympathetic to the 'neo-avant-garde', as he terms it, admits that 'The Irish neo-avant-garde poets may be seen to court accusations of wilful peripheralism in their admittedly overstated attacks on the hidebound traditionalism of modern Irish poetry, as they choose to depict it.' Davis, *A Broken Line*, p. 176.

24 Ibid., p. 176.

25 Goodby, *Irish Poetry*, p. 301.

26 Tom Raworth, *Collected Poems* (Manchester: Carcanet, 2003), p. 138. Henceforth referred to as *CP*.

27 William Wootten, 'Seeing through walls', *Guardian*, 22 March 2003, http://books.guardian.co.uk/review/story/0,12084,918470,00.html, accessed 21 September 2004.

28 Mark Rotella, 'Review of *Other: British and Irish Poetry Since 1970*', *Publishers Weekly*, vol. 245, no. 48, p. 67.

29 Tom Raworth, *That More Simple Natural Time Tone Distortion* (Storrs, CT: printed for a reading at University of Connecticut Library, 1975). This was an earlier and shorter version of the poem.

30 Email to author, 15 May 2005.

31 Kit Robinson, 'Tom Raworth', in *Dictionary of Literary Biography*, vol. 40, ed. Vincent B. Sherry, Jr (Detroit: Gale Research, 1985), pp. 459–68 (p. 467). Quoted by Tuma, *Fishing*, p. 234.

32 Davis, *A Broken Line*, p. 173.

33 Catherine Walsh, *idir eatortha and making tents* (London: Invisible Books, 1996), p. 39. Henceforth referred to as *ie*.

34 Catherine Walsh, interview in *Prospect into Breath*, p. 184.

35 Geraldine Monk, *Selected Poems* (Cambridge: Salt, 2003), p. 235. Henceforth referred to as *SP*.

36 Forward slashes are here used in the conventional way to indicate line breaks in the original text.

37 Marjorie Perloff, *Radical Artifice: Writing Poetry in the Age of Media* (Chicago: University of Chicago Press, 1991), p. 3.

38 Readers interested in further pursuing Reading's use of metre should consult Isabel Martin's impressive critical book, *Reading Peter Reading* (Newcastle: Bloodaxe, 2000).

39 Peter Reading, *Collected Poems 2: 1985–1996* (Newcastle upon Tyne: Bloodaxe, 1996), p. 164. Henceforth referred to as *CP2*.

40 Martin, *Reading Peter Reading*, p. 194.

41 The title comes from the words inscribed above the Gates of Hell in Dante's *Inferno*:

> Per me si va nella città dolente
> Per me si va nel eterno dolore
> Per me si va tra la perduta gente

Or, in Dorothy Sayers's English translation:

> Through me the road to the city of desolation;
> Through me the road to sorrows diuturnal;
> Through me the road among the lost creation.

The Divine Comedy, trans. Dorothy Sayers, vol. 1 (London: Penguin, 1949), p. 85.

42 Readers interested in pursuing the question of the political implications of Reading's work should look at the section on Reading in Sean O'Brien's *The Deregulated Muse*, in which he argues that Reading's poetry 'leaves a huge hole where causality ought to be' (*The Deregulated Muse: Essays on Contemporary British and Irish Poetry* (Newcastle upon Tyne: Bloodaxe, 1998), p. 131). One brief response can be found in Section 3 of John Matthias's 'British Poetry at Y2K'. See also the chapter on Peter Reading in David Kennedy's *New Relations: The Refashioning of British Poetry 1980–1994* (Bridgend: Seren, 1996), pp. 120–52.

43 Martin, *Reading Peter Reading*, pp. 191–2. Elegiac distich consists of a line of dactylic hexameter followed by a line made up of two hemiepes divided by a caesura. A single hemiepes is as follows –uu –uu –.

44 Peter Reading, *Collected Poems 3: 1997–2003* (Newcastle upon Tyne: Bloodaxe, 2003), p. 310.

45 Martin, *Reading Peter Reading*, p. 12.

46 Kwame Dawes, 'Dichotomies of reading "street poetry" and "book poetry" ', *Critical Quarterly*, vol. 38, no. 4 (1996), pp. 3–20 (p. 19).

47 Ibid., p. 3.

48 Jean Binta Breeze, Patience Agbabi, Jillian Tipene, Ruth Harrison and Vicki Bertram, 'A round-table discussion on poetry in performance', *Feminist Review*, no. 62 (1999), pp. 24–54 (p. 43).

49 Paul Beasley makes this point in 'Vive la différence! Performance poetry', *Critical Quarterly*, vol. 38, no. 4 (1996), pp. 28–38 (p. 37). Beasley also sees

connections on the level of the use of 'mantric, chant and incantatory forms' (p. 38).

50 Agbabi in 'A round-table discussion', p. 29.

51 Patience Agbabi, *Transformatrix* (Edinburgh: Payback Press, 2000), p. 11. Henceforth referred to as *T*.

52 My comments here are based on two performances of this poem which I have attended. Obviously every performance differs, and Agbabi may present this poem very differently in other contexts.

53 Patience Agbabi, *R.A.W.* (London: Izon Amazon, 1995), p. 56. Henceforth referred to as *R*.

Select Bibliography

Primary texts

This list covers the poetry, verse drama, libretti and film poems published by the poets discussed in this book, including significant pamphlets. It does not include poetry for children, or writings in other genres. In cases where authors have published a number of pamphlets, translations and so on, *and* where it is possible to make a clear distinction between 'major' poetry collections and other works, the titles of the major collections have an asterisk (*) at the beginning of the entry. In some cases it is not possible to make such distinctions.

Patience Agbabi

R.A.W. (London: Izon Amazon, 1995)
Transformatrix (Edinburgh: Payback Press, 2000)

Moniza Alvi

The Country at My Shoulder (Oxford: Oxford University Press, 1993)
A Bowl of Warm Air (Oxford: Oxford University Press, 1996)
Carrying my Wife (Newcastle upon Tyne: Bloodaxe, 2000)
Souls (Tarset: Bloodaxe, 2002)
How the Stone Found Its Voice (Tarset: Bloodaxe, 2005)

Simon Armitage

Zoom! (Newcastle upon Tyne: Bloodaxe, 1989)
Around Robinson (Nottingham: Slow Dancer, 1991)
Kid (London: Faber, 1992)
Xanadu (Newcastle upon Tyne: Bloodaxe, 1992)
Book of Matches (London: Faber, 1993)
The Dead Sea Poems (London: Faber, 1995)
CloudCuckooLand (London: Faber, 1997)
Killing Time (London: Faber, 1999)
Mister Heracles after Euripides (London: Faber, 2000)
Selected Poems (London: Faber, 2001)
The Universal Home Doctor (London: Faber, 2002)
Travelling Songs (London: Faber, 2002)

Eavan Boland

New Territory (Dublin: Allen Figgis, 1967)
The War Horse (London: Gollancz, 1975)

In Her Own Image (Dublin: Arlen House, 1980)
Night Feed (Dublin: Arlen House, 1982)
The Journey (Dublin: Gallery, 1982)
The Journey and Other Poems (Manchester: Carcanet, 1987)
Selected Poems (Manchester: Carcanet, 1989)
Outside History (Manchester: Carcanet, 1990)
Outside History: Selected Poems 1980–1990 (New York: Norton, 1990)
In a Time of Violence (Manchester: Carcanet, 1994)
Collected Poems (Manchester: Carcanet, 1995)
The Lost Land (Manchester: Carcanet, 1998)
Code (Manchester: Carcanet, 2001)
Against Love Poetry (New York: Norton, 2001)

Ciaran Carson

The New Estate (Belfast: Blackstaff, 1976)
The Lost Explorer (Belfast: Ulsterman Publications, 1978)
The Irish for No (Dublin: Gallery, 1987; Newcastle upon Tyne: Bloodaxe, 1988)
The New Estate and Other Poems (Loughcrew: Gallery, 1988)
Belfast Confetti (Loughcrew: Gallery, 1989; Newcastle upon Tyne: Bloodaxe, 1990)
First Language (Loughcrew: Gallery, 1993)
Letters from the Alphabet (Loughcrew: Gallery, 1995)
Opera Et Cetera (Newcastle upon Tyne: Bloodaxe, 1996)
The Alexandrine Plan: Versions of Sonnets by Baudelaire, Mallarmé, and Rimbaud
    (Oldcastle: Gallery, 1998)
The Twelfth of Never (London: Picador, 1999)
The Ballad of HMS Belfast: A Compendium of Belfast Poems (London: Picador, 1999)
The Inferno of Dante Alighieri: A New Translation (London: Granta, 2002)
Breaking News (Oldcastle: Gallery, 2003)

Gillian Clarke

Snow on the Mountain (Swansea, Llandybie: C. Davies, 1971)
The Sundial (Llandysul: Gomer Press, 1978)
Letter from a Far Country (Manchester: Carcanet New Press, 1982)
The King of Britain's Daughter (Manchester: Carcanet, 1993)
Five Fields (Manchester: Carcanet, 1998)
Selected Poems (Manchester: Carcanet, 1985)
Collected Poems (Manchester: Carcanet, 1997)
Making the Beds for the Dead (Manchester: Carcanet, 2004)

David Dabydeen

Slave Song (Mundelstrup: Dangaroo Press, 1984; Oxford: Dangaroo Press, 1986)
Coolie Odyssey (London/Coventry: Hansib Publishing and Dangaroo Press, 1988)
Turner: New and Selected Poems (London: Cape, 1994)

Carol Ann Duffy

Standing Female Nude (London: Anvil Press Poetry, 1985; new edition, 1988)
Selling Manhattan (London: Anvil Press Poetry, 1987)
The Other Country (London: Anvil Press Poetry, 1990)
Selected Poems (Harmondsworth: Penguin in association with Anvil, 1994)
Meantime (London: Anvil Press Poetry, 1993; new edition 1998)
The World's Wife (London: Macmillan, 1999)
Feminine Gospels (Basingstoke: Picador, 2002)

Tony Harrison

Earthworks (Leeds: Northern House, 1964)
Aikin Mata: The Lysistrata of Aristophanes, with James Simmons (Ibadan: Oxford University Press, 1966)
Newcastle is Peru (Newcastle upon Tyne: Eagle Press, 1969)
*The Loiners (London: London Magazine Editions, 1970)
The Misanthrope, by Molière, trans. Harrison (London: Collings, 1973; 2nd 1975)
Phaedra Britannica, after Racine (London: Collings, 1975)
Palladas: Poems, trans. Harrison (London: Anvil Press Poetry, 1975; 2nd edition, 1984)
Bow Down (London: Collings, 1977)
The Passion (London: Collings, 1977)
The Bartered Bride (New York: G. Schirmer, 1978)
*From 'The School of Eloquence' and Other Poems (London: Collings, 1978)
*Continuous: 50 Sonnets from 'The School of Eloquence' (London: Collings, 1981)
U.S. Martial (Newcastle upon Tyne: Bloodaxe, 1981)
The Oresteia, by Aeschylus, trans. Harrison (London: Collings, 1981)
A Kumquat for John Keats (Newcastle upon Tyne: Bloodaxe, 1981)
Yan Tan Tethera, with Harrison Birtwistle (London: Universal Editions, 1984)
*Selected Poems (London: Penguin, 1984) (expands *The School of Eloquence* to 67 sonnets)
*Selected Poems, 2nd edition (London: Penguin, 1987) (expands *The School of Eloquence* to 78 sonnets)
Anno Forty Two: Seven New Poems (London: Scargill Press, 1987)
The Mysteries (London: Faber, 1985)
'Medea: a sex-war opera' (1985), *in Dramatic Verse 1973–1985* (Newcastle upon Tyne: Bloodaxe, 1985), pp. 363–448
*V. (Newcastle upon Tyne: Bloodaxe, 1985; 2nd edition, 1989)
The Fire-Gap: A Poem with Two Tails (Newcastle upon Tyne: Bloodaxe, 1985)
The Big H (1984), in *Dramatic Verse 1973–1985* (Newcastle upon Tyne: Bloodaxe, 1985), pp. 321–61
V. and Other Poems (New York: Farrar Straus Giroux, 1990)
The Trackers of Oxyrhynchus (London: Faber, 1990; 2nd edition, 1991)
A Cold Coming: Gulf War Poems (Newcastle upon Tyne: Bloodaxe, 1991)
*The Gaze of the Gorgon (Newcastle upon Tyne: Bloodaxe, 1992)
The Common Chorus: A Version of Aristophanes' Lysistrata (London: Faber, 1992)
Square Rounds (London: Faber, 1992)

Poetry or Bust (Saltaire: Salts Estates, 1993)
Black Daisies for the Bride (London: Faber, 1993)
A Maybe Day in Kazakhstan (London: Channel 4 Television, 1994)
The Shadow of Hiroshima and Other Film Poems, introduction by Peter Symes (London: Faber, 1995)
Permanently Bard: Selected Poetry, ed. Carol Rutter (Newcastle upon Tyne: Bloodaxe, 1995)
The Prince's Play (London: Faber, 1996)
Prometheus (London: Faber, 1998)
*Laureate's Block (Harmondsworth: Penguin, 2000)
Under the Clock (London: Penguin, 2005)

Seamus Heaney

*Death of a Naturalist (London: Faber, 1966)
*Door into the Dark (London: Faber, 1969)
*Wintering Out (London: Faber, 1972)
*North (London: Faber, 1975)
Stations (Belfast: Ulsterman Publications, 1975)
*Field Work (London: Faber, 1979)
Selected Poems, 1965–1975 (London: Faber, 1980)
Sweeney Astray, a version of *Buile Suibhne* (Derry: Field Day, 1983)
*Station Island (London: Faber, 1984)
*The Haw Lantern (London: Faber, 1987)
The Cure at Troy: A Version of Sophocles' Philoctetes (London: Faber, 1990)
New Selected Poems 1966–1987 (London: Faber, 1990)
*Seeing Things (London: Faber, 1991)
The Midnight Verdict, based on translations of Ovid's *Metamorphoses* and Brian Merriman's *Cúirt an Mheán Oíche* (Oldcastle: Gallery, 1993)
*The Spirit Level (London: Faber, 1996)
Opened Ground: Poems 1966–1996 (London: Faber, 1998)
Beowulf: A New Translation (London: Faber, 1999)
*Electric Light (London: Faber, 2001)
The Burial at Thebes: Sophocles' Antigone (London: Faber, 2004)

Kathleen Jamie

*Black Spiders (Edinburgh: Salamander Press, 1982)
A Flame in Your Heart (Newcastle upon Tyne: Bloodaxe, 1986)
*The Way We Live (Newcastle upon Tyne: Bloodaxe, 1987)
The Autonomous Region: Poems and Photographs from Tibet, with Sean Mayne Smith (Newcastle upon Tyne: Bloodaxe, 1993)
*The Queen of Sheba (Newcastle upon Tyne: Bloodaxe, 1994)
*Jizzen (London: Picador, 1999)
Mr and Mrs Scotland are Dead: Poems 1980–1994, sel. Lilias Fraser (Tarset: Bloodaxe, 2002)
*The Tree House (London: Picador, 2004)

Jackie Kay

The Adoption Papers (Newcastle upon Tyne: Bloodaxe, 1991)
Other Lovers (Newcastle upon Tyne: Bloodaxe, 1993)
Off Colour (Newcastle upon Tyne: Bloodaxe, 1998)
Life Mask (Tarset: Bloodaxe, 2005)

David Kinloch

Dustie-fute, with drawings by W.N. Herbert (London: Vennel Press, 1992)
Paris-Forfar (Edinburgh: Polygon, 1994)
Un Tour d'Ecosse (Manchester: Carcanet, 2001)

Tom Leonard

Six Glasgow Poems (Glasgow: Other People Publications, 1969)
A Priest Came on at Merkland Street (Glasgow: Midnight Press, 1970)
Poems (Dublin: E. & T. O'Brien, 1973)
Bunnit Husslin (Glasgow: Third Eye Centre, 1975)
Three Glasgow Writers, with Alex Hamilton and James Kelman (Glasgow: Molendinar Press, 1976)
My Name is Tom (London: Good Elf Press, 1978)
Ghostie Men (Newcastle upon Tyne: Galloping Dog Press, 1980)
Intimate Voices: Selected Work 1965–1983 (Newcastle upon Tyne: Galloping Dog Press, 1984; London: Vintage, 1995; Buckfastleigh: Etruscan Books, 2003)
Situations Theoretical and Contemporary (Newcastle upon Tyne: Galloping Dog Press, 1986)
nora's place (Newcastle upon Tyne: Galloping Dog Press, 1990)
Reports from the Present: Selected Work 1982–1994 (London: Cape, 1995)
access to the silence: poems and posters 1984–2004 (Buckfastleigh: Etruscan Books, 2004)
inside looking in (Glasgow: Survivors Press, 2004)

Michael Longley

*No Continuing City (London: Macmillan, 1969)
*An Exploded View (London: Gollancz, 1973)
*Man Lying on a Wall (London: Gollancz, 1976)
*The Echo Gate (London: Secker & Warburg, 1979)
Poems 1963–1983, 2nd edition (London: Secker & Warburg, 1991)
*Gorse Fires (London: Secker & Warburg, 1991)
*The Ghost Orchid (London: Cape, 1995)
Broken Dishes (Newry: Abbey Press, 1998)
*The Weather in Japan (London: Cape, 2000)
*Snow Water (London: Cape, 2004)

Geraldine Monk

Long Wake (London: Writers Forum/Pirate Press, 1979)
Rotations (Sheffield: Siren Press, 1979)

Banquet (Sheffield: Siren Press, 1980)
La Quinta del Sordo (London: Writers Forum, 1981)
Tiger Lilies (Bradford: Rivelin Press, 1982)
Sky Scrapers (Durham: Galloping Dog Press, 1986)
Herein Lie Tales of Two Inner Cities (London: Writers Forum, 1986)
Animal Crackers (London: Writers Forum, 1988)
Quaquaversals (London: Writers Forum, 1990)
Walks in a Daisy Chain (Hebden Bridge: Magenta, 1991)
The Sway of Precious Demons: Selected Poems (Twickenham and Wakefield: North and South, 1992)
Interregnum (London: Creation Books, 1995)
Dream Drover (Cheltenham: Grattan Street Irregular, 1999)
Noctivigations (Sheffield: West House Books, 2001)
Insubstantial Thoughts on the Transubstantiation of the Text (Sheffield: West House Books and The Paper, 2002)
Mary Through the Looking Glass (Sheffield: Gargoyle Editions, 2002)
Absent Friends (Sheffield: Gargoyle Editions, 2002)
Selected Poems (Cambridge: Salt Publications, 2003)

Paul Muldoon

*Mules (London: Faber, 1977)
*Why Brownlee Left (London: Faber, 1980)
*Quoof (London: Faber, 1983)
Selected Poems, 1968–1983 (London: Faber, 1986)
The Wishbone (Dublin: Gallery, 1984)
*Meeting the British (London: Faber, 1987)
*Madoc: A Mystery (London: Faber, 1990)
Shining Brow (London: Faber, 1993)
*The Annals of Chile (London: Faber, 1994)
The Prince of the Quotidian (Oldcastle: Gallery, 1994)
Six Honest Serving Men (Oldcastle: Gallery, 1995)
New Selected Poems, 1968–1994 (London: Faber, 1996)
Kerry Slides, with photographs by Bill Doyle (Oldcastle: Gallery, 1996)
*Hay (London: Faber, 1998)
The Birds, by Aristophanes, trans. Paul Muldoon with Richard Martin (Oldcastle: Gallery, 1999)
Bandanna (London: Faber, 1999)
Vera of Las Vegas (Oldcastle: Gallery, 2001)
Poems, 1968–1998 (London: Faber, 2001)
*Moy Sand and Gravel (London: Faber, 2002)

Grace Nichols

i is a long memoried woman (London: Caribbean Cultural International, 1983; Karnak House, 1990)
The Fat Black Woman's Poems (London: Virago, 1984)

Lazy Thoughts of a Lazy Woman and Other Poems (London: Virago, 1989)
Sunris (London: Virago, 1996)

Don Paterson

*Nil Nil (London: Faber, 1993)
*God's Gift to Women (London: Faber, 1997)
The Eyes, a version of Antonio Machado (London: Faber, 1999)
*Landing Light (London: Faber, 2003)

Tom Raworth

The Relation Ship (London: Goliard Press, 1966)
Haiku (London: Trigram Press, 1968)
The Big Green Day (London: Trigram Press, 1968)
Lion Lion (London: Trigram Press, 1970)
Moving (London: Cape Goliard, 1971)
Act (London: Trigram Press, 1973)
From the Hungarian (Bowling Green, OH: privately printed, 1973)
Ace (London: Goliard Press, 1974)
Cloister (Paris and Northampton, MA: Blue Pig Press, 1975)
Common Sense (San Francisco: Zephyrus Image, 1976)
The Mask (Berkeley, CA: Poltroon Press, 1976)
Logbook (Berkeley, CA: Poltroon Press, 1976)
Skytails (Cambridge: Lobby Press, 1978)
Four Door Guide (Cambridge: Street Editions, 1979)
Nicht Wahr, Rosie? (Berkeley, CA: Poltroon Press, 1979)
Writing (Berkeley: The Figures, 1982)
Lèvre de Poche (Durham, NC: Bull City Press, 1983)
Heavy Light (London: Actual Size Press, 1984)
Tottering State: Selected and New Poems 1963–1984 (Berkeley, CA: The Figures, 1984)
Lazy Left Hand (London: Actual Size Press, 1986)
Visible Shivers (Oakland, CA: O Books, 1987)
The Vein (Gt Barrington, MA: The Figures, 1991)
All Fours (London: Microbrigade, 1991)
Blue Screen (Cambridge: Equipage, 1992)
Eternal Sections (Los Angeles: Sun & Moon Press, 1993)
Catacoustics (Cambridge: Street Editions, 1996)
Survival (Cambridge: Equipage, 1994)
Emptily (Gt Barrington, MA: The Figures, 1994)
The Mosquito and the Moon (Cambridge: Ankle Press, 1994)
Silent Rows (Gt Barrington, MA: The Figures, 1995)
Muted Hawks (Berkeley, CA: Poltroon Press, 1995)
Clean and Well Lit (New York: Roof Books, 1996)
Meadow (Sausalito, CA: Post-Apollo Press, 1999)
Landscaping the Future (Bologna: Porto dei Santi, 2000)
Collected Poems (Manchester: Carcanet, 2003)

Peter Reading

Water and Waste (Walton-on-Thames: Outposts Publications, 1970)
For the Municipality's Elderly (London: Secker and Warburg, 1974)
The Prison Cell & Barrel Mystery (London: Secker and Warburg, 1976)
Nothing for Anyone (London: Secker and Warburg, 1977)
Fiction (London: Secker and Warburg, 1979)
Tom o'Bedlam's Beauties (London: Secker and Warburg, 1981)
Diplopic (London: Secker and Warburg, 1983)
5x5x5x5x5, with David Butler (Sunderland: Ceolfrith Press, 1983)
C (London: Secker and Warburg, 1984)
Ukulele Music with *Going On* (London: Secker and Warburg, 1985)
Essential Reading, ed. Alan Jenkins (London: Secker and Warburg, 1986)
Stet (London: Secker and Warburg, 1986)
Final Demands (London: Secker and Warburg, 1988)
Perduta Gente (London: Secker and Warburg, 1989)
Shitheads (London: Squirrelprick Press, 1989)
3 in 1 (London: Chatto and Windus, 1992) (*Diploplic, C* and *Ukelele Music*)
Evagatory (London: Chatto and Windus, 1992)
Ukelele Music with *Perduta Gente* (Evanston, IL: Northwestern University Press, 1994)
Last Poems (London: Chatto and Windus, 1994)
Collected Poems 1: Poems 1970–1984 (Newcastle upon Tyne: Bloodaxe, 1995)
Collected Poems 2: Poems 1985–1996 (Newcastle upon Tyne: Bloodaxe, 1996), including *Eschatological* (1996)
Work in Regress (Newcastle upon Tyne: Bloodaxe, 1997)
Chinoiserie (Ryton: Bay Press, 1997)
Ob. (Newcastle upon Tyne: Bloodaxe, 1999)
Apophthegmatic (Ryton: Bay Press, 1999)
Repetitious ([n.p]: Laertides Press, 1999)
Copla a Pie Quebrado (Lake Worth, FL: Lannan Foundation, 1999)
Marfan (Newcastle upon Tyne: Bloodaxe, 2000)
[untitled] (Tarset: Bloodaxe, 2001)
Faunal (Tarset: Bloodaxe, 2002)
Collected Poems 3: Poems 1997–2003 (Tarset: Bloodaxe, 2003), including *Civil* (2002) and *ɤ* (2003)

Denise Riley

Marxism for Infants (Cambridge: Street Editions, 1976)
No Fee; a Line or Two for Free, with Wendy Mulford (Cambridge: Street Editions, 1978)
Some Poems, with Wendy Mulford (Cambridge: CMR Press, 1982)
Dry Air (London: Virago, 1985)
Stair Spirit (Cambridge: Equipage, 1992)
Four Falling, Poetical Histories no. 26 (Cambridge: P. Riley, 1993)
Mop Mop Georgette (London: Reality Street Editions, 1993)
Selected Poems (London: Reality Street Editions, 2000)

Catherine Walsh

Macula (Dublin: Red Wheelbarrow Press, 1986)
The Ca Pater Pillar Thing and More Besides (Dublin: hardPressed Poetry, 1986)
Making Tents (Dublin: hardPressed Poetry, 1987)
Short Stories (Twickenham and Wakefield: North and South, 1989)
Pitch (Durham: Pig Press, 1994)
Idir Eatortha and *Making Tents* (London: Invisible Books, 1997)
from City West (Guilford, VT: Longhouse, 1997)

Benjamin Zephaniah

Pen Rhythm (London: Page One, 1980)
The Dread Affair: Collected Poems (London: Arena, 1985)
Inna Liverpool (Liverpool: Africa Arts Collective, 1988)
City Psalms (Newcastle upon Tyne: Bloodaxe, 1992)
Propa Propaganda (Newcastle upon Tyne: Bloodaxe, 1996)
Too Black, Too Strong (Tarset: Bloodaxe, 2001)

Further reading

Acheson, James and Romana Huk (eds), *Contemporary British Poetry: Essays in Theory and Criticism* (Albany, NY: State University of New York Press, 1996)
Allen, Michael (ed.), *Seamus Heaney: Contemporary Critical Essays* (Basingstoke: Macmillan (now Palgrave Macmillan), 1997)
Andrews, Elmer (ed.), *Contemporary Irish Poetry: A Collection of Critical Essays* (London: Macmillan (now Palgrave Macmillan), 1992)
Andrews, Elmer, *Seamus Heaney: A Collection of Critical Essays* (London: Macmillan (now Palgrave Macmillan), 1992)
Astley, Neil (ed.), *Tony Harrison* (Newcastle upon Tyne: Bloodaxe, 1991)
Berry, James, 'The literature of the Black experience', in *The Language of the Black Experience*, ed. David Sutcliffe and Ansel Wong (Oxford: Blackwell, 1986), pp. 69–106
Bertram, Vicki (ed.), *Kicking Daffodils: Twentieth-Century Women Poets* (Edinburgh: Edinburgh University Press, 1997)
Byrne, Sandie (ed.), *Tony Harrison: Loiner* (Oxford: Clarendon, 1997)
Campbell, Matthew (ed.), *The Cambridge Companion to Contemporary Irish Poetry* (Cambridge: Cambridge University Press, 2003)
Childs, Peter, *The Twentieth Century in Poetry* (London: Routledge, 1999)
Collins, Floyd, *Seamus Heaney: The Crisis of Identity* (Newark, DE: University of Delaware Press, 2003)
Corcoran, Neil, *The Chosen Ground: Essays on the Contemporary Poetry of Northern Ireland* (Bridgend: Seren, 1992)
Corcoran, Neil, *English Poetry Since 1940* (London: Longman, 1993)
Corcoran, Neil, *The Poetry of Seamus Heaney: A Critical Study* (London: Faber, 1998)
Crawford, Robert, *Devolving English Literature* (Oxford: Clarendon, 1992)

Curtis, Tony (ed.), *The Art of Seamus Heaney*, 3rd edition (Bridgend: Seren, 1994)

Davis, Alex, *A Broken Line: Denis Devlin and Irish Poetic Modernism* (Dublin: University College Dublin Press, 2000)

Day, Gary and Brian Docherty (eds), *British Poetry from the 1950s to the 1990s: Politics and Art* (Basingstoke: Macmillan (now Palgrave Macmillan), 1997)

Donnell, Alison and Sarah Lawson Walsh (eds), *The Routledge Reader in Caribbean Literature* (London and New York: Routledge, 1996)

Gifford, Douglas and Dorothy McMillan (eds), *A History of Scottish Women's Writing* (Edinburgh: Edinburgh University Press, 1997)

Goodby, John, *Irish Poetry Since 1950: From Stillness into History* (Manchester: Manchester University Press, 2000)

Grant, Kevin (ed.), *The Art of David Dabydeen* (Leeds: Peepal Tree Press, 1997)

Gregson, Ian, *Contemporary Poetry and Postmodernism: Dialogue and Estrangement* (London: Macmillan (now Palgrave Macmillan), 1996)

Haberstroh, Patricia Boyle, *Women Creating Women: Contemporary Irish Women Poets* (Syracuse, NY: Syracuse University Press, 1996)

Hampson, Robert and Peter Barry (eds), *New British Poetries: The Scope of the Possible* (Manchester: Manchester University Press, 1993)

Hufstader, Jonathan, *Tongue of Water, Teeth of Stones: Northern Irish Poetry and Social Violence* (Lexington, KT: University of Kentucky Press, 1999)

Kelleher, Joe, *Tony Harrison* (Plymouth: Northcote House, 1996)

Kendall, Tim, *Paul Muldoon* (Bridgend: Seren, 1996)

Kendall, Tim and Peter McDonald (eds), *Paul Muldoon: Critical Essays* (Liverpool: Liverpool University Press, 2004)

Kenneally, Michael (ed.), *Poetry in Contemporary Irish Literature* (Gerrards Cross: Colin Smythe, 1995)

Kennedy, David, *New Relations: The Refashioning of British Poetry 1980–1994* (Bridgend: Seren, 1996)

Kinnahan, Linda A., 'Experimental poetics and the lyric in British women's poetry: Geraldine Monk, Wendy Mulford, and Denise Riley', *Contemporary Literature*, vol. 37 (1996), pp. 620–70

King, Bruce, *The Internationalization of English Literature*, Oxford English Literary History, vol. 13, 1948–2000 (Oxford: Oxford University Press, 2004)

Kirkland, Richard, *Literature and Culture in Northern Ireland Since 1965: Moments of Danger* (London: Longman, 1996)

Lloyd, David, *Anomalous States: Irish Writing and the Post-Colonial Moment* (Durham, NC: Duke University Press, 1993)

Lloyd, David T. (ed.), *The Urgency of Identity: Contemporary English-Language Poetry from Wales* (Evanston, IL: Northwestern University Press, 1994)

Ludwig, Hans-Werner and Lothar Fritz (eds), *Poetry in the British Isles: Non-Metropolitan Perspectives* (Cardiff: University of Wales Press, 1995)

McClure, J. Derrick, *Language, Poetry and Nationhood: Scots as a Poetic Language from 1878 to the Present* (East Linton: Tuckwell Press, 2000)

McDonald, Peter, *Mistaken Identities: Poetry and Northern Ireland* (Oxford: Clarendon Press, 1997)

Marks, Alison and Deryn Rees-Jones (eds), *Contemporary Women's Poetry: Reading/Writing/Practice* (Basingstoke: Macmillan (now Palgrave Macmillan), 2000)

Martin, Isabel, *Reading Peter Reading* (Newcastle upon Tyne: Bloodaxe, 2000)

Matthews, Steven, *Irish Poetry: Politics, History, Negotiation: The Evolving Debate, 1969 to the Present* (Basingstoke: Macmillan (now Palgrave Macmillan), 1997)

Michelis, Angelica and Antony Rowland (eds), *The Poetry of Carol Ann Duffy: 'Choosing Tough Words'* (Manchester: Manchester University Press, 2003)

Murphy, Andrew, *Seamus Heaney*, 2nd edition (Plymouth: Northcote House, 2000)

Narain, Denise deCaires, *Contemporary Caribbean Women's Poetry: Making Style* (London: Routledge, 2002)

O'Brien, Eugene, *Seamus Heaney: Searches for Answers* (London: Pluto Press, 2003)

O'Brien, Sean, *The Deregulated Muse: Essays on Contemporary British and Irish Poetry* (Newcastle upon Tyne: Bloodaxe, 1988)

O'Donoghue, Bernard, *Seamus Heaney and the Language of Poetry* (Hemel Hempstead: Harvester Wheatsheaf, 1994)

Peacock, Alan J. and Kathleen Devine (eds), *The Poetry of Michael Longley* (Gerrards Cross: Colin Smythe, 2000)

Rees-Jones, Deryn, *Carol Ann Duffy*, 2nd edition (Tavistock: Northcote House, 2001)

Roberts, Neil, *Narrative and Voice in Postwar Poetry* (Harlow: Addison-Wesley Longman, 1999)

Robinson, Alan, *Instabilities in Contemporary British Poetry* (Basingstoke: Macmillan (now Palgrave Macmillan), 1988)

Shaffer, E.S. (ed.), *Comparative Criticism: An Annual Journal, vol. 19: Literary Devolution: Writing in Scotland, Ireland, Wales and England* (Cambridge: Cambridge University Press, 1997)

Sheppard, Robert, 'Poetics and ethics: The saying and the said in the linguistically innovative poetry of Tom Raworth', *Critical Survey*, vol. 14, no. 2 (2002), pp. 75–89

Spencer, Luke, *The Poetry of Tony Harrison* (Hemel Hempstead: Harvester Wheatsheaf, 1994)

Stevenson, Randall, *The Last of England?*, Oxford English Literary History, vol. 12, 1960–2000 (Oxford: Oxford University Press, 2004)

Tuma, Keith, *Fishing by Obstinate Isles: Modern and Postmodern British Poetry and American Readers* (Evanston, IL: Northwestern University Press, 1998)

Vendler, Helen, *Seamus Heaney* (London: Fontana, 1999)

Wills, Clair, *Improprieties: Politics and Sexuality in Northern Irish Poetry* (Oxford: Oxford University Press, 1993)

Wills, Clair, *Reading Paul Muldoon* (Newcastle upon Tyne: Bloodaxe, 1998)

Wisker, Gina (ed.), *Black Women's Writing* (Basingstoke: Macmillan (now Palgrave Macmillan), 1993)

Index